Sustainable Logistics and Supply Chain Management

Second edition

Sustainable Logistics and Supply Chain Management

Principles and practices for sustainable operations and management

David B Grant, Alexander Trautrims
and Chee Yew Wong

KoganPage

First published in Great Britain and the United States in 2013 by Kogan Page Limited
Second edition published 2017

2nd Floor, 45 Gee Street	c/o Martin P Hill Consulting	4737/23 Ansari Road
London	122 W 27th St, 10th Floor	Daryaganj
EC1V 3RS	New York, NY 10001	New Delhi 110002
United Kingdom	USA	India

www.koganpage.com

© David B Grant, Alexander Trautrims and Chee Yew Wong, 2017

The right of David B Grant, Alexander Trautrims and Chee Yew Wong to be identified as the authors of this work has been asserted by them in accordance with the Copyright, Designs and Patents Act 1988.

ISBN   978 0 7494 7827 8
E-ISBN   978 0 7494 7828 5

British Library Cataloguing-in-Publication Data

A CIP record for this book is available from the British Library.

Library of Congress Cataloging-in-Publication Data

Names: Grant, David B., author. | Trautrims, Alexander, author. | Wong, Chee Yew, author.
Title: Sustainable logistics and supply chain management : principles and practices for sustainable operations and management / David B Grant, Alexander Trautrims and Chee Yew Wong.
Description: Second Edition. | New York : Kogan Page Ltd, [2017] | Revised edition of the authors' Sustainable logistics and supply chain management, 2015. | Includes bibliographical references and index.
Identifiers: LCCN 2017001791 (print) | LCCN 2017004774 (ebook) | ISBN 9780749478278 (pbk.) | ISBN 9780749478285 (ebook) .
Subjects: LCSH: Business logistics. | Production management.
Classification: LCC HD38.5 .G694 2017 (print) | LCC HD38.5 (ebook) | DDC 658.5–dc23
LC record available at https://lccn.loc.gov/2017001791

Typeset by Integra Software Services, Pondicherry
Print production managed by Jellyfish
Printed and bound by CPI Group (UK) Ltd, Croydon CR0 4YY

CONTENTS

LIST OF FIGURES AND TABLES

FIGURES

TABLES

ABOUT THE AUTHORS

David B Grant is professor of logistics at Hull University Business School and professor of supply chain management and social responsibility at Hanken School of Economics, Helsinki. His recent visiting appointments include the École Supérieure du Commerce Extérieur, Paris and Universidad de los Andes, Bogotá as the Silla Corona Distinguished Visiting Professor. David obtained his PhD from Edinburgh University and his thesis, which investigated customer service, satisfaction and service quality in UK food processing logistics, received the James Cooper Memorial Cup PhD Award from the Chartered Institute of Logistics and Transport (UK). His research interests include logistics customer service, satisfaction and service quality; retail logistics; and reverse, closed-loop and sustainable logistics. David's business experience includes retail, corporate banking, technical design and consulting, and recent applied research has investigated on-shelf availability and out-of-stocks, total loss and waste in food retailing, forecasting and obsolete inventory, service quality and fulfilment in internet retailing, and consumer logistics. David has over 200 publications in various refereed journals, books and conference proceedings and is on the editorial board of many international journals. Recent books include *Logistics Management* (Pearson) and *Fashion Logistics* (Kogan Page) with John Fernie.

Alexander Trautrims, BA (Hons), MSc, PGDip, PhD, is a lecturer in supply chain and operations management at Nottingham University Business School, UK. He also holds adjunct positions at Royal Holloway – University of London, and Copenhagen Business School.

His current research focuses on ethical issues and compliance in supply chains and the execution and implementation of responsible sourcing solutions in procurement. He is working closely with UK businesses and non-profit organizations on the implementation of the Modern Slavery Act and is the supply chain lead in the University of Nottingham's research priority area for Rights and Justice.

He is a member of the Council of Supply Chain Management Professionals (CSCMP), the Institute for Supply Management (ISM), the Logistics Research Network (LRN) in the UK and the German Logistics Association (BVL).

Chee Yew Wong is professor of supply chain management at Leeds University Business School, UK. His doctoral thesis investigated the coordination of supply chain planning across a toy supply chain in Europe. He teaches operations, logistics and supply chain management at undergraduate and postgraduate levels, and provides speeches, workshop facilitation and consulting to supply chain companies. Research interests include supply chain integration; sustainable supply chain management; reverse logistics; global value chains; service operations; and third-party logistics service. He has more than seven years' business experience in engineering, production, logistics sourcing and supply chain management in industries such as power, beverages, food, toys, retail, grocery and manufacturing. Recent applied research has investigated collaborative forecast and planning, centralization of warehouses, implementation of ERP systems, green practices in the service and manufacturing sectors, and transfer of supply chain management knowledge to small and medium-size companies. Chee Yew Wong has authored over 80 publications in various refereed journals, books and conference proceedings and is on the editorial board of three international academic journals. He is a member of the UK Logistics Research Network (LRN) and European Operations Management Association (EurOMA).

FOREWORD

In recent years, the subject of sustainability has garnered increased attention from individuals, companies and governments. Sustainability in sourcing; sustainability in manufacturing; sustainability in distribution; sustainability in marketing and sales; and sustainability in consumption and product disposition. There is not a single area of business that has not been impacted in some way by climate change, product stewardship, trying to do more with less, and improving energy consumption. The stakeholders of companies are demanding that firms employ sustainable practices in their manufacturing, supply chains, supplier relations, human resources, and other corporate responsibility efforts. For some firms, sustainability has become a requirement of doing business, whether that is in the B2B or B2C sectors. In today's omnichannel environment, sustainability has become a key initiative that is important in a firm's success, irrespective of whether the firm sells its products or services on the internet, through physical brick-and-mortar stores, or a combination of both options.

The paradigm of the 'Triple Bottom Line' that includes people, planet and profits, has become the watchword of many companies worldwide. And rightfully so, inasmuch as all aspects of the triple bottom line are important, both to the present and future wellbeing of the planet, its people, and the economies of the world. Logistics and supply chain management have significant sustainability impacts on people, the planet, and profits. The authors, in the second edition of their book, provide a good overview of the subject matter relating to the various roles that logistics and supply chain management play in the physical and fiscal health of individuals, companies and governments. The authors do a good job of highlighting the importance of sustainability. The book includes coverage of the major sustainability aspects of logistics and supply chain management, including transportation, warehousing, purchasing and procurement, product design, production, and notably, reverse logistics. Writers often ignore the role of reverse logistics, including product returns processing, in discussions of sustainability. To their credit, the authors of *Sustainable Logistics and Supply Chain Management: Principles and practices for sustainable operations and management* include that discussion as one of the chapters of their book.

The book can be used in the classes at all higher education levels, including both undergraduate and graduate courses. The book should be 'student friendly', given the writing styles of the authors, its logistics and supply chain sustainability coverage, and inclusion of highly topical mini case studies. The authors do an effective job in relating the theoretical concepts to practice and what is actually happening 'in the real world'. The book offers excellent insights into logistics and supply chain sustainability that will provide executives, students, and academics alike with information on how to manage, implement and control sustainability programmes, policies and procedures within companies. From a pedagogical perspective, this revised edition includes valuable supporting online materials, including PowerPoint presentations, chapter summaries, learning objectives, tips for teaching, and in-class activities.

James R Stock
Fulbright-Hanken Distinguished Chair in Business and Economics,
Hanken School of Economics (Finland)
Distinguished University Professor and Frank Harvey Endowed Professor
of Marketing, University of South Florida (USA)

Introduction

This second edition of our book discusses sustainability issues pertaining to logistics and supply chain management (SCM), and is different from other books as it takes a holistic view across the supply chain from point of origin through point of consumption and back within the reverse logistics chain. Logistics and supply chain activities permeate almost every aspect of our lives and thus their ability to impact the natural environment is of significant importance. This edition includes updated information and cases, as well as supplementary materials available at the Kogan Page website.

The objective of this book is to introduce principles and practices that facilitate responsible SCM and sustainable logistics operations in a holistic manner and consider factors of logistics and SCM affecting the natural environment beyond the usual factors of road miles, fuel use and carbon dioxide (CO_2) emissions that have been well discussed in freight transportation; see for example *Green Logistics: Improving the environmental sustainability of logistics* by McKinnon *et al* (2015), which is a good complement to this book. As an example of wider factors, globalization of business has meant that many products are not manufactured in national markets anymore; they are outsourced and manufactured in lesser-developed countries, particularly in Asia, and then shipped all around the world. How then does a national firm ensure sustainability in its global supply chain? Further, most seasonal fresh food such as fruit and vegetables is now available all year round due to sourcing in foreign markets or the use of sophisticated chilled storage and transport to prevent premature spoiling or ageing. So should consumer markets return to more seasonal goods to reduce the effects on the environment of continuous product availability?

The development of these types of activities and factors has increased the effects that logistics and SCM have on the natural environment. Accordingly, logistics and supply chain strategies and operations are discussed in this book in the context of raising awareness of, and shifting an emphasis to, responsible, ethical and sustainable practices. It is important for firms, consumers and societies to do so and be proactive in considering these issues. Otherwise, legislation may emerge to limit the impact of logistics and SCM on the environment, which may be more draconian than these three stakeholders would desire.

For example, the UK government considered and then abandoned a scheme of personal or individual 'carbon credits' in 2008 (BBC News, 2008). Under the scheme, individuals would have an annual carbon dioxide (CO_2) emission limit for fuel and energy use, which they could only exceed by buying credits in a secondary carbon-trading market from those who were under limit. The scheme was considered more progressive than taxation, as it would redistribute wealth from rich to poor, transparent and easy for everyone to understand, and fair, as everyone would get the same annual CO_2 limit. However, the government's initial studies found that the cost of introducing the scheme would be between £700 million and £2 billion, plus a further £1–2 billion a year to operate. There were also practical difficulties identified in deciding how to set annual limits, taking into account a person's age, location, health and activities such as business and personal travel. From a different sustainability perspective, many members of parliament admitted that the public were likely to be opposed to the scheme, but urged the government to be courageous in going ahead with it. With a general election less than two years away, the government decided to discontinue further tax-payer-funded research on the scheme while noting that the concept of personal carbon limits and trading had not been completely abandoned.

Today, individuals can calculate their own CO_2 emissions or 'carbon footprint' through websites such as **www.carbonfootprint.com**. Factors for this calculation include energy use in the home, personal and public transport including aeroplane flights, and lifestyle preferences such as in-season or organic food, packaging, recycling, and recreation. What this discussion about CO_2 emission limits and carbon taxes has highlighted is that environmental issues are complex, involve elements of logistics and SCM in many facets of everyday life, and are not easy to solve.

But, there is recent evidence that individual attitudes may be changing. For example, from 2010 to 2012 the percentage of US citizens who believed climate change was real increased from 57 to 70 per cent (Porter, 2012). And a study in the UK by Cardiff University in 2015 found that almost 88 per cent of respondents agree that the world's climate is changing, while 76 per cent of respondents reported a personal experience of climate change during their lifetime. About 75 per cent supported the UK signing up to international agreements to limit CO_2 emissions, with only 7 per cent opposing this idea (ESRC, 2015).

Further, hundreds of residents in the English village of Ashton Hayes banded together in 2005 to reduce CO_2 and other greenhouse gas emissions by using clotheslines instead of dryers, taking fewer flights, and installing solar panels and double-glazed windows to better insulate their homes (Schlossberg, 2016). These initiatives themselves are not unique, but what *is* unique here is that the residents of Ashton Hayes have done this without government suggestions or regulations. Because of that individual impetus, about 200 towns, cities and counties around the world have reached out to learn how they can also do so.

Finally, in late 2016, almost a year on from when the UK government introduced a 5 pence charge for plastic bags at retail stores – a very late move compared to other European countries – more than 9 in 10 people 'often' or 'always' carry their own bags, up from 7 in 10 before the charge came into effect (Vaughan, 2016). The number of plastic bags obtained in-store from retailers has fallen by 85 per cent, proving that behaviour regarding sustainability can be changed with the right incentive or disincentive in this case. The success of this programme has prompted a call for a charge on takeaway coffee cups.

The pathways for the nine chapters in this book are shown in Figure 0.1. Each chapter is designed to be read and considered on its own; however, the flow of the chapters is based on two basic premises in logistics and supply chain activities: transportation – or 'Go' – and storage/production – or 'Stop' (Grant, 2012) – that are further discussed in Chapter 1.

Chapter 1 discusses an overview of logistics and SCM activities and contemporary thought about sustainability as it pertains to logistics and SCM, including the impact of logistics and SCM activities on the natural environment and ecosystem and vice-versa. Topics include the nature of various logistical and supply chain activities, the increase in globalization that has lengthened supply chains, and the debate between being more lean and efficient versus a need to compress time and be more agile and responsive. New to this edition is a discussion of the growth of e-commerce and its effects on sustainability, as well as updated statistics and new case studies.

Chapter 2 then discusses the science of sustainability, the environmental and climate change debate, and the nature of the earth as a holistic ecosystem that must be in balance but also make sense for people and business, ie a 'triple bottom line' approach. Topics here include the earth's climate and sustainability as such an ecosystem, the greenhouse effect and related greenhouse gases such as carbon monoxide, sulphur dioxide and methane, and the impact of human activity on sustainability affecting the use of natural resources such as minerals, oil and gas, and water, as well as population growth and food production. Updated statistics and enhanced insights into

Figure 0.1   Chapter pathways in this book

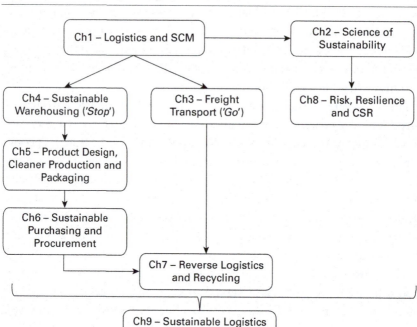

issues facing society as a result of current climate change challenges are new to this edition.

The following five chapters consider sustainability issues in depth as they relate to the main functional 'Go' and 'Stop' activities of logistics and SCM. Chapter 3 leads off by considering freight transport as the major contributor to the logistics and SCM environmental debate due to its overwhelming importance in the supply chain and its very visible presence. Topics include the nature of various freight transport modes, trends in global freight transportation issues of emissions, fuel consumption and congestion, and the evolution of technology to assist greener transport alternatives. The key principles of making transportation more sustainable have not changed much over the last decade. In practice, however, research and industry are trying new applications – some more successful than others – for the future of transportation. In particular, the search for more sustainable fuels is still in full swing. Electric vehicles and hydrogen fuel are currently the main considerations since biofuels fell out of fashion due to a potential increase in food prices if agricultural capacity is diverted to fuel production instead of food. The discussion is now on the implementation of more sustainable solutions with a particular focus on the provision of a new fuel infrastructure and the capital-intensive build-up of such infrastructure. An entirely new aspect in transportation is the advent of driverless technology. What this technology advancement will mean for the millions of transport workers around the world can today only be guessed.

Chapter 4 discusses sustainable warehousing; after transportation, storage facilities in the form of factories, warehouse and distribution centres contribute the second-largest logistical and supply chain impact on the natural environment. Topics here include designing green warehouses and inherited emissions from construction materials, reducing resources consumption in existing warehouses, location of warehouses and network design, and LEED and BREEAM certifications for sustainable facilities. Whereas the sustainability of warehouse construction and operations is improving only gradually, warehouses as workplaces have gained strong critical attention from the public. Chapter 4 includes a case study on the labour conditions at Sports Direct. Ethical aspects in modern supply chains have become an equally important sustainability dimension to environmental sustainability and they are very often closely linked to each other.

Chapter 5 takes the storage discussion further by considering issues related to product design, cleaner production and packaging that are the underlying tenets in producing sustainable products and services. Topics here include environmental product design to use fewer materials, ie design for the environment and be lighter and easier to transport; novel production methods which consume less energy/natural resources and produce less pollution; and packaging for logistics versus the environment, ie reusable packaging, recycling of packaging materials.

The next two chapters go one step beyond production and logistics and supply chain activities. Chapter 6 considers sustainable purchasing, procurement and supplier relationships that are important antecedents for the production process. Topics here include drivers and barriers for environmental or green purchasing, procurement frameworks and a product whole-lifecycle (or life cycle) assessment. A product's lifecycle assessment naturally includes a reverse element to recycle or dispose of unwanted products or components. Procurement departments became natural gatekeepers for many organizations and are hence facing increasing responsibility to protect the organization from risks and to ensure supply chain compliance. Legislation such as the California Transparency Act and the Modern Slavery Act in the UK are adding to these responsibilities but are also upgrading procurement departments to a crucial and more strategic role in the ambition to make supply chains more sustainable.

Chapter 7 discusses reverse logistics and recycling, which are important factors for transportation ('Go') and storage ('Stop') functions. Topics discussed include circular economy; reverse-loop product recovery options such as refurbishing, remanufacturing, upcycling, cannibalization and recycling; current regulatory frameworks; and issues surrounding these topics.

Chapter 8 then returns to a more holistic approach to consider issues of risk, resilience and corporate social responsibility (CSR) relating to logistics and SCM. Topics include the wider scope of corporate social responsibility including environmental sustainability and social responsibility; the different risks affecting a global supply chain including environmental disasters, ethical models and the notion of 'greenwash'; and global and industrial initiatives that promote economic, environmental and social sustainability.

Finally, Chapter 9 provides an overview of sustainable logistics and SCM strategy regarding how firms can incorporate environmental considerations into their overall corporate strategies, including accounting for the related costs and benefits. Topics include strategic planning for sustainability, the redesign of supply chain networks, sustainable logistics and supply chain performance measurement, and environmental cost trade-offs in logistics systems and supply chains. Enhanced discussions about assessing sustainability trade-offs and choices and a new case study on reducing emissions are included.

It has been our pleasure to write this second edition of our book and we sincerely hope you find it informative and inspiring regarding holistic environmental concerns as they apply to logistics and SCM.

References

BBC News (2008) MPs back personal carbon credits [online] available at: http://news.bbc.co.uk/go/pr/fr/-/1/hi/uk_politics/7419724.stm [accessed 1 January 2013]

ESRC (2015) Public belief in climate change reaches 10-year high [online] available at: http://www.esrc.ac.uk/...9d64b29b-eNews_FEB_2015&utm_medium=email&utm_term=0_4a06f0b327-429d64b29b-118568545 [accessed 13 February 2015]

Grant, D B (2012) *Logistics Management*, Pearson Education Limited, Harlow, UK

McKinnon, A, Browne, M, Whiteing, A and Piecyk, M (2015) *Green Logistics: Improving the environmental sustainability of logistics* (3rd edn), Kogan Page, London

Porter, H (2012) America's carbon tax offers a lesson to the rest of the planet, *Observer*, 2 December, p 40

Schlossberg, T (2016) English village leads a climate revolution, *International New York Times*, 23 August, pp 1, 3

Vaughan, A (2016) Shoppers in England now far more likely to use their own bags, *Guardian* [online] available at: https://www.theguardian.com/environment/2016/sep/29/shoppers-in-england-now-more-likely-to-use-their-own-bags-plastic?CMP=Share_iOSApp_Other [accessed 30 September 2016]

Logistics and supply chain management

01

The nature of logistics and supply chain management

Logistics and supply chain management (SCM) are far-reaching activities that have a major impact on a society's standard of living. In western developed societies, we have come to expect excellent logistics services and only tend to notice logistical and supply chain issues when there is a problem. To understand some of the implications for consumers of logistics activities, consider:

- the difficulty in shopping for food, clothing and other items if logistical and supply chain systems do not conveniently bring all those items together in one place, such as a single store or a shopping mall;
- the challenge in locating the proper size or style of an item if logistical and supply chain systems do not provide a wide mix of products, colours, sizes and styles through the assortment process;
- the frustration of not having an online order fulfilled if logistical and supply chain systems do not satisfactorily meet an agreed delivery time window.

These are only a few of the issues we often take for granted that illustrate how logistics touches many facets of our daily lives. However, the various activities associated with logistics and SCM also have an impact on environmental sustainability and this chapter provides an overview of logistics and SCM and such impacts.

We first need to define what is meant by logistics and SCM. The Council of Supply Chain Management Professionals (CSCMP) in the United States defines logistics management as (2016):

> ... that part of supply chain management that plans, implements and controls the efficient, effective forward and reverse flow and storage of goods, services and related information between the point of origin and the point of consumption in order to meet customers' requirements.

Logistics management activities typically include inbound and outbound transportation management, warehousing, materials handling, order fulfilment, logistics network design, inventory management, supply/demand planning, and management of third-party logistics (3PL) service providers. To varying degrees, the logistics function also includes sourcing and procurement, production planning and scheduling, packaging and assembly, and customer service. Until the turn of the Millennium, point of consumption meant point of sale, ie a retail store or some other form of outlet. Rapid advances in technology offering online shopping or other services through the Internet of Things (IoT) have now verified and validated the point of consumption notion.

The term 'supply chain management' or SCM was introduced by consultants in the 1980s and since then academics have attempted to give theoretical and intellectual structure to it. CSCMP (2016) defines SCM as encompassing:

> ... the planning and management of all activities involved in sourcing and procurement, conversion, and all logistics management activities. Importantly, it also includes coordination and collaboration with channel partners, which can be suppliers, intermediaries, third-party service providers, and customers. In essence, supply chain management integrates supply and demand management within and across companies.

SCM is thus considered an integrating function with a primary responsibility for linking major business functions and business processes within and across companies into a cohesive and high-performing business model. It includes all the logistics management activities noted above, as well as manufacturing operations, and drives the coordination of processes and activities with and across marketing, sales, product design, finance, and information technology, and is thus a more holistic view of a firm.

Nevertheless, there are some overlaps which have prompted some authors (Larson and Halldórsson, 2004) to consider whether SCM is merely a re-labelling of logistics due to a lack of understanding by academics and practitioners of what supply chains are and what supply chain managers do, an intersection between logistics and SCM as SCM represents a broad strategy across all business processes in the firm and the supply chain, or a union whereby logistics is a sub-set of SCM due to a wider supply chain

Figure 1.1 A simplified supply chain

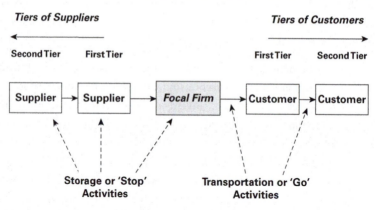

SOURCE Authors.

and business process perspective of SCM. The CSCMP definitions above represent a unionist view and this book adopts the CSCMP definitions and the unionist view as they appear intellectually sound and bring clarity to the sustainability debate.

A firm's simplified supply chain and its relevant features are shown in Figure 1.1. The immediate customers and suppliers of the firm under consideration (the focal firm), are known as first-tier customers and suppliers. The first-tier customer's first-tier customer and the first-tier supplier's first-tier supplier are the focal firm's second-tier customer and supplier respectively, and so on. Between each supply chain node, where a node is the focal firm, a supplier or a customer, goods are moved by transportation or 'Go' activities. Further, goods are stored and/or processed at each node in storage or 'Stop' activities. Essentially, logistics and SCM are about 'Go' or 'Stop' activities, although details surrounding each of them can be quite complex (Grant, 2012). However, it will be useful to consider this simple 'Go' or 'Stop' concept when discussing sustainability issues as they really occur during transportation or storage activities.

Logistics and SCM activities have a significant economic impact on countries and their societies. For example, these activities accounted for 8.3 per cent US gross domestic product (GDP) or US $1.45 trillion in 2014 (Wilson, 2015) and 6.8 per cent of GDP (€876 billion) across the European Union's (EU) 27 countries in 2012 (EC, 2015). Thus, a small percentage decrease in these activities would see major environmental impacts from reductions in the use of fuel, water and other natural resources and decreases in waste and emissions. An example of such an impact, together with the associated problems in measuring this impact, is discussed in the following box.

How should we reduce food miles?

What are the correct measures to use when assessing sustainability and logistics and SCM generally, or 'food miles' in particular? A UK study of food miles has determined that the globalization of the food industry, with increasing food trade and wider geographical sourcing of food within the UK and overseas, has led to a concentration of the food supply base into fewer, larger suppliers (Watkiss, 2005). This has happened for several reasons: to meet demand for bulk year-round supply of uniform produce; major changes in delivery patterns with most goods now routed through supermarket regional distribution centres (RDCs) and a trend towards use of larger heavy goods vehicles (HGVs); and a switch from more frequent food shopping on foot at small local shops to a concentration of sales at supermarkets by weekly shopping with cars. This rise in food miles has led to increases in environmental, social and economic impacts such as CO_2 emissions, air pollution, traffic congestion, accidents and noise and a growing concern over these impacts has led to a debate on whether to try to measure and reduce food miles.

The UK study also estimated that the annual amount of food tonne kilometres moved in the UK by HGVs has increased by over 100 per cent since 1974 and the average distance for each trip has increased by over 50 per cent. UK food transport – export, import and internal – accounted for 19 million tonnes of CO_2 emissions in 2002 with estimated direct costs of £9 billion, £5 billion of which related to traffic congestion.

And yet a US study, conducted by Carnegie Mellon University in the mid-2000s and using a lifecycle assessment, found that transportation accounts for only 11 per cent of the 8.1 metric tons of greenhouse gases generated by an average US household every year from food consumption – over 83 per cent comes from agricultural and industrial activity in growing and harvesting food (Whitty, 2008). The differences in these two emissions numbers suggests different factors are taken into account in each calculation. Also, the UK study found that the increase in UK food tonne kilometres has not been accompanied by an increase in HGV food vehicle kilometres due to increases in vehicle operating efficiencies and improvements in vehicle load factors.

Finally, the US study found that greenhouse gases from food miles per food product in the United States are as follows: red meat – 30 per cent; dairy products – 18 per cent; cereals and carbohydrates and fruit and vegetables – 11 per cent each; chicken, fish and eggs – 10 per cent; with beverages, oils, sweets, condiments and 'other' comprising the remaining 21 per cent. The US study's authors also found that switching to a totally local diet saves about 1,000 miles per year, but that the following dietary trade-offs are almost as effective in reducing food miles: replacing red meat once a week with chicken, fish or eggs saves 760 miles per year and eating only vegetables one day a week saves 1,160 miles per year.

The UK study concluded that a single indicator based on total food kilometres is an inadequate indicator of sustainability; the impacts from food transport are complex and involve many trade-offs between different factors. The study's authors recommended a suite of indicators be developed to take into account transport modes and efficiency, differences in food production systems and wider economic and social costs and benefits.

Shaw *et al* (2010) concluded that while logistics and supply chain performance measurement is a well-established area of research, green or environmental logistics and supply chain performance measurement is relatively under-researched in both the logistics/supply chain and environmental management literature. However, despite being an important and topical subject, the lack of clear direction and legislation on environmental management makes it difficult for firms to know exactly what they should measure and how to measure, whether it is food miles, emissions or recycling. More theoretical and empirical research needs to be undertaken to give firms and other stakeholders the tools to do so.

SOURCES Watkiss (2005); Whitty (2008); Shaw *et al* (2010).

Logistics and SCM trends affecting sustainability

Environmental issues have been an area of growing concern and attention for businesses on a global scale. Transportation, production, storage and the disposal of hazardous materials are frequently regulated and controlled. In Europe, firms are increasingly required to remove and dispose of packaging materials used for their products. These issues complicate the job of logistics and SCM, increasing costs and limiting options. Important logistics and SCM trends were discussed in the literature at the turn of this Millennium (for example Bowersox *et al*, 2000); however, Grant (2014) and Wieland *et al* (2016) have provided an update of the major trends, some of which significantly affect sustainability. Following is a discussion of these key trends and their impacts.

Globalization

Globalization has increased tremendously since the 1970s, primarily due to the development and widespread adoption of the standard shipping container, international trade liberalization, the expansion of international transport infrastructure such as ports, roadways and railroads, and production and logistics cost differentials between developed and developing countries. However, the geographical length of supply chains has increased along with the attendant environmental issues of fuel use and emissions.

The impact on logistics and SCM of globalization has been significant over the past several decades. For example, global container trade has increased on average 5 per cent per year over the last 20 years and at its peak in the mid-2000s comprised 350 million 20-foot equivalent units (TEU) a year (Grant, 2012). However, the impact of globalization doesn't only affect sea-borne containers. Worldwide demand and subsequent fulfilment of smart phones and tablets have led to an increase in air freight volumes and prices.

For example, every autumn when new Apple smartphones are released for sale, the prices for air freight spike upwards (Petersen, 2016). In 2015, air freight rates were at their lowest in spring and summer at about US $2.50 per kilogram. However, these rates rose dramatically to US $11.00 per kilogram by November. During the fourth quarter of 2015, Apple sold 74.4 million smartphones of which 40 per cent were sold in the United States.

Relationships and outsourcing

In concert with the logistics and SCM definitions above, there has been a need for increased collaboration and mutually beneficial relationships among customers, suppliers, competitors and other stakeholders in an increasingly interconnected and global environment, which can have positive benefits for sustainability. For example, two competitors could share transportation and warehousing facilities in an effort to avoid the empty running of trucks and also provide return or reverse logistics opportunities.

On the other hand, many firms have outsourced their logistics and SCM activities to 3PL specialists, such as DHL or XPO Logistics, to perform activities that are not considered part of a firm's 'core competencies'. The outsourcing/3PL market is now worth over US $166 billion in the United States (Wilson, 2015) and is estimated to be 50 per cent of all logistical expenditures in the EU or about €435 billion in Europe (EC, 2015). Across the globe, over 80 per cent of domestic and 75 per cent of international transportation or 'Go' and 74 per cent of warehousing or 'Stop' activities are outsourced, as is over 35 per cent of reverse logistics and product labelling, packaging and assembly activities (Langley and Capgemini Consulting, 2010).

Outsourcing can be very cost effective for firms, as they can efficiently concentrate on their core competencies, reduce capital expenditures and fixed assets related to transportation and storage infrastructure, reduce labour and internal operating costs, and enjoy the expertise and economies of scale provided by the 3PL service provider. However, firms lose control of those operations that they outsource, despite service level agreements and contracts, and thus may not have control over the sustainability efforts of 3PLs or their sub-contractors.

Technology

Technology is also an important factor in modern global supply chains as it enables better, faster and more reliable communication. Logistics and SCM have interfaces with a wide array of functions and firms, and communication must occur between the focal firm, its suppliers, customers and various members of the supply chain who may not be directly linked to the firm, and the major functions within the firm such as logistics, engineering, accounting, marketing and production. Communications are thus key to the efficient functioning of any integrated logistical or supply chain system.

The use of communications technology has increased remarkably during the last few decades due to increases in computing power and storage that have fostered the invention of personal and laptop computers, global positioning systems, 'smart' mobile phones and the most desirable Christmas gifts: tablets and iPads. Such technology has become increasingly automated, complex and rapid, and has enabled firms to develop faster and longer supply chains due to their ability to trace and track goods in production or storage or in-transit.

Order processing involves the systems that an organization has for getting orders from customers, checking on the status of orders and communicating to customers about them, and actually filling the order and making it available to the customer. Increasingly, organizations today are turning to advanced order-processing methods such as electronic data interchange (EDI) and electronic funds transfer (EFT) to speed the process and improve accuracy and efficiency, as well as advanced scanning technology such as radio frequency identification (RFID) to track and trace products across the entire supply chain. But technology that extends to the true point of consumption, allowing consumers to efficiently replenish basic household goods, is also on offer for consumers; a discussion follows about Amazon Dash as part of the IoT.

The Internet of Things and logistics/SCM: panacea or Pandora's Box?

Amazon launched its Dash buttons in the UK and parts of Europe in September 2016. For the price of £4.99 – redeemable from a first order – subscribers to Amazon's 'Prime' service are able to immediately order refills of basic or commodity household products, such as razor blades, condoms or washing powder, with the press of a button. Each of the 197 products that Amazon features for Dash has its own button, which means that an individual consumer might need to possess dozens of the plastic, high-tech buttons that work through an Internet connection.

The Dash is an example of the IoT (Internet of Things), where devices are Internet enabled to automate tasks. Another example is a smart thermostat that is connected to a home's heating system and which can be operated through the homeowner's smartphone, allowing the homeowner to turn the heat on or off from anywhere. There are also similar applications and IoT devices for controlling a home's lighting, and all these technologies are meant to add convenience and benefits to the lives of time-poor consumers who cannot get to the shops to replenish basic items or wish to control costs and their use of energy at home.

The IoT concept is also highly applicable to upstream supply chain management activities. Van Kranenburg (2008) discussed Heineken's Green Lanes project to efficiently move its beverage products through customs networks worldwide. Green Lanes reduces about 30 documents for one single container crossing a border through a unified data system that allows changes in information about product sizes, weight, name, price, classification, transport requirements and volumes to be immediately transmitted along the supply chain, ie online and in real time. Benefits include allowing shippers to immediately know if amounts of products stacked on pallets had changed or to give a retailer time to adjust shelf display space. Van Kranenburg quipped that:

You used to be able to spot one person taking one crate of Heineken from a pallet next to you, and you'd say: 'Hey, better leave that crate alone!' Well, now you sit in a control room in Rotterdam and if one crate disappears in Hong Kong, you know and alert your colleagues overseas. (2008: 29)

However, there are serious criticisms about aspects of IoT. Greenpeace's Gary Cook, cited in Boztas (2016), consider the Dash buttons:

a wasteful use of technology and a surprising step backwards for a company that prides itself on its innovative abilities... adding to the massive global e-waste problem with an electronic device that has such limited functionality is certainly not innovative.

Amazon spokesman Tarek El-Hawary countered that Dash buttons 'are fully recyclable and Amazon will cover the cost of recycling [and]... orders placed via Dash buttons are grouped together where possible, as with any order we fulfil'.

Van Kranenburg has focused on issues of security and privacy as regards a greater online interconnectedness and believes RFID technology is at a crucial point in terms of standards and policies, regulations and deployment and services. He considers that the increasing use of RFID and related technologies, such as near-field communications (NFC) to provide personal and business solutions also sees human beings 'distributing' themselves as data as such technology is being embedded in passports, bank/credit cards, employee access cards and other kinds of identification that identifies human beings by unique numbers. He concludes by noting that location-based, real-time services and applications are all possibilities within a wired or WiFi connected environment that need serious exploration and research.

SOURCES Belkin (2016); Boztas (2016); Honeywell (2016); Van Kranenburg (2008).

Time compression: the lean versus agile debate

Time compression refers to ways of 'taking time' out of operations. Longer lead times and process times create inefficiencies, require higher inventory levels, greater handling, storage, transportation and monitoring, incur a greater chance for error, and thus decrease the efficiency of the supply chain as a whole. Advanced logistics and supply chain activities and technology as discussed above help compress a firm's time by developing better relationships with suppliers and customers to share more real-time information and improve its accuracy. Thus, many firms have initiated time compression strategies to significantly reduce manufacturing time and inventory.

Retailers, particularly in the grocery sector where perishability is an issue, have been leaders in time compression, relying heavily on advanced computer systems involving bar coding, electronic point-of-sale (EPOS) scanning, and EDI to develop quicker responses for order processing. In fact, the grocery sector across the globe established efficient consumer response (ECR) in the 1990s to do just that (Fernie and Grant, 2008).

As a result of a need to be more efficient in production and manufacturing at an operational level and reduce times at a logistical and supply chain level, two different logistics and supply chain paradigms, 'lean' and 'agile', emerged during the 1990s (Purvis et al, 2014). The lean paradigm is based on the principles of lean production in the automotive sector where a 'value stream' is developed to eliminate all waste, including time, and ensure a level production system. Firms make to order and therefore speculate on the number of products that will be demanded by forecasting such demand. Thus, a firm assumes inventory risk rather than shifting it through developing economies from large-scale production, placing large orders that reduce the costs of order processing and transportation, and reducing stock-outs and uncertainty and their associated costs. Speculation very much fits a lean strategy.

The agile paradigm has its origins in principles of channel postponement. Under postponement, costs can be reduced by postponing changes in the form and identity of a product to the last possible point in the process, ie manufacturing postponement, and by postponing inventory locations to the last possible point in time since risk and uncertainty costs increase as the product becomes more differentiated from generic form, ie logistical postponement. Being agile means using market knowledge and information in what is known as a virtual corporation to exploit profitable opportunities in a volatile marketplace inventory.

The lean approach seeks to minimize inventory of components and work in progress and to move towards a 'just-in-time' (JIT) environment wherever possible. Conversely, firms using an agile approach are meant to respond in shorter time-frames to changes in both volume and variety demanded by customers. Thus, lean works best in predictable high-volume, low-variety environments while agility is needed in less predictable environments where the demand for variety is high.

Figure 1.2   A hybrid lean and agile supply chain

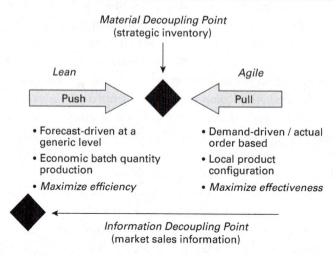

Material Decoupling Point
(strategic inventory)

Lean   *Agile*

Push   Pull

- Forecast-driven at a   • Demand-driven / actual
  generic level   order based
- Economic batch quantity   • Local product
  production   configuration
- *Maximize efficiency*   • *Maximize effectiveness*

Information Decoupling Point
(market sales information)

SOURCE Authors.

While the paradigms appear dichotomous, in reality, most firms likely have a need for both lean and agile logistics and supply chain solutions, suggesting a hybrid strategy. Such a strategy has also been called 'leagile' (Naylor *et al*, 1999) and Figure 1.2 illustrates this hybrid solution. The 'material decoupling point' represents a change from a lean or 'push' strategy to an agile or 'pull' strategy. The 'information decoupling point' represents the point where market sales or actual order information can assist forecasting efforts within the lean approach of this hybrid solution.

The impact of time compression on sustainability includes increased transportation or 'Go' and storage or 'Stop' activities in an agile supply chain, along with their associated environmental effects, in order to achieve levels of responsiveness and flexibility. Further, the location selection of transportation hubs and ports or storage and production sites may also be detrimental to the environment. For example, ports and surrounding areas will have to develop a strong environmental outlook and a public and ecological health approach. It has been estimated that 70 per cent of shipping emissions occur within 400 kilometres of land; thus, ships contribute significant pollution in coastal communities. Shipping-related particulate matter (PM) emissions have been estimated to cause 60,000 cardiopulmonary and lung cancer deaths annually, with most deaths occurring near coastlines in Europe, East Asia and South Asia (Corbett *et al*, 2007).

The rise of e-commerce

Electronic commerce, or e-commerce, in business to business (B2B), business to consumer (B2C) and consumer to consumer (C2C) exchanges has risen rapidly in importance for almost 20 years (Fernie and Grant, 2015). For example, retail e-commerce sales in the United States increased more than five-fold between 2002 and 2014 (Wilson, 2015). E-commerce sales in the United States and Canada in 2015 were US $349 billion and US $17 billion respectively, while in Europe, e-commerce sales in the UK, Germany, France, The Netherlands, Sweden, Italy, Poland and Spain grew almost 19 per cent from US $132 billion in 2014 to US $157 billion in 2015 (Centre for Retail Research, 2016).

This increase in e-commerce has significant relevance for the logistic and SCM sector as it imposes enormous pressure on areas of reliability, punctuality and expedition. Further, the impact of e-commerce on parcel deliveries and returns, the tracking of freight and vehicles and its management, and Cloud services which allow the sharing of data to make synchronous supply chains function, are likely to be of increasing importance in future (EC, 2015). All of these issues have an impact on the sustainability of transport.

Another development in the e-commerce phenomenon is omnichannel retailing, where a consumer's entire online shopping experience, ie both sales and fulfilment, is seamlessly and consistently integrated across all channels of interaction, including in-store, digital media including computers, mobiles and tablets, social media, catalogues and call centres (Fernie and Grant, 2015). From a supply chain perspective, omnichannel also means there should be complete visibility across channels, along with a holistic, unified view of the path to purchase. Thus, omnichannel increases complexity in e-commerce activities.

The 'one-way flow' of logistics and SCM

The logistical or supply chain flow of products is predominantly one way from raw materials/resources and producers to consumers. Reverse or return networks and systems are woefully underdeveloped and, for those networks that do have some development, the vagaries of the economy significantly affect those networks that have some maturity. For example, the UK was sending a lot of mixed paper and cardboard waste to China in the 2000s for reprocessing and reuse as new product packaging. However, the price of this waste fell from over £90 per tonne to £8 per tonne in late 2008 as a result of the economic recession (Sutherland and Gallagher,

2009). Consumer demand and thus Chinese production of new products slowed with a knock-on effect that demand for mixed paper and cardboard waste as well as container shipping, particularly from west to east, also fell precipitously.

At that point, none of Britain's 80 paper mills was accepting new stock and it was estimated that there was about 100,000 tonnes of local authority waste sitting in warehouses, which was set to double by March 2009. Another concern was that if paper is stored for longer than three months it will rot and attract vermin, rendering it worthless, and will then have to be incinerated or sent to landfill. The demand situation eased and by 2010 prices returned to around £75–80 per tonne. However, the market remains weak due to the lingering recession and by December 2012 prices had again fallen and were around £45–50 per tonne (letsrecycle.com, 2013).

Thus, globalization, technology, lean and agile techniques and a 'one-way flow' have all contributed to increased standards of living around the world, including in developing nations who benefit from better economic activity. However, parallel increases in logistical and supply chain activities related to this prosperity have been detrimental to the natural environment in terms of increased resource use, waste and pollution as well as inefficient movement and storage of goods. The following box provides an example of how this detriment could be addressed using a technological solution for retail fulfilment.

Empowering consumers in the 'last mile' for home deliveries

Online retail sales are increasing exponentially in the UK; however, delivery costs, missed deliveries and an inability to return goods are inconvenient and costly for consumers, retailers and parcel carriers. The cost of parcel delivery is a major factor in a consumer's decision to buy online and also erodes overall margins for online retailers with online grocery retailers losing £11–15 on every delivery. To minimize delivery costs, retailers fulfil online orders using a rigid methodology based on fixed delivery schedules and time windows, and during checkout, consumers are offered a few scheduling choices, generally with longer delivery windows, but based on a static model and assumptions about territorial demand. This approach is limiting, as many carriers require consumers to be at home to receive a delivery and consumers ideally want a more precise delivery time or options.

However, 31 per cent of deliveries fail due to consumers not being home and this costs retailers and carriers over £770 million a year, with a cost of £238 for each failed delivery attributable to increased administration/processes, decreased capacity utilization, and call centre overburden. The failure of a national UK delivery carrier, City Link, in 2014, illustrates how important but precarious costs are to deliveries and non-deliveries. It is estimated that time spent waiting at home to receive a delivery implicitly costs each consumer £177 a year and between 25 and 50 per cent of certain products sold online are returned, representing a value of £1.2 billion. There are also external sustainability costs including CO_2 emissions, fuel consumption, traffic congestion and fraud from stolen parcels.

A contributing factor is a lack of delivery time notification or communication and there needs to be a solution to provide a range of fulfilment options that consumers can select to ensure a flexible and tailored service and allow dialogue between consumers, retailers and carriers throughout the whole delivery process. The key problem is a lack of meaningful and accessible data against which all three parties can make decisions for everyone's benefit. The data exists but is disparate and sometimes private: consumers know their diaries, delivery preferences and the amount they will spend for a delivery to maximize convenience, retailers know their consumers, and carriers know their operational costs and constraints.

The issue is not about obtaining new data but integrating extant data securely and privately and analysing it to add value and maximize the effectiveness of each delivery within millions of deliveries for the benefit of that specific delivery and the whole delivery ecosystem. One solution for this issue is provided by ParcelSpace in the UK. The ParcelSpace mobile application system is a common software platform collecting data and connecting multiple consumers, retailers and carriers, allowing not just communication and tracking, but also the ability to manage deliveries in transit.

Consumers can use the ParcelSpace mobile application to track and amend any scheduled delivery. The process works as follows: the consumer first gets the application and registers with ParcelSpace to adjust default alert preferences, set up texts, and enter their home address. When they make an online purchase, they can enter the delivery's tracking number, select a delivery address and enter a receipt name. Then, if the consumer has to change the delivery for any reason they can access the retailer and/or carrier to amend the delivery.

ParcelSpace thus enables retailers, carriers and consumers to connect securely and privately during delivery, working well with one or more connections. This empowers consumers by meeting their online shopping demands, unlocks new delivery options while protecting brands, complements existing systems, reduces delivery queries and misdeliveries, increases sales due to consumer satisfaction, and is a more sustainable solution to redeliveries to the location or to a collection point.

SOURCES ChainLink Research (2013); Clipper Logistics (2015); *Logistics Manager* (2013); ParcelSpace (2016); TOA Technologies (2011).

Sustainable logistics and supply chains

Abukhader and Jönson (2004) posed two interesting questions regarding logistics and SCM and the natural environment:

1 What is the impact of logistics on the environment?

2 What is the impact of the environment on logistics?

The impact of logistics on the environment is the easier question to answer but the second question is a bit more difficult to conceptualize. However, an example should illustrate their point. Cotton does not grow naturally in many countries in northern latitudes. Thus, if people living in northern European countries or Canada desire cotton clothing or other cotton goods, then some form of logistics activity such as transportation and/or warehousing will be required to bring cotton to these markets. However, the main logistical/supply chain issue here is whether the cotton should be in the form of raw materials or finished goods. The answer to that issue will depend on the design of the particular logistical system and supply chain.

Abukhader and Jönson (2004) also posited there are three main 'themes' regarding sustainable or 'green' logistics and supply chain management:

1 reverse logistics;

2 assessment of emissions; and

3 the 'greening' of logistical activities and supply chains.

When Abukhader and Jönson wrote their article, there was little use of lifecycle assessment (LCA) in logistics and supply chain management and little consideration of environmental impacts beyond cost–benefit analysis. That situation has improved since then (Curran, 2006) and will be discussed further in Chapters 6 and 9, but it is important to remember that the sustainability agenda in general and its application to logistics and supply chain management in particular are still fairly recent and underdeveloped. However, some insights in this area were developed in the 1990s, as discussed in the following box.

The early days of sustainable logistics and SCM

While sustainability, 'green' and environmental issues are reasonably new to the logistics and SCM domain, early research in the 1990s considered both transportation processes in the lifecycle of a product, concentrating on the activities of the manufacturer, and reverse logistics.

An article by Stefanie Böge in 1995 was one of the first discussions regarding the impact of 'food miles' on consumer products, and her research also quantified the environmental impact of transport. Her study of a milk manufacturer in southern Germany examined all constituent parts of the manufacturer's strawberry yogurt in 150-gram recyclable glass jars, including ingredients of milk, jam, sugar and packaging of the glass container, paper label, aluminium cover, cardboard box and cardboard sheets, and glue and foil.

Böge found that the transport intensity to deliver 150-gram yogurt pots across German supply chains meant that 24 fully-packed trucks each had to travel 1,005 kilometres to distribution centres, collectively using over 10,200 litres of diesel fuel in the process. She further broke that down and noted that each yogurt pot moved a total of 9.2 metres, comprising 5.1 metres of movement related to sub-contractors, 3.1 metres for the manufacturer, and 1.0 metres for trade distribution, and used 0.004 litres of diesel.

She concluded that there were three basic options for manufacturers: use inputs from nearer sub-contractors, improve existing transportation vehicles, and shift to more environmentally sound freight shipment vehicles. These themes of closer sourcing, less environmentally intrusive vehicles and modal shift now have currency among those responsible for logistics and supply chain activities. However, at the time, Böge's work was not considered extensively by either academics or practitioners. Her article was published in a journal outside the mainstream logistics and SCM domain which today is an open access Internet journal published by Eco-Logica Ltd in the UK (see http://www. eco-logica.co.uk/index.html).

In 1998, Dale Rogers and Robert Tibben-Lembke at the University of Nevada Reno and James Stock at the University of South Florida wrote a monograph and book respectively on reverse logistics. Notions of recycling consumer products such as bottles and cans and product recovery management in the manufacturing domain for remanufacture or cannibalization (see Thierry *et al*, 1995) had been around since the 1950s, but little previous work existed on issues related to reverse logistical flows. The next section and Chapter 7 consider these issues more fully, but the Rogers/Tibben-Lembke and Stock works were pioneering in this area.

SOURCES Böge (1995); Rogers and Tibben-Lembke (1998); Stock (1998); Thierry *et al* (1995).

Reverse logistics

Reverse logistics is not a new concept, as noted above. The return, recovery and recycling of products have been practised for decades. However, it is a growing area in logistics and SCM, particularly for retail returns in an era of growing omnichannel e-commerce as discussed above. Work by Rogers and Tibben-Lembke and Stock in 1998 set the stage for this impetus. Reverse logistics has been defined (Rogers and Tibben-Lembke, 1998, p 2) as:

> ... the process of planning, implementing, and controlling the efficient, cost-effective flow of raw materials, in-process inventory, finished goods and related information from the point of consumption to the point of origin for the purpose of recapturing value or proper disposal.

Note that this definition is very similar to the CSCMP definition of logistics above, with only the latter part changed. Reverse logistics encompasses all of the activities in the CSCMP definition of logistics; however, the difference is that reverse logistics activities occur in the opposite direction, ie against the one-way flow. Reverse logistics also includes processing returned merchandise due to damage, seasonal inventory, restock, salvage, recalls and excess inventory.

There are four primary questions regarding reverse logistics from a strategic perspective:

- What types of materials may be returned, recovered or recycled?
- How are responsibilities defined in a reverse logistics supply chain?
- What is it reasonably possible to return, recover or recycle?
- How are economic value and ecological value determined?

There are also some key differences between new product and reverse logistics supply chains:

- There is uncertainty in the recovery process regarding reverse product quality or condition, quantity and timing.
- Return forecasting is an even greater problem than demand forecasting.
- There is uncertainty in consumer behaviour:
  - the consumer has to initiate the return as opposed to simply disposing of the products;
  - the consumer has to accept and purchase recovered and refurbished products;
  - the price offered and value placed by the consumer on returning or recycling goods is not clear.
- The number of collection points is greater and uncertain in location or viability and there may be delayed uplift of products as time is not critical, ie no time compression.
- Returned products often have poor packaging and small consignment sizes, and the clarity of information, traceability and visibility may be poor.
- Inspection and separation of products are necessary and are very labour intensive and costly.

However, providing proper refurbished or remanufactured goods can provide a competitive advantage for firms and brand credibility and quality for consumers. For example, Fujifilm launched single-use cameras in 1986 under the brand name QuickSnap after market research determined that a growing segment of Japanese consumers only wanted to take pictures on an occasional basis (Grant and Banomyong, 2010). QuickSnap quickly became a popular consumer convenience product and a million cameras were sold in its first six months in the marketplace. However, at the beginning of the 1990s, several stakeholder groups attacked the product's disposable nature, which resulted in a negative impact on the brand's image and sales. Consumers began to refer to QuickSnap as 'disposables' or 'throwaways' and the media reported environmental groups' concerns regarding their wastefulness.

In response to these environmental pressures, Fujifilm initiated a voluntary take-back programme and began recycling the cameras by utilizing a highly developed and original recycling programme. They also redesigned the camera to use various techniques of product recovery management, with design characteristics that prevent it being reused or resold without undergoing them. Waste management is almost non-existent in the QuickSnap 'inverse manufacturing system', as an almost 100 per cent recycling rate can be achieved, even with components such as packaging for the product. In doing this, Fujifilm established one of the first, fully integrated closed-loop or reverse logistics systems for FMCG products and has since reversed much of the poor environmental image of the QuickSnap product.

The topics of reverse logistics and product recovery management are dealt with further in Chapter 7; however, the use of recycled products can also be used to achieve other sustainable goals as discussed in the following box.

Recycling rubber to meet other environmental objectives

As traffic grows around the globe, there is a comparable increase not only in the use of rubber tyres but also in road noise, which is one external form of pollution affecting humans' wellbeing. One noise abatement technique is the use of roadside barriers; however, they are expensive, costing up to US $600,000 per kilometre, can generate wind tunnels, and may not be aesthetically pleasing.

However, two Swedish scientists are among several across Europe who are investigating the use a poroelastic road surface (PERS) in an attempt to reduce traffic noise. PERS is a wearing course or layer that has a porous structure and has several advantages over normal 'rubberized' asphalt or tarmac that contains 'rubber crumbs' recycled from used tyres as an additive to the bitumen and crushed stone.

The Swedish experiments used a PERS made up of rubber particles bound with polyurethane as an additive to create a 30mm-thick structure that contained 30–35 per cent interconnecting air voids. Laboratory experiments on test specimens indicated very low wear from exposure to studded tyres and emissions particles in the air but showed rolling resistance comparable to that of a conventional asphalt surface. Adhesion to a base asphalt course and skid resistance received particular attention and the laboratory experiments indicated satisfactory performance.

Field tests conducted on a Stockholm street carrying a mixture of light and heavy traffic in the region indicated road noise was reduced by 8–11 decibels at A weighting or dB(A), rolling resistance and braking resistance were the same as on normal asphalt, and there was no significant wear on the PERS surfaces even with studded tyres used in winter. However, there were some technical issues beyond the cost of five times asphalt: the PERS materials significantly absorbed water, which would necessitate better drainage under the surfaces, and wear through the use of snow ploughs was significant.

If cost and technical issues can be resolved, then surfaces like PERS offer some unique sustainability benefits: reducing the externality of road noise from traffic and using recycled materials instead of virgin asphalt.

SOURCES Sandberg and Kalman (2005); *The Economist* (2012).

Assessment of emissions

How do transportation and storage activities compare to other activities in society with respect to their environmental impact? Both are users of energy, for example fuel and electricity, and both produce carbon dioxide (CO_2) emissions as a result of using this energy. The World Economic Forum (2009) estimates that logistics activity accounts for 2,800 mega-tonnes of carbon dioxide emissions annually or about 6 per cent of the total 50,000 mega-tonnes produced by human activity, so it is not surprising that non-energy companies are beginning to assess the energy consumption of their supply chains as a way to reduce their overall carbon emissions.

The UK's domestic CO_2 emissions, excluding international aviation and shipping, are generated from four main sectors: energy supply at 40 per cent, transportation at 23 per cent, industry including manufacturing, retailing, service and warehousing at 18 per cent and residential at 15 per cent (Commission for Integrated Transport, 2007).

Examining the transportation sector's 23 per cent of emissions in more detail, private automobiles are the primary source of CO_2 emissions at 54 per cent, followed by heavy goods trucks or lorries and vans at 35 per cent.

Thus, road freight transportation accounts for just over 8 per cent of the UK's total CO_2 emissions. This is consistent with the World Economic Forum's (2009) findings.

On the energy input side, vehicle engines are becoming more efficient in terms of fuel use and emissions and there are ongoing efforts to consider alternative fuels such as biodiesel or bioethanol, hydrogen, natural gas or liquid petroleum gas, and electricity. However, these developments are still in their infancy and also have their own environmental impacts. For example, the growth of crops for biofuels requires the use of arable land, which displaces the growing of crops for food. A response to that situation might see farmers cultivating more forests and grasslands for food production, thus possibly negating the positive effects of greenhouse gas emissions reductions from using biofuels.

Turning to warehousing as one aspect of the industrial sector, the World Business Council for Sustainable Development (2007) notes that buildings account for 40 per cent of worldwide energy use. Initiatives to increase the efficiency of building in using energy and reducing emissions have been developed by the Leadership in Energy and Environmental Design certification programme (LEED) in the United States and the Building Research Establishment Environmental Assessment Method (BREEAM) in the UK.

Aspects of transportation emissions assessment and performance measurement will be discussed further in Chapters 3 and 9 respectively, while further consideration of warehouses and buildings, including LEED and BREEAM, will be discussed in Chapter 4.

The 'greening' of logistical activities and supply chains

The 'greening' of logistics activities and supply chains means ensuring that these activities are environmentally friendly and not wasteful, and particularly focus on reducing carbon emissions across the entire supply chain. The World Economic Forum (2009) argued that a collaborative responsibility for 'greening' the supply chain resides with three groups: logistics and transport service providers; shippers and buyers as recipients of such services; and both government and non-government policy makers. They presented specific recommendations for these three groups as follows.

Transportation, vehicles and infrastructure networks

Logistics and transport service providers should increase adoption of new technologies, fuels and associated processes by implementing where there is a positive business case, deploy network reviews of large closed networks to ensure efficient hierarchies and nodal structures, look to integrate opti-mization efforts across multiple networks, enable further collaboration between multiple shippers and/or between carriers, and look to switch to more environmentally friendly modes within their own networks. Shippers and buyers should build environmental performance indicators into the contracting process with logistics service providers, work with consumers to better support their understanding of carbon footprints and labelling where appropriate and make recycling easier and more resource efficient, support efforts to make mode switches across supply chains and begin to 'de-speed' the supply chain. Policy makers should promote further expan-sion of integrated flow management schemes for congested roads and make specific investments in congested nodes or sections of infrastructure around congested road junctions, ports and rail junctions, mode switches to rail, short sea and inland waterways, and consider re-opening idle rail lines, waterways and port facilities with government support.

Green buildings

Logistics and transport service providers should encourage wider indus-try commitment to improve existing facilities through retrofitting green technologies and work towards industry-wide commitments to boost invest-ment into new building technologies, and develop new offerings around recycling and waste management, working collaboratively with customers. Policy makers should encourage industry to commit to improvements that consider the boundaries of possibilities with current and future technolo-gies, through individual and sector-wide actions.

Sourcing, product and packaging design

Shippers and buyers should determine how much carbon is designed into a product through raw material selection, the carbon intensity of the production process, the length and speed of the supply chain, and the carbon characteristics of the use phase. Shippers and buyers can take decisions which actively drive positive change up and down the supply chain. Shippers and buyers should agree additional standards and targets around packaging light weighting and elimination and seek cross-industry agreements on modularization of transit packaging materials. They should also develop sustainable sourcing policies that consider the carbon impact of primary production, manufacturing and rework activities, and integrate carbon emissions impact into the business case for near-shoring projects.

Administrative issues

Logistics and transport service providers should develop carbon offsetting solutions for their own operations and clients as part of a balanced suite of business offerings. Policy makers should work with them to develop universal carbon measurement and reporting standards, build an open carbon

Table 1.1 Four aspects of eco-efficiency and supply chain initiatives

Aspect	Description	Supply chain application
Dematerialization	Substitution of material flows with information flows	Substituting information for inventory so as to avoid premature deployment of goods before demand is known
	Product customization	Any form of production or logistics postponement allows firms to more closely meet actual demand with less anticipatory stock – therefore less use of materials and energy
Production loop closure	Closed-loop systems and zero-waste factories, ensuring that every output can be returned to become an input into the production of another product, or returned to natural systems as a nutrient	Closed-loop supply chains are being increasingly adopted as firms look to recapture their products for refurbishment, remanufacture, and sales in primary or secondary markets; this requires product recovery strategy and facilitated by Design-for-Disassembly or Design-for-Environment strategies
Service extension	In demand-driven economies firms need to develop customized responses to customer needs; this is increasingly being accomplished through leasing goods rather than outright purchase	Asset recovery programmes are employed to manage the return of products at the end of lease; this requires reverse logistics and reprocessing capabilities upon receipt
Functional extension	'Smarter' products with enhanced functionality; associated services further enhance products' functional value	Product design initiatives to enhance product life with upgrade and service enhancements

trading system, review tax regimes to remove counter-productive incentives, and support efforts to move towards further carbon labelling. Further, they should ensure that the full cost of carbon is reflected in energy tariffs across all geographies and all modes of transport.

Another view on 'greening' the supply chain was provided by Mollenkopf (2006). She argued there are four aspects of eco-efficiency, based on earlier work by the World Business Council on Sustainable Development, that provide strategic guidance for firms operating in knowledge-based economies. These aspects, along with related supply chain applications, are presented in Table 1.1.

An approach to using these guidelines should begin with a firm considering why it should develop a sustainable supply chain strategy. The major factors might include regulatory changes, market demand and competitive pressures, such as Wal-Mart Canada's development of a sustainable warehouse discussed in the following box.

Techniques for 'greening' a warehouse

Wal-Mart Canada opened a 400,000-square-foot fresh and frozen food warehouse in Balzac, Alberta in November 2010 to serve about 100 retail outlets in Western Canada. The facility is expected to reap CAD $4.8 million in energy cost savings through 2015, but will also become the model for the company's future warehouse and DC design and development.

The warehouse generates electricity from a combination of on-site wind turbine generators and roof solar panels and the refrigerated building uses low-energy, solid-state light-emitting diode (LED) lights, an advantage for the retailer because solid-state illumination keeps the facility cooler than does traditional incandescent lighting. Even though the LED lights cost an additional CAD $486,000, Wal-Mart expects annual savings of CAD $129,000 from that approach.

Wal-Mart has also custom-designed dock doors to minimize the loss of cool air from the refrigerated warehouse and the company monitors cooling loss from the dock doors daily with the use of thermal imaging cameras to ensure that dock doors are not opened unnecessarily. The facility is also using hydrogen fuel cells to power its fleet of lift trucks and material handling equipment. The hydrogen-powered vehicles cost Wal-Mart CAD $693,000 more than conventional vehicles, but they are expected to generate nearly CAD $269,000 per year in operational savings.

Lift trucks powered by hydrogen fuel cells are also considered more efficient because they don't have to be taken out of service for battery replacement and recharging. Warehouse workers can refuel a hydrogen fuel cell vehicle as it moves around the warehouse in as little as two minutes.

SOURCE *CSCMP's Supply Chain Quarterly* (2011).

Product development and stewardship impacts all stages of logistics and SCM. Suppliers may need to get involved in the product development process in order to design appropriately for the environment. An understanding of the lifecycle of the product is critical as to when it reaches end of use and end of life as well as the costs and environmental impacts of the product at each stage. Table 1.1 suggests that the four external environments may act as drivers to developing a sustainable supply chain as well as providing the context in which the supply chain operates. Therefore, a solid understanding of these factors and the ability to monitor them as they change over time is paramount to developing successful sustainable strategies. For example, the EU Waste Electrical and Electronic Equipment (WEEE) Directive has caused many manufacturers to reassess their production and supply chain activities in order to be compliant with the changes in the regulatory environment.

A sustainable supply chain must also consider both upstream and downstream firms. Supplier requirements and codes of conduct can be employed to ensure that suppliers and customers behave in socially and environmentally responsible ways. Further, sustainability is also about ensuring the source of the product. For example, do wood products that consumers purchase come from certified, sustainable forests as endorsed by Forest Stewardship Council (FSC) guidelines? Traceability and chain of custody capabilities are necessary to ensure this is the case, and this must be demonstrable to customers.

Internal operations are at the core of a firm's activities. Transformation and logistics activities provide a plethora of opportunities for firms to reduce their 'environmental footprint' through better waste management, reduction of hazardous substances, packaging reduction, efficient reverse logistics, and appropriate transportation.

Many firms are now using design for the environment programmes so that the environmental impact of their products at end-of-life will be minimized. Product stewardship means that a supply chain must increasingly accommodate the re-acquisition of product and the return flow of product/

parts up the supply chain for further disposition. These activities need to be designed into a sustainable supply chain from the earliest stages of product development.

Summary

Logistics and SCM have a major impact on the global economy as well as everyday life. The concepts of transportation or 'Go' and storage or 'Stop' activities enable the right products to be in the right place in an efficient and effective manner. However, while the trends of increased globalization, increased outsourcing and deeper relationships, more use of technology, lean and agile supply chain processes, and a one-way flow in the supply chain have assisted logistics and SCM activities, they have also been detrimental from a sustainability perspective. Emissions of greenhouse gases, use of fuel and other natural resources, other forms of pollution, and increased levels of waste from packaging are just some of these detriments.

There are several recurring themes regarding sustainable logistics and SCM that stem from works discussed above that tie in to these current trends for logistics and SCM. First, firms need to recognize that sustainability needs to form part of their logistics and supply chain strategies and for the right reasons – this theme is developed further in Chapters 8 and 9. Second, internal operations including transportation, warehousing and production need to be conducted as efficiently as possible. These elements of this theme feature in Chapters 3, 4 and 5 respectively. Third, relationships with upstream suppliers and downstream customers need to embrace sustainability. Chapter 6 discusses relationships with suppliers in the context of sustainable purchasing and procurement. Finally, what goes downstream in the supply chain must also come back upstream; hence reverse logistics is important and will be discussed in Chapter 7.

Some issues of sustainable logistics and supply chain activities have been examined over the past 15 years. However, they are becoming more important due to a realization that economic and environmental sustainability issues require urgent attention and that logistics and supply chain activities have a significant impact on the natural environment. The science of sustainability and its relationship to logistics and SCM will be discussed next in Chapter 2.

This domain is growing rapidly and many initiatives are underway to increase efficiencies in sustainability, particularly energy use and emissions. However, it is still under-developed and under-researched, particularly regarding tradeoffs between a sustainable supply chain and current logistical and supply chain practices that involve long, global one-way supply chains dependent on technology, outsourcing and time compression to meet ever-increasing customer demand for more and better products in a timely manner.

References

Abukhader, S M and Jönson, G (2004) Logistics and the environment: is it an established subject? *International Journal of Logistics: Research and Applications*, 7 (2), pp 137–149

Belkin (2016) WeMo home automation [online] http://www.belkin.com/us/Products/home-automation/c/wemo-home-automation/ [accessed 27 September 2016]

Böge, S (1995) The well-travelled yogurt pot: lessons for new freight transport policies and regional production, *World Transport Policy & Practice*, 1 (1), pp 7–11

Bowersox, D J, Closs, D J and Stank, T P (2000) Ten mega-trends that will revolutionize supply chain logistics, *Journal of Business Logistics*, 21 (2), pp 1–16

Boztas, S (2016) Amazon Dash: does the world really need more little pieces of plastic? *Guardian* [online] https://www.theguardian.com/sustainable-business/2016/sep/02/amazon-dash-buttons-plastic-waste-sustainable-consumption?CMP=Share_iOSApp_Other [accessed 8 September 2016]

Centre for Retail Research (2016) Online retailing: Britain, Europe, US and Canada 2016 [online] http://www.retailresearch.org/onlineretailing.php [accessed 19 August 2016]

ChainLink Research (2013) Home delivery for retailers: more sales, less cost [online] http://www.ChainLinkResearch.com/ [accessed 15 August 2015]

Clipper Logistics (2015) Boomerang: the future of returns management [online] http://www.clippergroup.co.uk/services/boomerang-the-future-of-returns-management/ [accessed 16 August 2015]

Commission for Integrated Transport (2007) *Transport and Climate Change: Advice to government from the Commission for Integrated Transport*, Commission for Integrated Transport, London

Corbett, J J, Winebrake, J J, Green, E H, Kasibhatla, P, Eyring, V and Laurer, A (2007) Mortality from ship emissions: a global assessment, *Environmental Science & Technology*, 41 (24), pp 8512–18

CSCMP (2016) http://www.cscmp.org/ [accessed 15 September 2016]

CSCMP's Supply Chain Quarterly (2011) A peek inside Wal-Mart Canada's 'green distribution center' [online] http://www.supplychainquarterly.com/print/20111221inside_walmarts_green_dc/ [accessed 26 December 2011]

Curran, M A (2006) *Life Cycle Assessment: Principles and practice*, EPA/600/ R-06/060, US

EC (2015) *Fact-finding studies in support of the development of an EU strategy for freight transport logistics Lot 1: Analysis of the EU logistics sector*, Contract Number FV355/2012/MOVE/D1/ETU/SI2.659384, European Commission, Brussels

Economist (2012) When the rubber hits the road, 30 June, p 78

Fernie, J and Grant, D B (2008) On-shelf availability: the case of a UK grocery retailer, *International Journal of Logistics Management*, **19** (3), pp 293–308

Fernie, J and Grant, D B (2015). *Fashion Logistics*, Kogan Page, London

Grant, D B (2012) *Logistics Management*, Pearson Education Limited, Harlow, UK

Grant, D B (2014) Trends in logistics and supply chain management: a focus on risk, *Journal of Supply Chain Management: Research and Practice*, **8** (2), pp 1–12

Grant, D B and Banomyong, R (2010) Design of closed-loop supply chain and product recovery management for fast-moving consumer goods: the case of a single-use camera, *Asia Pacific Journal of Marketing & Logistics*, **22** (2), pp 233–46

Honeywell (2016) Smart home technology: WiFi thermostats, Smarthome [online] http://www.smarthome.com/wifi-thermostat.html [accessed 27 September 2016]

Langley, C J and Capgemini Consulting (2010) 15th annual third-party logistics study [online] www.3plstudy.com/ [accessed 15 October 2012]

Larson, P D and Halldórsson, Á (2004) Logistics versus supply chain management: an international survey, *International Journal of Logistics: Research and Applications*, **7** (1), pp 17–31

letsrecycle.com (2013) Paper prices archive [online] http://www.letsrecycle. com/news/latest-news/paper/waste-paper-markets-see-fall-in-prices [accessed 5 January 2013]

Logistics Manager (2013) £53 billion cost of failed deliveries [online] http://www. logisticsmanager.com/Articles/20208/53+billion+cost+of+failed+deliveries.html [accessed 15 August 2015]

Mollenkopf, D (2006) Environmental sustainability: exploring the case for environmentally sustainable supply chains, *CSCMP Explores*, **3**, Fall/Winter, CSCMP, Lombard, IL

Naylor, J B, Naim, M M and Berry, D (1999) Leagility: integrating the lean and agile manufacturing paradigms in the total supply chain, *International Journal of Production Economics*, **62**, pp 107–18

ParcelSpace (2016) https://www.parcelspace.com/ [accessed 26 September 2016]

Petersen, R (2016) The iPhone's impact on air freight prices, *Flexport* [online] https://www.flexport.com/blog/the-iphones-impact-on-air-freight-prices/ [accessed 28 September 2016]

Purvis, L, Gosling, J and Naim, M M (2014) The development of a lean, agile and leagile supply network taxonomy based on differing types of flexibility, *International Journal of Production Economics*, **151**, pp 100–111

Rogers, D S and Tibben-Lembke, R S (1998) *Going backwards: reverse logistics trends and practices*, Reverse Logistics Executive Council, Reno, NV

Sandberg, U and Kalman, B (2005) *The poroelastic road surface: results of an experiment in Stockholm, Project Report SILVIA-VTI-006-WP4-030605*, Swedish National Road and Transport Research Institute (VTI), Linköping

Shaw, S, Grant, D B and Mangan, J (2010) Developing environmental supply chain performance measures, *Benchmarking: An International Journal*, **17** (3), pp 320–39

Stock, J R (1998) *Development and Implementation of Reverse Logistics Programs*, Council of Logistics Management, Oak Brook, IL

Sutherland, K and Gallagher, I (2009) Recycling crisis: taxpayers foot the bill for UK's growing waste paper mountain as market collapses, *Daily Mail* [online] http://www.dailymail.co.uk/news/article-1104741/Recycling-crisis-Taxpayers-foot-UKs-growing-waste-paper-mountain-market-collapses.html [accessed 5 January 2013]

Thierry, M, Salomon, M, Van Nunen, J and Van Wassenhove, L (1995) Strategic issues in product recovery management, *California Management Review*, **37** (2), pp 114–35

TOA Technologies (2011) Cost of waiting report [online] www.toatech.com [accessed 12 August 2015]

Van Kranenburg, R (2008) The Internet of Things: a critique of ambient technology and the all-seeing network of RFID, *Institute of Network Cultures* [online] http://www.networkcultures.org/_uploads/notebook2_theinternetofthings.pdf [accessed 19 September 2016]

Watkiss, P (2005) *The validity of food miles as an indicator of sustainable development: final report for the Department for Environment, Food & Rural Affairs (Defra) ED50254 Issue 7*, AEA Technology, Didcot, UK

Whitty, J (2008) Food miles and your carbon footprint, 21 April, *Mother Jones* [online] http://www.motherjones.com/blue-marble/2008/04/food-miles-your-carbon-footprint [accessed 19 November 2012]

Wieland, A, Handfield, R B and Durach, C F (2016) Mapping the landscape of future research themes in supply chain management, *Journal of Business Logistics*, **37** (3), pp 205–12

Wilson, R (2015) 26th Annual State of Logistics Report: freight moves the economy in 2014, *CSCMP* [online] http://www.cscmp.org/ [accessed 16 June 2016]

World Business Council for Sustainable Development (2007) Energy efficiency in buildings: business realities and opportunities [online] www.wbcsd.org [accessed 25 December 2012]

World Economic Forum (2009) *Supply Chain Decarbonization: The role of logistics and transport in reducing supply chain carbon emissions*, World Economic Forum, Geneva

Science of sustainability

02

Concepts of sustainability

Collins English Dictionary (1998) provides two definitions for sustainability: (1) capable of being sustained, ie of economic development, energy sources, etc, and (2) capable of being maintained at a steady level without exhausting natural resources or causing severe ecological damage, ie sustainable development. These two separate meanings highlight an important point that 'green is green', ie a firm's sustainability initiatives for the natural environment, or being green, need to be considered in conjunction with the economic case for long-term firm corporate sustainability, ie green being the colour of money. The placement of these definitions has not changed in almost 20 years. Collins Online (2016) still records them in the same order, but also provides a trend curve showing increasing usage of the word since the late 1980s – before that, the word was not in use at all.

Further, the second definition of sustainability relating to development raises the issue of consumption not only today but also for tomorrow. The philosopher John Rawls (1999) termed this issue 'intergenerational equity' whereby societies must justly determine how much of the earth's resources they will sacrifice or not use today in order that future generations will be able to access and enjoy such resources. This view helped shape a more widely used definition of sustainable development by Brundtland (1987) as development that meets the needs of the present without compromising the ability of future generations to meet their own needs.

Sustainability is linked to corporate social responsibility, as a socially responsible firm should ensure its impact on the natural environment is minimized. But CSR goes beyond the natural environment to include aspects of fair trade, good employment practices, and appropriate relationships with customers, suppliers and other stakeholders. The topic of CSR is discussed further in Chapter 8; however, the linkage with sustainability is manifested in John Elkington's (1994) 'triple bottom line' or TBL concept encompassing profits, the planet and people. The TBL posits that firms should focus on maximizing shareholder wealth or economic value they create while ensuring that they also add environmental and social value to achieve long-term natural environment security and proper working and living standards for all human beings. The TBL concept has found wide acceptance across firms, governments and non-governmental organizations (NGOs).

The natural environment has received attention for the past 40 years since the first UN Conference on the Human Environment at Stockholm in 1972. Since then there have been a number of events and meetings to raise the profile of the environment and climate change around the world including, inter alia, the Brundtland (1987) Commission, the initial UN 'Earth Summit' at Rio de Janeiro in 1992 which declared that polluters should pay the cost of pollution, the 1997 Kyoto Protocol which determined greenhouse gas emissions reduction targets for the world, and follow-on events such as the 2000 New York Millennium summit, the 2002 Johannesburg summit, the 2009 Copenhagen climate change conference and the 2012 Rio+20 conference.

Many of the later summits have not been considered successful; however, at the summit held in late 2015 in Paris, known as COP 21, nearly 200 countries signed a legal agreement that set ambitious goals to limit temperature rises to below 2 degrees Celsius, and to strive to keep temperatures at 1.5 degrees Celsius, above pre-industrial levels (Goldenberg et al, 2015). The agreement commits countries to peak greenhouse gas emissions as soon as possible, which likely means bringing down greenhouse gas emissions to net zero by 2030, and to seek a balance between human-caused emissions and removals by carbon sinks.

Wealthier nations also agreed to raise US $100 billion a year by 2020 to help developing nations transform their economies. For example, India has committed that at least 40 per cent of its electricity will be generated by non-fossil fuel sources by 2030, which will likely include 175 gigawatts (GW) of renewable energy capacity by 2022 (Associated Press, 2016). Manish Bapna, executive vice-president and managing director of the World Resources Institute, said India 'has one of the boldest renewable energy targets in the world, making it destined to be a major player in solar and wind markets'. However, funding will be crucial to achieving these targets; as India noted, it will need over US $2.5 trillion to meet them, and will depend on other countries giving it money and discounts on new technology.

Brundtland (1987) defined five key areas related to sustainability: species and ecosystems, energy, industry, food, and population and urban growth. These areas, plus the area of fresh water, form a holistic view of sustainability and will now be discussed in turn, including their respective relationship to logistics and SCM.

Species and ecosystems

Brundtland (1987) noted that the conservation of living natural resources – plants, animals, and micro-organisms and the non-living elements of the environment on which they depend – is crucial for development and that the conservation of wild living resources is now on the agenda of governments.

The climate system is a complex, interactive system consisting of the atmosphere, land surface, snow and ice, oceans and other bodies of water, and living things. For example, humans and animals require oxygen to breathe and live and exhale CO_2, whereas plants absorb CO_2 and convert it into oxygen in a process known as photosynthesis. This activity should maintain an ecosystem balance, but the removal of plants and trees or the extinction of species puts the ecosystem into imbalance.

Climate change can occur as a result of internal variability within the climate system and external variability (natural or anthropogenic). Natural variability includes phenomena such as volcanic eruptions and solar variations. Anthropogenic variability includes human-induced changes in the composition of the atmosphere, for example a change in the concentration of greenhouse gases (GHGs).

The greenhouse effect is a naturally occurring phenomenon and without it, life on earth could not exist, as it acts as a natural thermostat for the earth's atmosphere. Without a natural greenhouse effect, the temperature of the earth would be zero degrees F (–18°C) instead of its present 57°F (14°C) and a decline of 8–10°C would plunge Europe and North America into an ice age. Climatic observations over the past 150 years have shown that temperatures at the earth's surface have risen globally, with important regional variations. Most of the observed increase in global average temperatures since the mid-20th century is considered to be due to an observed increase in greenhouse gas concentrations (Shaw *et al*, 2010).

However, this may not be a new phenomenon. Cline (2014) argues that climate change, manifested by droughts and famines, has contributed to global conflict and the collapse of civilizations for over 3,000 years. One of Cline's most vivid examples comes from the Late Bronze Age – around

1200 BC – where a centuries-long drought in the Aegean and Eastern Mediterranean regions contributed to (if not caused) widespread famine, unrest and ultimately the destruction of many prosperous cities. Cline noted that research scientists have recently determined the length and severity of the drought by examining ancient pollen as well as oxygen and carbon isotope data drawn from alluvial and mineral deposits; their conclusions were corroborated by correspondence, inscribed and fired on clay tablets, dating from that time. Ancient letters from the Hittite kingdom (now modern-day Turkey) '... beseeched neighbouring powers for shipments of grain to stave off famine caused by the drought... one letter, sent from a Hittite king, pleads for help: It is a matter of life or death!' National security for the powers of the age was also affected. A letter sent to the king of Ugarit (on the coast of modern-day Syria) advised '... be on the lookout for the enemy and make yourself very strong!' This advice probably came too late as another letter from the same time notes: '... when your messenger arrived, the army was humiliated and the city was sacked... our food in the threshing floors was burned and the vineyards were also destroyed... our city is sacked... may you know it!' Cline concludes that we live in a world that has more similarities to that of the Late Bronze Age than one might suspect, including an 'increasingly homogeneous yet uncontrollable global economy and culture' where 'political uncertainties on one side of the world can drastically affect the economies of regions thousands of miles away'. Whether our civilization collapses like the Late Bronze Age into the Dark Ages remains to be seen, but it is useful to note the parallels.

An article appearing in an issue of *Nature* (Farman *et al*, 1985) documented a large seasonal disappearance of ozone from the earth's atmosphere over Antarctica. Immediately following the *Nature* publication, 20 nations signed the Vienna Convention which established a framework for negotiating international regulations on ozone-depleting substances. In 1988, the Intergovernmental Panel on Climate Change (IPCC) was set up jointly by the World Meteorological Organization and the United Nations Environment Programme (UNEP) to provide an authoritative international statement of scientific understanding of climate change. This action and subsequent work have determined that the need to reduce GHG emissions is the greatest long-term ecosystem challenge facing the world today.

The six major greenhouse gases (Shaw *et al*, 2010) include CO_2, methane (CH_4), nitrous oxides (N_2O), hydrofluorocarbons (HFC), perfluorocarbons (PFC) and sulphur hexafluoride (SF_6). CO_2 is the most significant of these greenhouse gases and is the main contributor to global warming. The 1997

Kyoto Protocol, the initial meeting of the world's nations to address climate change issues, legally bound industrialized nations to reduce emissions of GHGs, particularly CO_2, to an average of 5.2 per cent below 1990 baseline levels by 2012. The aim of this legislation, as well as various climate change bills in the EU and UK, is to maintain global carbon dioxide levels below 450 parts per million (ppm) and limit the temperature rise to no more than 2 degrees Celsius by 2012. These goals have been superseded by subsequent conferences and the COP 21 summit in Paris in 2015, as discussed above, and a sense of urgency has been posited by some.

Kahn (2016) considers that history will 'look back on September 2016 as a major milestone for the world's climate... at a time when atmospheric carbon dioxide is usually at its minimum, the monthly value failed to drop below 400 parts per million.' September is usually the month when CO_2 is at its lowest after a summer of plants growing and absorbing it in the northern hemisphere. As the autumn commences, those plants lose their leaves, which in turn decompose and release the stored CO_2 back into the atmosphere. At Mauna Loa Observatory, the world's primary site for monitoring CO_2, the indications were that levels were already above 400 ppm before the process began. Further, 2016 was also set to be the hottest year on record and the earth has edged up against the 1.5 degrees Celsius warming threshold, which is a key metric in the Paris COP 21 agreement.

The UK government committed to reducing GHG emissions to at least 12.5 per cent below the Kyoto baseline by the same dates, but then also set a tougher long-term goal in the Climate Change Act of 2008 to reduce CO_2 emissions by 80 per cent by 2050 through five budget periods. The UK is currently in the second budget period of the Act (2013–17) where emissions must be 27 per cent lower than 1990 and has made good progress towards its targets. It has achieved almost a 38 per cent reduction in emissions since 1990, which is ahead of the third budget and also substantial when compared with cuts achieved by other nations (HSBC, 2016). Much of this reduction has been generated through better energy efficiency and the retirement of coal- and oil-fired power stations.

Concerns in the logistics and SCM space about increased greenhouse gases such as pollution, traffic congestion, global warming, disposal and the clean-up of hazardous materials have led to a number of environmental laws and EU directives that affect logistics systems design and strategies. GHG emissions, particularly CO_2, have been the focus of much work in logistics and SCM, particularly consumer and freight transport. The UK's domestic carbon dioxide emissions, excluding international aviation and shipping, are generated from four main sectors (Commission for Integrated

Transport, 2007): the energy supply sector (40 per cent), all modes in the transport sector (25 per cent), the industrial sector including manufacturing, retailing, services and warehousing (20 per cent) and the residential sector (15 per cent).

Examining the transport sector in more detail, private automobiles are the primary source of carbon dioxide emissions (54 per cent) followed by heavy goods trucks or lorries (22 per cent) and vans (13 per cent). Thus, truck and van freight transportation in the UK accounts for less than 9 per cent of total carbon dioxide emissions. This is consistent with worldwide estimations of 8 per cent for transport; warehousing and goods handling worldwide are estimated to add about 4 per cent to that total (McKinnon *et al*, 2012).

However, the UK's total transportation emissions have risen 11 per cent from the Kyoto baseline of 1990; faster than any other sector, despite efficiencies in fuel use and emissions. This situation is due primarily to the growth in freight transport activity and is again consistent with predicted growth in freight transport, particularly road freight, all over the globe (World Business Council for Sustainable Development, 2007a). Freight transport issues will be discussed in depth in Chapter 3, while warehousing and manufacturing and production will be discussed in Chapters 4 and 5 respectively.

Climate change due to GHGs is continually being discussed by the media and at international conferences, and major reports are issued regularly on the steps to combat it by organizations such as the IPCC. However, proper and accurate measurement, particularly regarding alternative trade-offs and decisions, remains difficult. A recent study to determine an economic value for carbon storage and CO_2 is discussed in the following box.

Banking on carbon: the economic impact of the natural environment

A report by the David Suzuki Foundation based in Vancouver, Canada has demonstrated the economic value of maintaining a massive carbon storehouse of trees and plants to reduce carbon through the photosynthesis process (Tomalty, 2012). A massive greenbelt in southern Ontario, Canada encompasses some 750,000 hectares (1.8 million acres) around the western end of Lake Ontario in an area known as the Greater

Golden Horseshoe (GGH). The GGH greenbelt contains natural features such as Niagara Falls and the adjacent Niagara Escarpment that runs north towards Lake Huron and the Oak Ridges Moraine system north of Toronto.

Within and surrounding these natural features are farms, forests and wetlands. The forests comprise about 24 per cent of the greenbelt and are estimated to 'bank' 40 million tonnes of carbon or the equivalent of 147 million tonnes of carbon dioxide while the wetlands 'bank' about almost 7 million tonnes of carbon or 25 million tonnes of CO_2. The total amount of CO_2 from both these sources is equivalent to the annual emissions of 33 million cars and trucks.

The study in the report estimated there are about 87 million tonnes of carbon being stored in the GGH greenbelt. Using an average peer-reviewed estimate of CAD $53 per tonne of carbon, this greenbelt's carbon value is about $4.5 billion. Considered as an annuity over 20 years, the carbon value is $370 million per year. Further, the GGH greenbelt's 'natural capital' produces $2.6 billion a year in critical ecosystem services, for example water storage and filtration, and plant pollination, or about $3,470 per greenbelt hectare.

These values allow for cost trade-offs to be considered when alternative land use is proposed. Removing any parts of the GGH greenbelt for other use such as industry or housing will release its banked or stored carbon into the atmosphere and thus have a negative impact on the natural environment. The GGH region is under tremendous pressure for growth; the report notes that by 2031 the population is expected to grow from its current 9 million to 11.5 million and an additional 107,000 hectares (257,000 acres), or just over 14 per cent of the current GGH greenbelt, will be urbanized.

Conversely, any attempt to increase the GGH greenbelt's ability to store carbon also represents a positive environmental value that can be accounted for as 'carbon offsets' and traded against carbon release or generation.

For example, there are around 7,100 farms in the greenbelt that generate CAD $1.5 billion in annual earnings. If the Ontario provincial government introduces a carbon cap and carbon-trading system, farmers could create carbon offsets by planting more trees or adopting no-till farming techniques to plant crops and control weeds without turning the soil and thus releasing carbon.

However, caution must be used when considering any such initiatives. Although golf courses provide carbon capture and storage through their vegetative land cover, ongoing maintenance operations including cutting regularly and applying fertilizers and pesticides generate CO_2 emissions. Golf courses also use large amounts of water for irrigation, often drawing this resource directly from rivers, streams or groundwater. Such water use puts strain on existing hydrologic systems. The Oak Ridges Moraine system, which serves as an essential groundwater discharge and recharge area for millions of Ontarians and a direct drinking water source for over 250,000 residents, already has 41 golf courses in place and plans for more would exacerbate ecological issues.

The David Suzuki Foundation report is useful as it provides a methodology to enhance discussions about the measurement of carbon and CO_2 and alternative strategies in order to provide an economic and ecological balance in southern Ontario society, as well as provide a framework for application in other areas around the globe.

SOURCES Kidd (2012); Tomalty (2012).

Energy

Energy is necessary for daily survival as it provides heat for warmth, cooking and manufacturing, or power for transport and mechanical work. Conventional energy sources for these services have included fossil fuels such as oil and gas, coal, nuclear, wood and other primary sources such as solar, wind, or water power. Primary energy sources used around the globe continue to be mainly non-renewable: oil, natural gas, coal, peat, and nuclear power. The resources used for such sources, ie crude oil, coal, peat and uranium, will eventually run out through depletion.

An important question that relates to Rawls' 'intergenerational equity' is 'when will the point occur where these resources are used up?' Certainly, as these resources become scarcer the cost to extract them and thus market prices and costs for users will both increase, prompting what economists call a 'threshold price' or the point where users will switch to a lower-cost alternative. There has been a concern over the past 40 years that daily production of oil and natural gas will soon be exceeded by daily demand, ie the concept of 'peak oil'; however, the following box suggests otherwise.

When will we run out of oil?

The concept of peak oil argues that global oil production will peak relative to increasing demand such that supply will be insufficient for all needs, which would trigger massive price increases and perhaps rationing. However, while oil prices increased during the early 2000s and widespread oil reservoir depletion suggested that the globe had passed the peak oil point, it is not yet clear if that is in fact the case.

Some argue that we have seen this all before: in 1975, MK Hubbert, a Shell geoscientist, successfully predicted a decline in US oil production and suggested that global supplies would peak in 1995, while in 1997 the petroleum geologist Colin Campbell estimated it would happen before 2010. And now a report by Leonardo Maugeri published by the Harvard Kennedy School argues that a new oil boom is taking place. Maugeri's thesis is that price rises in the early 2000s stimulated exploration in higher-cost, marginal oil fields and that a net additional capacity of over 17 million barrels of oil per day (mbd) to around 110 mbd will be added to global supplies by 2020. Average global production in 2015 was about 95.7 mbd, or about 102 per cent of 2015's average demand of 93.4 mbd. Daily production in 2011 was about 88 mbd.

Conventional oil production is continuing to grow throughout the world, although some areas of the world such as the United States, Canada and the North Sea are witnessing an apparently irreversible decline in conventional production. These areas, however, are enjoying a boom in unconventional oil production from tar sands and shale oil. It is estimated that the Bakken shale oil reservoir in the US state of North Dakota contains almost as much oil as Saudi Arabia, although much of this oil cannot be extracted. However, the application of shale oil extraction technologies, such as horizontal drilling and hydraulic fracturing, to conventional oilfields could further increase the world's oil production.

Maugeri argues that a 'revolution' in environmental and emission-curbing technologies is required to sustain the development of most unconventional oils along with strong enforcement of existing rules. Without such a revolution, a continuous clash between the oil industry and environmental groups will force governments to delay or constrain the development of new projects with the average price of oil hovering around US $45 per barrel in 2016. The Carbon Tracker Initiative foresaw in 2015 that any oil price slide would make many unconventional and high-cost oil projects uneconomical. It identified US $1.1 trillion of potential capital expenditure for projects over the next 10 years that would require a market price of over US $95 per barrel to provide an acceptable rate of return and which may be deferred or cancelled. For example, Norway's Statoil has relinquished three exploration licences off Greenland's west coast, Chevron has put its Arctic drilling plans on hold, and in the Canadian oil sands oil companies have cancelled or deferred billions of dollars' worth of projects (Hobley, 2016). In contrast, renewable energy has exhibited falling costs, zero price volatility, lower carbon emissions and superior security of supply as an indigenous energy source for many countries including the UK. Investment in clean energy through 2014 beat expectations despite the falling oil price. Surges in investment in offshore wind in Europe and solar in China and the United States helped to increase global clean energy investment by 16 per cent to US $310 billion.

Some of the major geopolitical consequences of Maugeri's report include Asia becoming the reference market for the bulk of Middle East oil with China becoming a new protagonist in the political affairs of the whole region. At the same time, the western hemisphere could return to a pre-World War II status of theoretical oil self-sufficiency and the United States could dramatically reduce its oil import needs. However, quasi-oil self-sufficiency will not insulate the United States from the rest of the global oil market and world oil prices. Further, Canada, Venezuela and Brazil may decide to export their oil and gas production to markets other than the United States for purely commercial reasons, making the notion of western hemisphere self-sufficiency irrelevant.

Thus, Maugeri concludes that oil is not in short supply from a purely physical point of view; there are huge volumes of conventional and unconventional oils still to be developed with no 'peak oil' in sight. He suggests instead that real problems concerning future oil production are 'above the surface, not beneath it, and relate to political decisions and geopolitical instability'. While the age of 'cheap oil' is over, it is still uncertain what the future level of oil prices might be as technology may turn today's expensive oil into tomorrow's cheap oil.

However, George Monbiot worries that the automatic environmental correction mechanism – resource depletion destroying the machine that was driving it – is not going to happen. The problem of too much instead of too little oil generates a conflict between the planet's natural systems and industrial and consumer capitalism as there are no obvious means or reasons to prevail upon governments and industry to leave oil in the ground to prevent climate breakdown, as evidenced by the collapse of multilateral discussions at the UN Conference on Sustainable Development (Rio +20) in June 2012. In summary, when will the earth run out of oil? And more importantly, how will that uncertainty affect environmental issues going forward?

SOURCES Hobley (2016); Maugeri (2012); Monbiot (2012); US Energy Information Administration (2016).

Renewable sources include wood, plants, dung, falling or gravity-fed water for hydroelectric or mechanical energy, geothermal sources, solar, offshore and onshore wind, biomass or biofuels, and tidal and wave energy. The latter five sources are relatively new, with only about 20–30 years of operational experience at the most, and are still higher-cost alternatives until economies of scale take effect.

Each source has its own economic, health and environmental costs, benefits and risk factors that interact strongly with other governmental and global priorities. Key factors for energy sustainability include sufficient growth of energy supplies to meet human and industrial needs, energy efficiency and conservation measures so that the waste of primary resources is minimized, public health by recognizing safety risks inherent in energy sources such as radiation from nuclear sources, and protection of the biosphere by prevention of pollution.

The growth of global primary energy demand in response to industrialization, urbanization, and societal affluence has led to a greater than 35 per cent increase in total consumption from all sources of just under 10,000 million tonnes of oil equivalent (Mtoe) in 2000 to about 13,500 Mtoe in 2015 (Enerdata, 2016). There is also an uneven distribution of energy consumption across the globe as shown in Tables 2.1 and 2.2. The highest energy-consuming countries by far in 2011 were China with 3,101 Mtoe and the United States with 2,196 Mtoe. The lowest-consuming countries were New Zealand with 21 Mtoe and Portugal with 22 Mtoe.

Table 2.1 Highest energy-consuming countries in 2015

Country	Energy Consumption (Mtoe)
China	3,101
United States	2,196
India	882
Russia	718
Japan	435
Germany	305
Brazil	299
South Korea	280
Canada	251
France	246

SOURCE Enerdata (2016).

Table 2.2 Lowest energy-consuming countries in 2015

Country	Energy Consumption (Mtoe)
Sweden	47
Uzbekistan	45
Czech Republic	40
Kuwait	38
Chile	38
Colombia	34
Romania	33
Norway	32
Portugal	22
New Zealand	21

SOURCE Enerdata (2016).

Halldórsson and Svanberg (2013) note that there are two purposes for energy. One is to power various operations processes such as storage (or 'Stop') and production and transportation of goods (or 'Go') for use and consumption. On the energy input side of logistics and SCM, trucks and vans use fuel-burning engines as their motive source. However, vehicle engines are becoming more efficient in terms of fuel use and emissions and there are ongoing efforts to consider alternative fuels such as biodiesel or bioethanol, hydrogen, natural gas or liquid petroleum gas, and electricity (McKinnon *et al*, 2015). Some of these developments are still in their infancy, just like newer sources of renewable energy, and also have their own environmental impacts. For example, growing crops for biofuels requires the use of arable land which displaces growing crops for food. A response to that situation might see farmers cultivating more forests and grasslands for food production, thus possibly negating the positive effects of greenhouse gas emissions reductions from using biofuels.

The second purpose (Halldórsson and Svanberg, 2013) is energy that is embedded in physical products, eg electricity through assembly such as energy consumption for vehicle assembly, or via their material content such as oil used in consumer products. These purposes also affect service provision. For example, energy includes mobility, eg transport, heating, eg households and warehouse facilities, and cooling, eg storing of drugs and food.

The World Business Council for Sustainable Development (2007b) notes that warehousing, as one aspect of the manufacturing and industrial sector, accounts for 40 per cent of worldwide energy use. Initiatives to increase the efficiency of building in using energy and reducing emissions have been developed by the Leadership in Energy and Environmental Design certification program (LEED) in the United States and the Building Research Establishment Environmental Assessment Method (BREEAM) in the UK (McKinnon *et al*, 2015). Such accreditations consider the following categories of building sustainability: the indoor environment quality including lighting, the materials and resources used in construction, the energy source and building atmosphere including electricity use, sustainable building sites, and water use efficiency. The ultimate goal for a sustainable building is a net zero operation where a building uses little or no outside energy or resources at all, for example by generating its own electricity through solar power, recycling and reusing waste water. This topic will be further discussed in Chapter 4.

Industry

Industry is central to the economies of modern societies and is an important engine of growth. It is also essential for developing countries to widen their development base and meet growing needs, for example China and India in the last decade. Essential human 'needs' such as food, shelter, clothing and white goods or appliances, as well as non-essential 'wants' such as luxury goods and package vacations, can be met only through goods and services provided by industry.

Economic development is fundamentally a process of structural transformation and involves the transformation of productive factors from traditional to modern agriculture, industry and services, and the reallocation of those factors among industrial and service sector activities. This process involves shifting resources from low- to high-productivity sectors to be successful in accelerating economic growth (UN Department of Economic and Social Affairs, 2007). Essentially, sustained economic growth is associated with the capacity to diversify domestic production structure, ie to generate new activities, strengthen economic linkages within the country, and create domestic technological capabilities.

Since the end of the World War II, modern industrial policies have led to rapid growth in the developing world through such diversification of production into manufacturing and services. The business management mantra of outsourcing manufacturing to low-cost, global producers during the 1960s and 1970s, coupled with a reduction in transportation and communication costs combined with corresponding increases in technological power especially computing and data processing power, has led to a physical disintegration of production. Because of lower transaction costs, different components of final product are now manufactured in several different countries. The product may then be assembled in yet another country and finally distributed worldwide. This means that, to get products or services to the market, it is now important to tap into the global production and supply chains now operating in the 21st century (UN Department of Economic and Social Affairs, 2007). This structural transformation is also known as the two great 'unbundlings'.

The first unbundling is the end of the necessity to produce goods close to consumers. This transformation has been accelerated by the rapid decline in transportation regulation and costs during the last four decades, particularly with the widespread use of containers and bulk carriers. Thus, the impact has been that much manufacturing production, especially of the more standard and labour-intensive goods, has been transferred to developing countries with lower labour costs. The second unbundling is the end of the need to perform most manufacturing stages near each other. This has been made possible by rapidly falling costs of telecommunications, the possibility of codifying and digitizing tasks and increasing data processing power to turn such data into information. The resultant impact has been that many service tasks supporting manufacturing as well as other services, such as back-office accounting and customer service support, have been sent offshore to countries with lower labour costs.

Table 2.3 Comparison estimated gross domestic product (purchasing power parity) in 2015

Country	GDP (US $ trillion)	Percentage World GDP
World	113.7	100.0
China	19.4	17.1
European Union 28	19.2	16.9
United States	18.0	15.8
India	8.0	7.0
Japan	4.8	4.2
Germany	3.8	3.3
Russia	3.7	3.2
Brazil	3.2	2.8

SOURCE CIA (2016).

The shift to offshore facilities has led to significant growth in developing countries such as China, India and Southeast Asia. Total gross domestic product (GDP) at purchasing power parity, representing the sum value of all goods and services produced in the country valued at prices prevailing in the United States, was estimated across the globe in 2015 at US $113.7 trillion, as shown in Table 2.3 (CIA, 2016). The three major geographic regions that account for the bulk of this economic activity are China with 17.1 per cent of world GDP, the 28 member states of the European Union (EU) with 16.9 per cent, and the United States with 15.8 per cent. However, three other countries worthy of note are India (7.0 per cent), Russia (3.7 per cent) and Brazil (3.2 per cent). These three plus China make up the so-called 'BRIC' group that have been presented over the last decade as rapidly developing countries. In fact, China has been the best performer of the four and now leads the world ahead of the EU and United States in terms of GDP.

A method to compare the logistics performance of various countries to their GDP performance is the World Bank Logistics Performance Index (Arvis *et al*, 2016) or LPI. The LPI is a multidimensional assessment of logistics performance rated on weighted average scale of individual country scores on six key dimensions with a maximum score of 5.0 (one being the worst and five being the best). The six dimensions are the efficiency of clearance processes, quality of trade and transport-related infrastructure, the ease of arranging competitively priced shipments, the competence and quality of logistics services, the

Table 2.4   World Bank logistics performance index 2016

Country	Rank	LPI Score
Germany	1	4.23
Luxembourg	2	4.22
Sweden	3	4.20
Netherlands	4	4.19
Singapore	5	4.14
Belgium	6	4.11
Austria	7	4.10
United Kingdom	8	4.07
Hong Kong SAR, China	9	4.07
United States	10	3.99
Norway	7	3.96
Japan	10	3.91
China	27	3.66
India	35	3.42
Brazil	55	3.09
Russian Federation	99	2.57

SOURCE Arvis *et al* (2016).

ability to track and trace consignments, and the timeliness of shipments in reaching their destination within a scheduled or expected delivery time. In 2016, the top five countries as shown in Table 2.4 were Germany (4.23 LPI score), Luxembourg (4.22), Sweden (4.20), Netherlands (4.19) and Singapore (4.14). In comparison, the four BRIC countries were ranked as follows: China 27th (3.66), India 35th (3.42), Brazil 55th (3.09) and Russia 99th (2.57).

One way of considering these differences is that those countries that have both high GDP and LPI values are highly efficient in terms of production and logistics and SCM. However, both the EU and the United States are more efficient in their logistics activities as represented by LPI scores and in economic performance as represented by their GDP standings. Further, that does not necessarily translate into efficient or better sustainability. The countries emitting the most CO_2 in 2012 according to the US Energy Information Administration were China and the United States at 8.0 and 5.5 billion tonnes respectively (EIA, 2015). Hence, it is significant that both were signatories to the COP 21 agreement in Paris in late 2015.

Industrial processes themselves remain very much the same, albeit enhanced by recent manufacturing techniques such as lean production and just-in-time (JIT). Industry extracts materials from the natural resource base, such as minerals and energy resources discussed above and, coupled, with financial and human resources, develops products for market. However, coupled with this activity is the production and distribution of pollution into the human environment.

Issues of depletion also affect non-energy inputs for industry, such as iron, copper and rare earth elements, and the concept of 'peak' also applies to them. The British Geological Survey (2016) publishes an annual Risk List for chemical elements or element groups that possess economic value and are necessary to maintain our economy and lifestyle. The numerical ranking value on the Risk List is an index score reflecting seven criteria: scarcity, production concentration, reserve distribution, recycling rate, substitutability, and governance of both the top-producing and reserve-hosting nations.

In 2012 those elements considered at high or very high risk, ie with index scores greater than 8.5, were rare earth elements: antimony, bismuth, germanium, vanadium and gallium. The top reserve holder and leading producer for all these elements except germanium and gallium is China. China is also the leading global producer of all the elements listed above and in fact is the leading producer of 15 of the top 20 high-risk elements on the Risk List.

The Risk List gives an indication of which elements or groups may be subject to supply disruption resulting from human factors such as geopolitics, resources nationalism, strikes, accidents and lack of sufficient reserves. The British Geological Survey's message for firms and countries is to develop diversified supplies of primary resources and make full use of secondary or substitute resources and recycling to reduce intensity of resource use. Such activities will also impact current logistics and supply chain designs and operations.

Food

The UN's Food and Agriculture Organization (2012) reported that about 870 million people in the world suffered from undernourishment in the period 2010–12, representing 12.5 per cent of the global population or one in eight people. While still unacceptably high, this overall amount is a decrease from amounts at the turn of the millennium. However, there are considerable differences among regions and individual countries remain, as about 852 million undernourished people live in developing countries.

For the periods between 1990–92 and 2010–12, the shares of southeastern and eastern Asia saw the most marked decline, from 13.4 to 7.5 per cent and from 26.1 to 19.2 per cent respectively, while Latin America also declined from 6.5 to 5.6 per cent. Meanwhile, shares increased from 32.7 to 35.0 per cent in Southern Asia, 17.0 to 27.0 per cent in sub-Saharan Africa, and 1.3 to 2.9 per cent in Western Asia and Northern Africa.

However, the effects of climate change may prevent further declines in undernourishment due to crop failures, drought and rising prices. World cereal production declined in 2012/13 to 2.27 billion metric tonnes as a result of summer drought, particularly in the United States. By harvest time in late 2012, the US Department of Agriculture estimated that the production of corn, soybeans, sorghum and hay was down 27.5 per cent, 16 per cent, 26.5 per cent and 9 per cent respectively. However, world production has since recovered and estimates for 2015/16 were 2.47 billion metric tonnes (Statista, 2016).

The most severe and extensive drought in 25 years seriously affected US agriculture in 2012, with impacts on the crop and livestock sectors and with the potential to affect food prices at the retail level (USDA Economic Research Service, 2012). The drought destroyed or damaged a significant portion of US agriculture in 2012 – about 80 per cent of agricultural land and 60 per cent of farms – which was more extensive than any drought since the 1950s. This drought led to increased retail prices for beef, pork, poultry, and dairy products well into 2013. But in the short term, drought conditions also led to herd culling in response to higher feed costs with resulting short-term meat supply increases.

Lawrence (2016) argues that overuse of agrochemicals in intensive farming practices to increase farm yields has contributed to losses in biodiversity and pollinators vital to food as increases in pest resistance threaten to reverse previous gains in yields. She notes that while research has found that over a short period yields per hectare for individual crops are greater in intense agricultural systems, over a longer period more mixed and diverse farming produces more when considering total farm output. As an example of this intensity, British farmers typically treat each wheat crop over its growing cycle with four fungicides, three herbicides, one insecticide and one chemical to control molluscs. They buy seed that has been pre-coated with chemicals against insects, spray the land with weedkiller before and after planting and apply chemical growth regulators to control the height and strength of the grain's stem. They spray against aphids and mildew during the growing season and often spray just before harvesting with the herbicide glyphosate to desiccate the crop which saves energy costs of mechanical drying.

Lawrence proposes there are other different and more ecological visions for future farming and food. One example is a large-scale horticultural export company based on Kenya's Lake Naivasha in Africa. The company, Flamingo Homegrown, has abandoned its use of chemical pesticides in response to a campaign highlighting their effect on workers' health and also in recognition they were on a losing treadmill of spraying and pest resistance. Flamingo have reinvented their agriculture by employing groups of highly trained African scientists to study and reproduce in labs the fungi and mycorrhizae present in healthy soil that form intricate links with plant roots. Thus, they are working to harness the land's immensely complex ecosystems rather than waging chemical war on it, and have built vast greenhouses dedicated to breeding and harvesting ladybirds to control pests biologically rather than chemically.

Coupled with such production issues, Tristram Stuart (2009) noted that approximately 40 million tonnes of food are wasted by households, retailers and food services each year. This amount of food would be enough to satisfy the hunger of every one of the 870 million people worldwide suffering from undernourishment. Further, irrigation water used globally to grow food that is wasted would be enough for the domestic needs of 9 billion people at 200 litres per person per day, or the number expected on the planet by 2050. Trees planted on land currently used to grow unnecessary surplus and wasted food would theoretically offset 100 per cent of GHG emissions from fossil fuel combustion.

Stuart (2009) argues that the United States and Europe, including the UK, have nearly twice as much food as is required for the nutritional needs of their populations and that up to half the entire food supply is wasted between the farm and the fork. Further, UK households waste 25 per cent of all the food they buy. The fishing industry is also not immune to waste, according to Stuart. Around 2.3 million tonnes of fish are discarded in the North Atlantic and the North Sea each year; 40 to 60 per cent of all fish caught in Europe are discarded either because they are the wrong size, species, or because of the European quota system.

While Stuart is an activist, the facts behind his arguments have cogency and are voiced by others. One element of waste that is not discussed in depth is the inefficiency of logistics and supply chain activities to deal with this food. For example, France has legislated that supermarkets must donate unsold food to charities or for animal feed rather than destroying or throwing it away (Chrisafis, 2015). This was sparked by official estimates that the average French person throws out 20.3 kilograms (kg) of food per year, of which 7 kg is still in its original packaging. The 7.1 million tonnes wasted across France comes primarily from consumers (67 per cent), restaurants (15 per cent) and shops (11 per cent). An example of using food that would otherwise be wasted in the supply chain for people in poverty in Austria is discussed in the following box.

Social supermarkets to prevent food waste and poverty

Nearly 80 million people, or 16 per cent of the European Union's population, live below a 'poverty line', where their monthly resources do not allow them to afford basic goods for living, including sufficient amounts of nutritious food. The Austrian government has defined its national poverty threshold as a monthly net income of 900 Euros for a one-person household and about 13 per cent of its population belongs to that group. One development undertaken to address the food issue is social supermarkets (SSMs), the first of which was opened in Linz in 1999 as a private initiative by four families.

The objectives of an SSM are to prevent consumable food and household products from turning into waste, to help people who are financially at risk or in poverty, and to support the re-integration of unemployed people into society. SSMs are similar to traditional supermarkets as they sell food and consumer products and offer similar in-store services, as opposed to 'food banks' that simply give food away. However, there are three main differences between an SSM and a traditional supermarket.

First, SSMs provide a very limited assortment of food and household products such as cosmetics or cleaning products. Their offered merchandise is surplus products given for free by food producers, processors and retailers. These products are still consumable, but are no longer merchantable as they are too close to an expiration date, have wrong labelling, or have slightly damaged packaging. Second, access to an SSM is limited to people at risk of poverty or who are already below the poverty threshold; this access is controlled with the help of identification cards that are issued according to the official income status and card holders are only able to spend a maximum of 30 Euros over a maximum of three visits per week. Lastly, shelf prices are significantly lower, with approximately 50–70 per cent off regular supermarket prices.

Services in an SSM are provided by volunteers as well as employees who are part of specific employment programmes; the key objective with the latter is to re-integrate people who are long-term unemployed.

The training and knowledge needed to run a supermarket operation are provided by suppliers and retailers, who later welcome employees of SSMs into their internal training programmes. The number of SSMs has increased to 80, located in every major Austrian city, with about 20 mobile SSMs supplying rural areas; the seventh SSM opened in Vienna in early 2012. SSMs represent a 1.5 per cent national share when compared to the 5,600 mainstream supermarkets in Austria.

From a sustainability perspective, large amounts of food and consumer products end up in Austria's public waste system. The Austrian Institute of Ecology has found that some 70 tonnes of food, or about 40 kilograms per capita, are thrown away in Vienna alone every year. Food waste stemming from private households comprises leftovers from preparing meals. However, the majority of food waste is products in original packaging or broken-up packaging.

Food waste from food producers or supermarkets usually comes in very large quantities of one kind, eg milk products, fruits or vegetables. It has been estimated that between 3 and 8 per cent of the value of food products along the entire food supply chain has the potential to be rescued for further consumption.

From a supply chain management point of view, SSM activity takes place at the very end of the supply chain process. This supply chain is more about onward distribution to a new location for the further use of products and waste reduction than it is about reverse logistics. However, the process involves a complex logistical redistribution of goods and many of the reverse logistics issues discussed in Chapter 8 will apply in this context.

SSMs have merit from a corporate and social responsibility perspective; they offer people in or near poverty a real opportunity to eat healthily and maintain dignity while reducing the vast amount of perfectly consumable food that goes to waste due to operational considerations.

SOURCES National Public Radio (2013); Holweg and Lienbacher (2010).

Population and urban growth

The current world population is almost 7 billion and the UN's median population forecast is 9.3 billion by 2050, with a variance range 2.5 billion – the total world population in 1950 – depending on the methodology used.

Every new person on earth requires additional food, water and energy and produces additional waste and pollution, thus increasing the total impact on the planet and decreasing everyone else's share (Martin, 2011).

The point is that indefinite population growth is physically impossible on a finite planet – it will certainly stop at some point. Maurice Strong, secretary general of the 1992 Earth Summit in Rio noted that either we reduce our population numbers voluntarily or nature will brutally do it for us. On a finite planet, the optimum population providing the best quality of life for all is clearly much smaller than the maximum, which only permits bare survival. An expansion in population can also increase the pressure on resources as noted above and slow the rise in living standards in areas where deprivation is widespread. Though the issue is not merely one of population size but of the distribution of resources, sustainable development can only be pursued if demographic developments are in harmony with the changing productive potential of the ecosystem as discussed above.

Growth has no set limits in terms of population or resource use and beyond that ecological disaster lies in wait. There are different limits for the use of energy, other resources, water and land. Many of these will manifest themselves in the form of rising costs and diminishing returns, rather than in the form of any sudden loss of a resource base. Also, the accumulation of knowledge and the development of technology can enhance the carrying capacity of the resource base. But there are ultimate limits and sustainability requires that long before these are reached the world must ensure equitable access to constrained resources and reorient technological efforts to relieve bottlenecks through better management or substitution.

Urbanization, the demographic transition from rural to urban, is associated with shifts from an agriculture-based economy to mass industry, technology and service. For the first time ever, the majority of the world's population lives in a city, and this proportion continues to grow. One hundred years ago, two out of every ten people lived in an urban area, but as of 2010, this accounts for more than half of all people. By 2030, six out of every ten people will live in a city, and by 2050, this proportion will increase to seven out of ten people, or 6.5 billion of the 9.3 billion predicted. Currently, around half of all urban dwellers live in cities with between 100,000 and 500,000 people, and fewer than 10 per cent of urban dwellers live in megacities, which are defined by UN HABITAT as a city with a population of more than 10 million.

Almost all urban population growth during the next 40 years will occur in cities of developing countries. Between 1995 and 2005, the urban population of developing countries grew by an average of 1.2 million people per week, or around 165,000 people every day. By the middle of the 21st century, it is estimated that the urban population of these countries will more than double, increasing from 2.5 billion in 2009 to almost 5.2 billion in 2050 (World Health Organization, 2012).

The satisfaction of human needs and wants is the major objective of development. The essential needs of vast numbers of people in developing countries for food, clothing, shelter and jobs are not being met, and beyond their basic needs, these people have legitimate aspirations for an improved quality of life. A world in which poverty and inequity are endemic will be prone to ecological and other crises, and sustainable development requires meeting the basic needs of all and extending to all an opportunity to satisfy their aspirations for a better life.

Meeting essential needs depends in part on achieving full growth potential, and sustainable development clearly requires economic growth in places where such needs are not being met. Elsewhere, it can be consistent with economic growth, provided the content of growth reflects the broad principles of sustainability and non-exploitation of others. Hence, sustainable development requires that societies meet human needs both by increasing productive potential and by ensuring equitable opportunities for all.

Logistical and supply chain challenges in urbanized environments and for an increasing population include traffic congestion, fulfilling needs through provision of goods to markets, demanding a share of finite resources such as fossil fuels and metals for vehicles and warehouses, and adding to pollution from all these sources.

Water

Global water use grew at more than twice the rate of population growth in the last century. While the world's population tripled in the last century, the use of fresh water grew six-fold. Water use comprises about 70 per cent for irrigation, about 22 per cent for industry, and about 8 per cent for domestic use such as cleaning, cooking and bathing. With the world's population forecast to grow by 40 per cent in the next 50 years, much more water will be needed to produce food and supply drinking water, particularly in heavily populated regions. Further, the volumes of fresh water needed to support the growth in energy production are not available with today's water management policies and practices, and ageing water-delivery systems compound these issues (International Council of Academies of Engineering and Technological Sciences, 2009).

The world's almost 7 billion people are appropriating 54 per cent of all the accessible freshwater contained in rivers, lakes and underground aquifers. And water withdrawals are predicted to increase by 50 per cent by 2025 in developing countries and 18 per cent in developed countries. Over 1.4 billion people currently live in river basins where the use of water exceeds minimum recharge levels, leading to the desiccation of rivers and depletion of groundwater. By 2025, 1.8 billion people will be living in countries or regions with absolute water scarcity, and two-thirds of the world population could be under stress conditions (UN Water, 2012).

On the supply side, climate change presents important challenges for local and global water resource management. Rainfall levels in many regions are already impacted, evidenced by increasing frequency and severity of floods and droughts that also have a serious impact on the aquatic ecosystems that support the sustainable supply of food and fresh water. The capability of global climate models to predict precipitation is poor, and the understanding of regional catchment scale impacts remains highly uncertain.

Since the Carbon Disclosure Project or CDP (2012) launched its first global water report in 2010, water and its relationship with business have rarely been out of the news. For example, the Swedish retailer H&M reported a 30 per cent fall in profits for the first quarter of 2011, largely because the price of cotton doubled in the previous 12 months as a result of increased global demand and disruption to supplies caused by drought and floods in cotton-producing countries like Pakistan. Also, about one-third of the world's hard disk drive production for computers is currently located in Thailand and severe floods in that region in late 2011 caused a shortage in the supply of hard disks around the world. Corporate responses to CDP's 2011 water disclosure questionnaire revealed that the supply chain is largely uncharted territory when it comes to water. Only 26 per cent of respondents require their key suppliers to report water use, risks and management plans while 38 per cent of respondents did not know if their supply chain is exposed to water-related risk.

However, there is recent evidence of corporate awareness for water issues, particularly in logistics and SCM. IGD, the UK food and grocery sector's trade association, formed a Water Stewardship Working Group (IGD, 2012) to run workshops exploring the impact of a drought crisis on the UK food and grocery industry. The workshops found that risks posed by changes in water availability and water quality, and their potential impacts on business, were a significant motivation for delegates to understand more about how to manage these risks. However, despite this motivation, delegates agreed there were insufficient financial or legislative drivers for the industry to embrace a collaborative approach to managing these risks, and considered that a crisis was the most likely driver for a collaborative water stewardship approach to be developed as this would create the financial impetus needed. Core recommendations from the workshop were that the food and grocery industry needs a water resilience framework to facilitate increasing levels of collaboration and the adoption of a water stewardship approach across the industry embracing water users and stakeholders, as well as long-term planning and actions to ensure greater resilience in the industry.

Summary

Economic growth and prosperity are fundamental imperatives in today's competitive and globalized marketplace and aspirations for all citizens of the world. However, the science of sustainability has taken on a sense of urgency in recent years as mounting evidence suggests that climate change and its effects of drought and reduced agricultural yields, as well as the depletion of energy, other natural resources and water, are beginning to affect the quality of human existence and its own sustainability. All of these issues have logistics and supply chain management implications due to the impact these activities have on the natural environment.

It has been suggested that these issues must be addressed very soon in order to ensure that what Elkington (1994) defines as economic, environmental and human sustainability, ie his triple bottom line, are in balance. By doing so, the two dictionary definitions of sustainability presented at the start of this chapter will be met. Further, the intergenerational concepts posited by Brundtland (1987) and Rawls (1999) of development meeting present needs without compromising the needs of future generations provides for temporal equity and fairness.

However, there remains some confusion over what trade-offs and interdependent strategies must be employed to achieve such balance. An increase in economic growth suggests better standards of living across the globe, which in turn leads to increased and healthier populations, which will demand more food and water. These issues are not minor and at present are not insurmountable but the will to embrace and address them is sometimes lacking in government, business and society. However, it is important that logisticians and supply chain managers do so in order to be the vanguards of sustainability and effect real change.

References

Arvis, J-F, Saslavsky, D, Ojala, L, Shepherd, B, Busch, C, Raj, A and Naula, T (2016) *Connecting to Compete 2016: Trade logistics in the global economy*, World Bank, Washington, DC

Associated Press (2016) India to ratify Paris climate change agreement at UN, *Guardian* [online] available at: https://www.theguardian.com/environment/2016/oct/02/india-paris-climate-change-agreement-un-narendra-modi?CMP=Share_iOSApp_Other [accessed 2 October 2016]

British Geological Survey (2016) Risk List 2015 [online] available at: www.bgs.ac.uk/mineralsuk/statistics/riskList.html [accessed 1 October 2016]

Brundtland, G B (ed) (1987) *Our Common Future: Report to the World Commission on Environment and Development*, Oxford University Press, Oxford

Carbon Disclosure Project (2012) *CDP Supply Chain Report 2012 – A New Era: Supplier management in the low-carbon economy*, Accenture on behalf of CDP, London

Chrisafis, A (2015) France orders supermarkets to donate unsold food to charity in war on waste, *Guardian*, Saturday 23 May, p 3

CIA (2016) The World Factbook [online] available at: https://www.cia.gov/library/publications/the-world-factbook/index.html [accessed 21 July 2016]

Cline, E H (2014) Climate change doomed the ancients, *International New York Times*, Thursday 29 May, p 6; also at http://www.nytimes.com/2014/05/28/opinion/climate-change-doomed-the-ancients.html [accessed 1 October 2016]

Collins English Dictionary (1998) *Collins English Dictionary: Millennium (4th) Edition*, HarperCollins, Glasgow, p 1543

Collins Online (2016) available at: http://www.collinsdictionary.com/dictionary/english/sustainability [accessed 26 September 2016]

Commission for Integrated Transport (2007) *Transport and Climate Change: advice to government from the Commission for Integrated Transport*, Commission for Integrated Transport, London

EIA (2015) United States and China advance policies to limit CO_2 emissions (18 November) [online] available at: http://www.eia.gov/todayinenergy/detail.php?id=23812 [accessed 15 September 2016]

Elkington, J (1994) Towards the sustainable corporation: win-win-win business strategies for sustainable development, *California Management Review*, **36** (2), pp 90–100

Enerdata (2016) Enerdata Global Energy Statistical Yearbook [online] available at: http://yearbook.enerdata.net/ [accessed 1 October 2016]

Farman, J C, Gardiner, B G and Shanklin, J D (1985) Large losses of total ozone in Antarctica reveal seasonal ClO_x/NO_x interaction, *Nature*, 16 May, **315** (6016), pp 207–10

Goldenberg, S, Vidal, J, Taylor, L, Vaughan, A and Harvey, F (2015) Paris climate deal: nearly 200 nations signal the end of the fossil fuel era, *Guardian* [online] available at: https://www.theguardian.com/environment/2015/dec/12/paris-climate-deal-200-nations-sign-finish-fossil-fuel-era?CMP=Share_iOSApp_Other [accessed 26 January 2016]

Halldórsson, Á and Svanberg, M (2013) Energy resources: trajectories for supply chain management, *Supply Chain Management: An International Journal*, **18** (1), pp 66–73

Hobley, A (2016) How the oil price collapse can deliver the boost the green economy needs, *Carbon Tracker* [online] available at: http://www.carbontracker.org/how-the-oil-price-collapse-can-deliver-the-boost-the-green-economy-needs/ [accessed 29 September 2016]

Holweg, C and Lienbacher, E (2010) Social supermarkets: a new challenge in supply chain management and sustainability, *Supply Chain Forum: An International Journal*, **11** (4), pp 50–58

HSBC (2016) *Sustainable Financing Newsletter Edition 2 – September 2016*, HSBC, London

IGD (2012) The impact of crisis on water stewardship in the UK food and grocery industry, [online] available at: http://www.igd.com/Research/Sustainability/The-impact-of-crisis-on-water-stewardship-in-the-UK-food-and-consumer-goods-industry/ [accessed 2 October 2012]

International Council of Academies of Engineering and Technological Sciences (2009) *Global Natural Resources – Management and Sustainability: A CAETS statement*, CAETS, Calgary

Kahn, B (2016) The world passes 400 ppm threshold. Permanently, Climate Central [online] available at: http://www.climatecentral.org/news/world-passes-400-ppm-threshold-permanently-20738 [accessed 30 September 2016]

Kidd, K (2012) Suzuki puts a price on greenbelt, *Toronto Star*, 15 August, p A4

Lawrence, F (2016) Agrichemicals and ever more intensive farming will not feed the world, *Guardian* [online] available at: https://www.theguardian.com/commentisfree/2016/oct/02/agrichemicals-intensive-farming-food-production-biodiversity?CMP=Share_iOSApp_Other [accessed 2 October 2016]

Martin, R (2011) Why current population growth is costing us the earth, *Guardian* [online] available at: www.guardian.co.uk/environment/2011/oct/23/why-population-growth-costs-the-earth-roger [accessed 12 October 2012]

Maugeri, L (2012) *Oil: The next revolution*, Discussion Paper 2012–10, Belfer Center for Science and International Affairs, Harvard Kennedy School, Cambridge, MA, June

McKinnon, A, Browne, M, Whiteing, A and Piecyk, M (2015) *Green Logistics: Improving the environmental sustainability of logistics* (3rd edn), Kogan Page, London

Monbiot, G (2012) We were wrong on peak oil. There's enough to fry us all, *Guardian*, 3 July, p 28

National Public Radio (2013) Social supermarkets a 'win-win' for Europe's poor [online] available at: http://www.npr.org/sections/ thesalt/2013/12/11/250185245/social-supermarkets-a-win-win-win-for-europes-poor [accessed 19 December 2016]

Rawls, J (1999) *A Theory of Justice*, Oxford University Press, Oxford

Shaw, S, Grant, D B and Mangan, J (2010) Developing environmental supply chain performance measures, *Benchmarking: An International Journal*, **17** (3), pp 320–39

Statista (2016) Total global grain production from 2008/2009 to 2015/2016 [online] available at: https://www.statista.com/statistics/271943/total-world-grain-production-since-2008-2009/ [accessed 19 December 2016]

Stuart, T (2009) *Waste: Uncovering the global food scandal*, Penguin, London

Tomalty, R (2012) *Carbon in the Bank: Ontario's greenbelt and its role in mitigating climate change*, David Suzuki Foundation, Vancouver, August

UN Department of Economic and Social Affairs (2007) *Industrial Development for the 21st Century: Sustainable development perspectives*, United Nations, New York

UN Food and Agriculture Organization (2012) *The State of Food Insecurity in the World 2012*, United Nations, Rome

UN Water (2012) Statistics: graphs and maps [online] available at: http://www.unwater.org/statistics/en/ [accessed 8 October 2012]

USDA Economic Research Service (2012) 'US drought 2012: farm and food impacts [online] available at: www.ers.usda.gov/newsroom/us-drought-2012-farm-and-food-impacts.aspx [accessed 12 October 2012]

US Energy Information Administration (2016) Global petroleum and other liquid fuels [online] available at: https://www.eia.gov/forecasts/steo/report/global_oil.cfm [accessed 18 September 2016]

World Business Council for Sustainable Development (2007a) Mobility for development [online] available at: www.wbcsd.org [accessed 8 October 2012]

World Business Council for Sustainable Development (2007b) Energy efficiency in buildings: business realities and opportunities [online] available at: www.wbcsd.org [accessed 8 October 2012]

World Health Organization (2012) Global Health Observatory [online] available at: www.who.int/gho/en/ [accessed 8 October 2012]

Freight transport 03

Freight transport is arguably the most visible issue in the discussion on making logistics activities in supply chains greener. Although the proportion of environmental impact of transport and transport intensity varies strongly between supply chains, every goods supply chain and almost every services supply chain contains transport activities. The World Economic Forum (2009) estimates that most of the carbon emissions from logistics activities are caused by freight transport. Nevertheless, other environmental costs and emissions from freight transport include wider issues such as noise, vibration and accidents. Increasingly the reduction of pay, labour rights and a constant performance monitoring pressure of transport workers also brings the ethical dimension of sustainability into discussion.

With supply chains becoming increasingly global, freight transport disproportionately outgrew economic development over recent decades and – particularly for international transport – continues to grow despite temporary reductions related to economic decline (FTA, 2015; OECD, 2015). Much of this can be related to offshoring and further specialization in supply chains leading to increased international trade. The ongoing debate on the downsides of globalization, supply chain risks and the higher responsiveness of local supply might mitigate this trend to some extent; however, it can be expected that a growing world economy will lead to an even higher growth in transport services. Even relatively simple products are now characterized by increasingly complex and long supply chains. The access to international trade and economic opportunities – and the consequent uplift out of poverty – for vast parts of the developing world appear to be connected to an environmental cost.

Impact of freight transport

The transport sector has been the biggest single energy user in the UK with a share of 38 per cent of all energy consumption in the country. Although some transport modes reduced their energy intensity during recent decades, the overall strong growth of transport and the increasing proportion of road transport in the modal split keep carbon emissions from transport on the rise (Department of Energy and Climate Change, 2009; Eurostat, 2016).

Looking at ambitious governmental commitments to reduce greenhouse gas emissions in most developed countries as part of international sustainability goals, the transport sector will undoubtedly need to contribute to such reductions.

Externalities

Although this chapter focuses on the greenhouse gas emissions, it is worth noting that freight transport has a wider impact than only atmospheric emissions. We therefore have a brief look into the external pollution aspects of noise and accidents, and the impact on societal sustainability before we focus again on the greenhouse gas aspect.

Noise

The vast majority of the population today experiences traffic noise, using both objective measures via the decibel levels that citizens are exposed to (den Boer and Schroten, 2007) and citizens' subjective perception of traffic noise (Lambert and Philipps-Bertin, 2008). In 2000, more than 44 per cent of Europe's population experience road traffic noise at a level of annoyance and 7 per cent were exposed to noise at such a level from rail transport. The exposure to noise impacts negatively on citizens' health and the social costs are conservatively estimated to be at least €40 billion. A reduction of noise can be achieved through a mix of central (European) and local regulation, and the application of already available technology (den Boer and Schroten, 2007; Lambert and Philipps-Bertin, 2008). The FEHRL report (2006) recommends European regulation for tyres and road construction to reduce traffic noise, with the improvement of tyres being seen as the most cost-effective measure for traffic noise reduction. It also suggests that innovation in the area of traffic noise reduction can be encouraged only through tightening regulation.

In the public debate, large transport infrastructure projects, such as airport expansions and new train lines, increasingly face opposition from local residents due to noise concerns. These often lead to restrictions of operating hours, for example restrictions on night flights at Heathrow, Frankfurt and Zurich airports.

Accidents

An often-ignored environmental impact of transportation is casualties from accidents. Road freight transport vehicles share roads and motorways with common road traffic, cyclists and pedestrians and are therefore more at risk of being involved in accidents than rail or water transport which use railway tracks or waterways exclusively. Due to the heavy weight of road freight transport vehicles, the severity of accidents is worse and the rate of fatal incidents is higher than for cars. The casualty rate varies strongly between countries due to road safety and vehicle maintenance standards, age of vehicles, etc (Cullinane and Edwards, 2010). A new aspect of road safety is the discussion around whether electric vehicles should be equipped with noise-emitting devices as there is a fear that electric vehicles may not be noticed by other traffic participants due to their low noise emittance at low speed (SWOV, 2011).

Workers in the transport sector

The workplaces of transport workers have changed drastically with the advance of new technology that allows permanent tracing of vehicles and performance monitoring. Telematic systems not only know where a vehicle currently is, but also analyse fuel efficiency, harsh braking by the driver and scrutinize delays with traffic data (Wenner and Trautrims, 2012). This is often combined with video recording to improve driving and produce evidence for legal disputes. Although such technology is used to optimize routing and improve driving behaviour for fuel efficiency and accident avoidance, it can also put drivers under constant pressure and disempower them and de-skill their profession by shifting all responsibility away from drivers.

More recently, delivery drivers are facing an increasingly pressured work environment, with low employment security and a direct or indirect pressure to work unreasonably long hours and on a per-delivery pay structure (Heywood, 2016).

Transport modes

By far the most emissions in freight transport stem from road transport. However, this has to be seen in the light that road freight transport has by far the largest share in tonne-kilometres of all inland transport modes, in Europe about three-quarters of all freight transport and in the United States around 70 per cent (Eurostat, 2016; US DoT, 2016). The choice of transport mode is influenced by the characteristic of the mode, operational factors and consignment factors, and cost and service requirements (Rushton *et al*, 2006).

Sea freight, whether in containers or in bulk, is generally a slow but cheap option for the transportation of mainly low-value, high-volume items. Shipping rates can vary extremely between busier and less busy routes. As ships are long-term investments and take a long time to build, capacity only adjusts slowly to changes in the economic cycle, leading to extreme variation in the profitability of the shipping industry. Usually there is always a need for double handling, as goods have to be brought to and away from the port. Although the emissions per tonne-kilometre are low, journeys are usually long and most ships burn bunker fuel, which is considered as one of the most pollutant fuels.

Rail freight is considered as a rather slow method of inland transport. It uses a fixed infrastructure, which makes it less prone to disruptions, but also means that goods have to be brought to a rail terminal if a site has no connection to the railway network. A common application for rail freight is transport of steady and heavy bulk loads, for example coal for coal fire stations or steel mills. The expensive infrastructure is often provided by state-owned companies, but many of the carriage operators have been privatized in European and other developed countries. Trains can be powered by electricity or traditional fuels. It is usually considered as a 'greener' mode than road transport, but that depends strongly on journey characteristics and backhauling.

Road freight is particularly popular for its accessibility and flexibility. The road network allows access to most industrial sites and is usually the first access mode that is constructed. It also requires little investment, which makes it popular for short- and medium-term solutions for which otherwise alternative modes would be more suitable from a long-term perspective. The road freight market is also very competitive and fragmented, with few large logistics companies but many small haulage companies of three or fewer lorries (Department for Transport, 2011). Road freight is usually classified as Full Truckload (FTL) or Less Than Truckload (LTL). Another classification occurs in the size of vehicles. The European Union separates between Light Commercial Vehicles (LCVs) which weigh less than 3.5 metric tonnes and Heavy Goods Vehicles (HGVs) of over metric 3.5 tonnes.

Air freight is surely the fastest available transport mode over long distances. However, it is also the mode that emits the most carbon, as aircraft burn a large amount of fuel per tonne-kilometre. Due to the fuel consumption, it is also relatively expensive, which makes it a more suitable transport mode for items of high value density or when a short lead time is of importance.

Pipelines are mainly used to transport large quantities of liquids or gas. Due to the high investment, it is used in situations of high volume and predictable demand. Not only does production and maintenance of pipelines result in emissions, but the operation also needs energy for pumping and sometimes temperature control.

The following figure shows the carbon emissions per tonne-km by transport mode; for airfreight in particular the assumed journey distance influences emissions drastically.

Using figures from Figure 3.1 above, one needs to be aware that they are averages based on many assumptions. The emission calculations depend on loading factors, engine efficiency, etc, which can vary hugely between countries and transport situations. Additionally, it is not uncommon that transport industry groups issue their own studies, naturally portraying their own member companies' offered transport mode in a more favourable light.

Factors to consider when choosing the transport mode

Whilst some transport modes are more harmful to the environment than others, we need to understand the commercial and logistical considerations for their selection by businesses and other organizations.

Figure 3.1 CO_2e emissions by transport mode

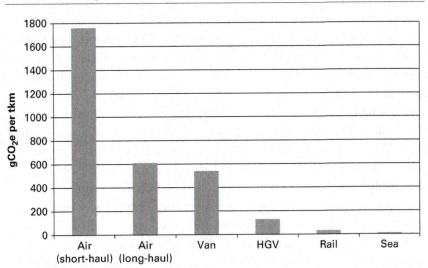

SOURCE Based on Defra (2011).

Operational factors

External factors affect the choice of transport mode. The availability and quality of infrastructure differ between countries and transport modes, as does the availability and quality of vehicles and logistics service providers. In addition, local law, regulations towards transport and the price for transport will impact the choice, with many developed countries trying to encourage transport modes of lower emission impact, for example through fuel taxation, aviation tax in the UK, or tax reductions for environmentally friendlier vehicles. Local climate becomes an issue when, for example, rainy seasons affect some transport modes more than others.

The availability of infrastructure needs to be seen in connection to the location where the goods need to be delivered. Accessibility by water or rail determines whether these modes can be considered as options in the choice of transport. Sea and rail transport very often need some road transport for the final leg of the journey.

Cost and service requirements

Customer requirements towards cost and service impact the selection of transport mode. Larger order sizes and longer order cycles make the use of less flexible transport modes worth consideration. An example would be a product such as white undershirts, which are a common low-value item sold in larger quantities and not subject to fashion changes. They would usually be shipped in sea freight containers from the Far East to markets in Europe or North America, as shipping by sea is a rather cheap way of transporting these large, low-value quantities.

Drivers for the growth of road freight transport in the past were the logistics strategies of 'just-in-time' (JIT) manufacturing, 'efficient consumer response' (ECR) in retailing and a trend towards centralization of operations and warehousing. JIT reduces inventory holding by having items delivered to an assembly line when they are needed, thus avoiding storage and inventory holding. Deliveries will therefore be optimized from an assembly line perspective, with sometimes short notice periods. This usually results in more frequent but smaller orders and transport, requiring flexibility that can usually only be provided by road transport. ECR is a common strategy in grocery retailing, and requires high levels of flexibility and responsiveness. It aims to replenish quickly what customers have bought at the store. Customer demand can be volatile and ECR uses a high frequency of store deliveries in response to this volatility. This way it increases the number of journeys and the proportion of less-than-truckload deliveries.

Product characteristics

The value density and weight density of transported items as influencing factors towards the choice of the transport mode have already been mentioned, but other product characteristics can also influence this choice. Perishable products will put a focus on speed of delivery if their ripening cannot be delayed. Bananas exported to western markets, for example, are harvested unripe and then transported in temperature-controlled ships to the destination countries. The same, however, is not possible for fresh flowers, which therefore have to be transported by aeroplane. The transport of hazardous goods is usually regulated, affecting the speed of delivery and the choice of transportation mode to protect the public from potentially harmful accidents.

Consignment factors

Whether a consignment can actually fill the size of a standardized unit of transportation has a significant impact on the price for freight transport. The loading factor (or utilization) for a transport mode, however, will be important for the environmental assessment. Whether the vehicle returns empty or other goods can be hauled back changes the calculation tremendously. Loads may also be incorporated into an already planned trip or may contribute to the utilization of an existent system, which may be financially and environmentally more attractive than setting up the use of a new system. For example, much air freight arrives on passenger planes, which would be serving a route anyway to transport passengers. The allocation of emissions for freight transport on a passenger plane is difficult, as the flight would have been scheduled anyway.

The carbon emissions of transport modes depend on the type of fuel and engine that is used. Electrified transport modes – using electricity generated at a power station – such as the train services in many Continental European countries have lower carbon intensity than those transport modes run on fossil fuels.

Although sea transport is relatively low in energy intensity per tonne-km, the bunker fuel burnt by ocean vessels is considered as being particularly pollutant and can therefore lead to the concentration of emissions and to respiratory health problems in port cities. One way of reducing the environmental impact on port communities is therefore to supply ships with energy from the grid whilst they are in port or to enforce a change in the fuel that is being used. The Baltic Sea region is an example of a shift to less polluting ship fuel.

Table 3.1   Comparison of greenhouse gas emissions by transport mode

	gCO_2e per tkm			
	CO_2	CH_4	N_2O	Total
Van	537.0	0.16	3.71	540.9
HGV	127.2	0.4	1.91	129.2
Rail	28.5	0.05	3.06	31.6
Sea (general cargo, 100+ TEU)	11.0	0.00	0.08	11.1
Air (long-haul)	610	0.00	10	610
Air (short-haul)	1740	0.00	20	1760

SOURCE Defra (2011).

The emissions from individual fuel types differ hugely between various pollutants. To make the discussion more transparent and measures comparable, the guidelines for company greenhouse gas reporting use $CO_2e - CO_2$ equivalence – as a measure. The figures from this guideline are to be used to estimate the environmental impact of a company's logistics activities in the lifecycle assessment of a supply chain.

The figures in Table 3.1 above were calculated based on average loading factors in the UK. The figures for air freight also considered the proportions of freight on passenger planes and on pure freight aircraft. This means, however, that the numbers are averaged across the entire country and individual performances may differ strongly. The guidelines are therefore quite detailed and they provide numbers based on different fuel types, vessel size, vehicle type, etc.

Additional complexity to the discussion is added by a report from PE International (2010) arguing that water and rail are not always greener than road freight transport. The study compares road and rail modes in several scenarios with various assumptions. When the comparison includes all factors like emissions from producing electricity and diesel, loading factors, type of goods to be transported, length of train, proportion of the journey from factory to freight terminals etc, it can in some scenarios show lower emissions for the lorry. In one scenario of light goods, river barge transport even has the highest emissions of all three compared modes. Since the study was conducted in Germany, comparisons in future also need to consider the reduction of nuclear energy in the electricity mix. If nuclear energy is replaced with energy from coal or other highly polluting ways of energy production, the environmental performance of electricity-powered trains will decrease.

Options to reduce the environmental impact of transport operations are to reduce the emissions from the current mode of transport, shifting freight towards less polluting modes of transport, and the overall reduction of freight transport. These options are now discussed in more detail.

Strategies to reduce environmental impact of freight transport

The selection of a transport mode and the resulting emissions can differ significantly between individual circumstances. However, the considerations and thought processes between individual solutions are similar. But nevertheless, the feasibility and availability of greener options varies. In the following paragraphs, we introduce the strategic decisions behind emission reductions in transport.

Change of transport mode

The move to alternative transport modes is subject to access to them. We have already discussed how water and rail transport sometimes need heavy investment into infrastructure. Regardless of whether these investments are made by governments or private investors, they need to make economic sense. The investment into 'greener' transport infrastructure therefore requires a certain number of users to utilize it. Since water and rail freight are particularly suitable for heavy, low-value density items, such infrastructure is mainly present in areas of manufacturing and heavy industry. The movement into a services-dominated economy and the consequent decline of sizeable manufacturing in the UK reduced the share of freight moved by water and rail. In contrast to this, the People's Republic of China, for example, invested more than US $200 billion from its 2008 stimulus package into the development of rail, waterway and grid networks to support the manufacturing sector (Park *et al*, 2012). To make use of these freight transport modes, potential users who are not based in a port and have no own rail terminal need to apply multi-modal solutions. Multi-modal refers to the use of more than one transport mode through the trip of a consignment. Using several transport modes means that the freight is handled when moved from one mode to another. This handling can be made much easier through the design of intermodal solutions whereby the infrastructure and equipment are prepared for the use of several transport modes.

The handling between transport modes became much easier through the widespread use and increasing standardization of pallets and containers. Before the development and acceptance of shipping containers, general cargo vessels were loaded and unloaded manually in a slow and labour-intensive process. Today there are also standardized containers for bulk loads and liquids. Containers allow a faster shifting of larger quantities onto rail carriages or trucks with a suitable body. A major obstacle for multi-modal transport is whether a loading unit (eg a container) can be used for the entire journey, avoiding double-handling of goods. The major unit in international container shipping is the TEU, a 20-foot equivalent unit, referring to a container 20 feet in length. However, 40- and 45-foot container units also exist. In a similar way, work swap-bodies can be used for the road and rail mode. The swap-body's dimensions need to adhere to the regulations of both modes and therefore are different to the shipping container. Unlike the shipping container, it cannot be stacked. Slightly different to the swap-body is a concept for a road–rail trailer where an entire articulated semi-trailer is put onto a modified rail wagon; the trailer is modified so the wheels can be pulled in to fit onto the rail wagon.

Another form of enabling multi-modal transport is the use of intermodal vehicles. RORO (roll-on roll-off) ferries allow road vehicles (and sometimes trains) to use water transport. The land-based version of this is trains that can carry lorries. These are, for example, used for freight traffic through Switzerland.

Some of the intermodal applications require special handling equipment and facilities. Intermodal terminals are needed for road–rail transport, with special cranes and ramps, and inland ports are built to connect waterway barges to the road and rail network; ferries also need terminals to connect with land transport modes.

Reduction of freight transport

Besides shifting freight to 'greener' transport modes, emissions can be reduced by avoiding freight transportation in the first place.

Much of the increase in emissions from freight transport is caused by what is commonly called 'globalization'. International trade grew through the reduction of trade barriers and the stronger participation of emerging economies. The availability of cheap and effective transportation across the globe, labour cost differences, and more specialization in the production of complex products supported the growth in international trade and the resulting increase in freight transport.

Hereby many of the emissions were shifted abroad through offshoring manufacturing from developed countries that were moving towards service-driven economies to developing countries (Peters, 2011) where environmental regulation is often less strict and enforced less rigorously. Some of the emissions from manufacturing would still also occur if the product was manufactured closer to the point of consumption, but the emissions from freight transport could be minimized by sourcing locally. Although this doesn't allow taking advantage of lower labour costs elsewhere, it reduces risks in the supply chain and makes supply chains more agile and responsive. The higher labour costs can sometimes be more than compensated for by a more efficient production and workforce, better quality, the savings achieved through the reduction of freight transport and the reduction in inventory caused by long lead times and necessary buffer stock in global supply chains (BCG, 2011; Roland Berger, 2011). As a combination of the advantages of close-by suppliers and low labour costs, the concept of 'nearshoring' evolved. Nearshoring locates manufacturing in low-wage countries near or next to the place of consumption. The main advantages of this concept are the reduction of lead times and uncertainties in the supply chain, and the consequent freeing up of cash flow for other company activities (Chow, 2010).

The decision for local sourcing or nearshoring is strongly influenced by the cost of freight transportation. As discussed earlier in this chapter, the costs for freight transport differ between the various transport modes. However, the freight transport charges are very volatile due to demand/supply mismatches and the cost of fuel.

In the recent economic slowdown, overcapacities in global container shipping suddenly appeared, but since the shipping companies had already placed orders for new ships, capacity increased further despite falling freight charges. Capacity in this market could not be adjusted quickly enough against the decline in demand and all major container liners announced financial losses in this period of very low freight rates. Overcapacities can also occur due to directional imbalances; for example, the shipment of a container from Europe to China much cheaper than vice versa because there is much less demand for shipping goods in this direction. A major cost factor for transport providers is fuel or the energy that goes into providing the transport service. The price for freight transport therefore depends strongly on the global fuel and oil prices, which fluctuate extensively. As ships can transport large numbers of products, the proportion of transport costs per item can be near negligible in many cases.

Reduction of emissions from current mode

In many cases, a shift to more environmentally friendly transport modes may be impossible, as the available infrastructure or product characteristics demand a particular mode of transport. But even if a shift to a 'greener' mode is not possible there is still much scope for reducing the emissions from the mode in use.

The greenhouse gas emissions of transport operations stem mainly from the burning of fuels. There are also emissions embedded in the manufacturing process of the vehicles and the disposal of the vehicles at the end of their lifecycle; nevertheless, the focus during the operations will be on the fuel consumption. Fuel consumption is relatively easy to measure across transport operations. Fuel is also a main cost factor in transportation and fuel savings therefore usually mean cost savings for operators, making the reduction of fuel consumption an attractive focus for 'greening' transport operations.

Alternative fuels

With rising oil prices in the past and political willingness to reduce the dependency on oil, several alternative fuels were brought to the fuel market. Their environmental balances vary tremendously and since most of them are relatively new in their application to the wider transport industry it is worthwhile to keep a holistic and critical perspective. A prime example of hidden issues is the political promotion of biofuels. Political leaders in Europe and elsewhere promoted the use of biofuel as a way to reduce greenhouse gas emissions whilst at the same time providing a new income stream for rural communities. The European Union even demands that petrol contains 10 per cent biofuel. To produce more biofuel, agricultural land previously used for food production was often converted to grow biofuel crops. Additionally, forest areas were converted into farmland for the growth of biofuel crops. The implications of the promotion of biofuel are therefore increased land use and a threat to biodiversity, and also increasing food prices leading to civil unrest – as during the so-called 'tortilla crisis' in Mexico in 2008 – in countries where citizens spend a large proportion of their income on food. Furthermore, the harvest of crops to make biofuel relies on weather conditions. After a serious drought in the United States, the world's major producer of corn, the United Nations asked the country to change its biofuel laws, which demand 40 per cent of the corn production to be used to make ethanol biofuel, amid fears of rising food prices worldwide (BBC, 2012). The use of agricultural products and land for biofuel which would otherwise be used for food therefore leads to a serious ethical dilemma, and biofuel development has since diverted more into using waste and uneatable crops and by-products from food production as a source of raw material.

Similarly, the promotion of bioenergy in generating electricity needs to be seen critically. Although electric vehicles are considered environmentally friendly and particularly suitable for short-distance urban travel, their 'fuel' – electricity – may be produced from different sources. Electricity from wind power and solar power is sustainable, but these sources are also very unreliable and volatile, and therefore other sources of energy are needed to ensure sufficient provision of electricity. These sources must come from fossil fuels, nuclear energy or biomass. Whilst fossil fuels show high levels of emissions and nuclear power is often unpopular, the use of biomass can only be considered as sustainable if it comes from waste products and by-products that are occurring anyway. If biomass is specially grown for the purpose of energy production it cannot be considered as a sustainable source of energy due to the ethical implications, the use of energy in the biomass supply chain itself, and the extremely low conversion from biomass into eventual electricity (Leopoldina, 2012). Whenever electric power is used to run vehicles it is necessary to investigate how the electricity is generated, as this will be the main determinant of whether it is a 'sustainable' mode or not.

Liquefied natural gas (LNG) is a fossil fuel too, nevertheless it burns with lower emissions than most oil-based products. So far it hasn't gained a huge market share as a fuel for cars as the distribution infrastructure does not exist yet. However, it is expected to be increasingly used in international shipping. The International Maritime Organization (IMO) has limited the nitrogen content in ship fuel for ships operating in the North Sea and the Baltic Sea to 0.1 per cent from 2015 onwards. This low level of nitrogen cannot be achieved with the bunker fuel commonly used in international shipping. Using higher-quality, oil-based fuels or cleaning the exhausted fumes would be more costly for operators than the use of LNG. Fuelling infrastructure for LNG already exists to some extent around the North and Baltic Seas and is currently extended to ports around this area. Currently only a few vessels are operating on LNG and there is doubt whether the conversion of vessels to LNG is viable. More likely, only newly built ships will use LNG as a fuel and therefore the market share of this ship fuel will be increasing gradually over the coming decades (Tankstellenmarkt, 2012; Germanischer Lloyd, 2012). Although only 95 vessels are currently operating with LNG fuel worldwide (56 of them in Norway), shipbuilders' orderbooks, political support – particularly from the European Union – and the establishment of standards by the International Maritime Organization give reason to expect a rising number in the near future (WPCI, 2016).

Compared to the fuel market for road vehicles, the ship fuel market in this case has the advantage that only a relatively small number of refuelling stations need to be built with some infrastructure already in place for local ferries, particularly along the Norwegian coast and in ports. Although the number of potential consumers is rather small, the consumed quantities make it worthwhile erecting a sufficient infrastructure. And lastly, there is regulatory pressure on the operators to switch to a lower-emission fuel (Germanischer Lloyd, 2012).

Figure 3.2 shows a comparison of greenhouse gas emissions for different fuel applications for cars and light-duty vehicles in the United States. The emissions differ significantly, and as discussed above, all fuels have their particular issues in their production.

Figure 3.2   Well-to-wheels greenhouse gases emissions for future mid-size car

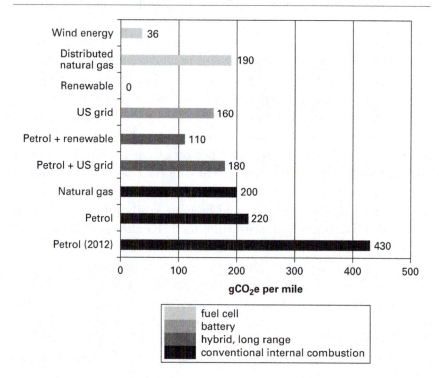

Infrastructure for hydrogen fuel

Hydrogen can be used as an alternative fuel in most applications where fossil fuels are consumed today. It can be applied in two ways: as a fuel in a 'traditional' tank in a vehicle or within fuel cells where it is converted into electric power. These hydrogen-powered vehicles are less noisy than conventional engines and the only emission from the consumption of hydrogen is water. Hydrogen can be sourced conventionally as a chemical by-product, from coal or from natural gas (in which case hydrogen fuel's environmental balance is not as good as the one from renewable sources, but still lower in CO_2 emissions than fossil fuels). But it can also be produced from biological processes or from solid and liquid biomass, or biogas. Either way, the production of hydrogen by electrolysis consumes significant amounts of energy. The environmental balance of hydrogen fuel therefore depends not only on whether it stems from a conventional or a renewable source, but also on the source of energy for its production. If electricity from renewable sources can be used (for example from wind power or solar power at times when demand is much lower than production) hydrogen becomes a renewable fuel itself.

Already today applications for hydrogen power include cars, buses, forklifts and even submarines. Whilst hydrogen-powered submarines are already in full operation and hydrogen-powered engines exist for cars, lorries and other vehicles, the use of hydrogen is still at an infant stage. The major obstacles for a wider application of hydrogen fuel are the availability of sufficient energy from renewable sources, which is expected to change at a global level over the coming decades, and a distribution network for hydrogen fuel to the wider population.

As with other alternative fuels, customers will only switch to hydrogen if they can fuel up their vehicle conveniently at a 'petrol station' nearby. The distribution network also needs sufficient geographic coverage so that drivers do not have to worry about refilling their vehicle during a longer journey. Due to the lack of refuelling infrastructure, applications naturally started with vehicles coming back to a base after an operation cycle. This is certainly the case for the submarines, but also for buses that come back to the depot at the end of a tour and forklifts that are fuelled up at the operating site.

Local transit agencies in California are using fuel cell-operated buses. From their initial pilot to their second-generation project, the price for specially amended buses halved and the number of participating agencies increased. The acceptance of hydrogen fuel vehicles depends on the extra purchase price for the vehicle and the availability of fuel. Yet at the same time, fuelling stations will only offer hydrogen fuel if there is a marketable number of vehicles consuming hydrogen.

The next step for public acceptance of hydrogen fuel is the development of a distribution infrastructure. In an initiative called 'H2 mobility', car manufacturers, energy companies, petrol station operators and hydrogen producers are collaborating to erect a hydrogen fuelling infrastructure with the overall aim of installing at least 400 hydrogen pumps at petrol stations across Germany. Each hydrogen pump installation is estimated to cost approximately 1 million Euros. The supply to the fuelling stations is planned to use conventional trailers transporting liquefied hydrogen under pressure, but there are also thoughts towards a decentralized production network.

SOURCE Linde Group Gases Division, www.linde.com/hydrogen.

After the choice of transport mode and the choice of fuel, freight transport's emissions can also be reduced through operational optimization, improvements in the network design and further technology that can support these improvements.

Operational options to reduce emissions

One way of operating transport vehicles and vessels on less fuel is to run them at their engines' optimal level. In international shipping this concept is called 'slow steaming' and came up during the economic downturn in 2007. Usually the world's fleet engines are designed to run at full load, but that is not the most fuel-efficient way to run these engines. With the existing overcapacities during the economic turmoil, shipping lines started to run their ships at slower speeds to save fuel (Delft, 2012; MAN, 2012). A ship like the *Emma Maersk* – currently the world's largest container ship – would save about 4,000 tonnes of bunker fuel on a trip from Europe to Singapore. When a ship runs at lower speed it needs longer to accomplish a journey. A ship running from Hong Kong to Rotterdam that was scheduled to take 21 days would take 23 days using slow steaming. Using extra days means a ship can make fewer journeys in a given amount of time, but due to the overcapacities in the global shipping market, this issue became less important. A side benefit of slow steaming is the increased reliability of shipping schedules, as the slow steaming provides a natural buffer for delays (A P Møller Maersk, 2011).

Another economically attractive operational improvement is the reduction of empty running in transport fleets. As shown in the discussion of transport modes, the environmental performance depends strongly on loading factors and the utilization of operating vehicles. Transport companies naturally have an interest in finding a load for the way back anyway and the question is therefore more about why empty running occurs and how transport companies can be supported in finding backloading opportunities. An increase in utilization and a reduction of empty journeys will consequently reduce the total number of journeys and therefore reduce emissions.

The discussion on backhauling has two aspects: the issue of empty running and the underutilization of vehicles. Both can happen for the same reasons.

Logistics strategies like just-in-time can be a factor when the arrival within the correct time window is more important than the availability of suitable backhauling opportunities. Many goods also have special transport characteristics, which means they are not compatible to be transported in the same vehicle as other goods, for example livestock and pharmaceuticals. Also, tankers transporting chemicals can only backload the same product or need to be cleaned before loading other chemicals. Vehicles may also be running underutilized because they follow a particular schedule; for example, aircraft and ships usually need to follow a schedule regardless of their loading factor on a particular journey. Also, transport equipment may not be suitable for other goods and there may be directional imbalances. For example, timber logs are usually transported on special trailers. First, those trailers are designed for timber logs and cannot be used for many other goods, and second, there is a lack of goods that need to be transported back to the place where timber is harvested. Imbalances in schedules can also cause underutilization. Delivery patterns vary and there is less demand for freight transport during the weekend. Many countries will also limit freight transport during times when the road network is particularly busy, for example during public holidays.

Transport operators may also often not be aware of backloading opportunities. Electronic platforms give transport companies easier access to potential backhauling. Opportunities to improve vehicle utilization can also exist in their own supply chain with customers and suppliers, but also with competitors. Despite being competitors, Nestlé and United Biscuits in the UK collaborate in their freight transport on one route where both own sites at either end. By combining their freight transport, they save on annual basis around 95,000 litres of diesel, 250 tonnes of CO_2 and around £300,000. Although such collaboration needs to cross many barriers and results in additional management effort, these are outweighed by the savings (IGD, 2009).

Underutilization can be caused by these directional imbalances, but also by product characteristics. If goods cannot be stacked on top of each other, the operator cannot use the full volume of the vehicle. Similarly, if a product is very heavy – for example steel – the vehicle will be quite empty, but it's already at the maximum weight capacity. The same problem applies to very light products, which may fill an entire trailer, but do not by far reach weight capacity. Vehicles are regulated in their dimensions and weight capacity and a load can only rarely perfectly match these determinants. As the dimensions of vehicles are regulated, initiatives to introduce larger and heavier lorries evolved. After initial pilot tests, 'gigaliners' are currently being further tested for approved use in Germany. These vehicles have a length of 25.25 metres and a capacity of 44 tonnes (the maximum length for lorries at the moment being 18.75 metres) and have been used in the less-populated Nordic countries for some time. The gigaliners are expected to save up to 20 per cent of CO_2 compared to the usual HGVs. Nevertheless, critics fear damage to the infrastructure and, due to the length of the trailer, additional congestion and an increased risk of accidents when overtaking the gigaliners (*Süddeutsche Zeitung*, 2015).

Vehicle design improvements within the regulated dimensions can also contribute to the reduction of emissions. Modern vehicles emit much fewer greenhouse gases, but there is a limit to the fuel efficiency that vehicles can achieve using traditional diesel engines. The aim of fuel efficiency is also in a trade-off with the emissions of other exhauster fumes. Regulations usually give priority to the reduction of health-damaging gases over the reduction of CO_2, leaving an estimated residue of 7–10 per cent increase in fuel efficiency.

Another aspect of vehicle design is aerodynamic profiling, where the vehicle shape is designed in a way that the air flows as smoothly as possible around the vehicle to minimize the air resistance. Such design can for example be seen in 'teardrop' trailers, which show a slight arc when looking at them from the side. But additional spoilers and shields around the trailer also add weight to the vehicle, offsetting some of the fuel savings. This is also in contrast to the aim of minimizing the weight of the vehicle. The lighter a vehicle, the less energy is needed to move it when it's empty and it also allows the loading of more weight onto it. In Europe, the maximum loaded weight is restricted to 40 tonnes, meaning that the weight saved on the vehicle can be used to load extra freight.

Information technology

Developments in the areas of information technology and mobile communication have opened huge potential for operational optimization in freight transport. On the one hand, software can optimize the routing, scheduling and loading of vehicles and online platforms make it easier to find backloading opportunities. On the other hand, this information can also be communicated to the operating vehicle through so-called telematic systems. In road freight, transport telematic systems connect the vehicle with the dispatching office. This way, operations can be optimized dynamically whilst they are running. Real-time routing can also consider and avoid motorway congestion and traffic accidents. By taking advantage of these opportunities, telematic systems can save miles, increase backhauling and reduce fuel consumption through which overall emissions are reduced at the same time (Wenner and Trautrims, 2012).

Telematic systems can also be used for monitoring vehicles and driver behaviour. Monitoring the vehicle allows the above-mentioned dynamic optimization and also provides information to the company and its customers about where a particular consignment is located. The information can also be used to comply with regulations, for example maximum driving hours, or to check on non-moving vehicles. Through monitoring driver behaviour, telematic systems allow the comparison of performances between drivers. Behaviour such as avoiding harsh braking, using the right gear and turning off the engine at idle times saves fuel and monitoring drivers' performance can therefore be used to encourage environmentally friendly driving performance. However, telematic systems are a significant investment for hauliers. Their use is most common in larger fleets operating in markets that require frequent route optimization and communication between vehicle and office. Smaller haulage companies – the majority of the road freight transport providers – are much less likely to use telematic systems (Wenner and Trautrims, 2012). Nevertheless, telematic systems only cover the monitoring side of driver behaviour. Positive environmental effects can only be achieved if drivers are trained about fuel saving.

Other measures to reduce fuel consumption are properly inflated tyres or automatic tyre inflation and automatic idle engine turn-off. However, measuring the potential fuel saving of all operational improvement actions is difficult as fuel savings can stem from numerous sources and are subject to many factors, for example the proportion of the journey time on motorways or the incline of roads. Comparing fuel efficiency between different fleets or countries is therefore difficult due to the specific situations and their influencing factors.

Alternative jet fuel

The greenhouse gas emissions from aviation are an omnipresent topic in the debate about transport's impact on global warming. With increased globalization, air transport became a regular feature of travel and supply chain routine, with the growth of air transport also increasing the emissions generated by it. Not only do aeroplanes burn a lot of fuel per tonne-kilometre, they also emit greenhouse gases at a very high altitude, which increases their effect on global warming.

Together with major airlines and biofuel producers, the European Commission established the European Advanced Biofuel Flightpath, an agenda towards the use of biofuel in aviation. The initiative aims to develop supply chains for its infrastructure, production and distribution that enable the availability and use of biofuel in the aviation sector.

Although the Flightpath initiative starts with relatively modest goals of making 10 per cent of the aviation fuel used by the three largest European airline groups (3–4 per cent of the total market in 2020) biofuel, the result from this stage will be the establishment of an infrastructure for alternative jet fuel to overcome logistical and infrastructure barriers to its use. The long-term goal is to increase the proportion of biofuel blended into the jet fuel to a level of 40–50 per cent. A key advantage of drop-in biofuel is that it does not require much new handling and infrastructure for operators.

So far flights using fuels from renewable sources have mainly used a blend of traditional jet fuel with biofuel, so-called drop-in fuel. Biofuel can be produced from various sources, and industry and government initiatives aim for sources that do not compete with food production. At the same time, the biofuel needs to have a high enough energy density, as aircraft carry the fuel (and therefore weight) with them over sometimes long distances. Through these considerations, the choice of usable currently available biofuels is limited.

Additionally, jet engines must be able to cope with the new fuel, hence the introduction of biofuel as a drop-in fuel and not as a pure biofuel variety. Every new type of jet fuel needs to be tested and authorized before it can be rolled out for wider application in aviation. The development of new engine types and aircraft that are more fuel efficient and can cope with a higher biofuel mix are hence also crucial to a reduction of carbon emissions from aviation.

The higher cost of biofuel compared to traditional jet fuel, however, is the main barrier to widespread use by airlines. Even a large-scale production of biofuel is not expected to be competitive with traditional jet fuel and governmental intervention through taxation or regulation may be necessary.

SOURCES European Commission; IATA Sustainable Aviation Fuel Roadmap; Sustainable Aviation Fuel Users Group.

Infrastructure

The growth in transport puts increasing demand on existing infrastructure. As freight transport infrastructure elements like ports, roads and railway tracks are significant financial investments that also come with sometimes extensive planning and consultation periods, the infrastructure is often not adjusted quickly enough to increased traffic demand and shifts in transportation. Insufficient capacity in the infrastructure automatically leads to congestion.

Congestion means that transport vehicles are not utilized well, as they spend much time queuing – and burning fuel – in traffic jams or waiting for a port terminal or a landing slot to become available. Land vehicles caught up in congestion do not operate at optimal speed, meaning their engines are burning more fuel than necessary. Continual accelerating and braking in traffic jams or in front of railway signals leads to high fuel consumption whilst at the same time the vehicle is not moving much of a distance.

The problem of congestion can be addressed in two ways: reducing traffic demands or increasing capacity. Extending transport infrastructure can face political obstacles. On the one hand, congestion in road transport leads to avoidable emissions, but on the other hand, an extension of the road network might lead to making the mode even more attractive for users. Furthermore, citizens will be affected by an extension of infrastructure. It may therefore be politically undesirable, as can be seen in the discussion about a third runway for Heathrow Airport.

In cities, however, an extension of the road infrastructure is often hard to achieve. Particularly in densely populated city areas and historic city centres, new road developments may be in contrast to the protection of historic sites and the quality of life of residents. Solutions can therefore only optimize the existing road network and its utilization, shift transport to other modes, reduce overall traffic or mitigate the impact on citizens.

Whilst freight transport is hard to shift to other transport modes in urban areas, government can encourage the reduction of freight transport and the use of low-emission vehicles. Across Europe, cities are seeing access restrictions for 'environmental zones' for vehicles that do not comply with specified levels of emission exhaustions. London introduced a congestion charge for road traffic in 2003, and since 2011, the charge has been related to the emission levels of a vehicle. Through this measure, traffic through London can be reduced and the use of cleaner vehicles be encouraged.

Shifting freight transport to off-peak times can be a way of reducing congestion. Nevertheless, night-time deliveries are unpopular with residents, because of an increase in noise at unpleasant hours. A variety of delivery hours across the same city also adds more complexity to the delivery schedule of logistics companies and may lead to non-compliance or more journeys. One way of reducing the number of delivery journeys in urban areas is the use of consolidation centres for city centre locations. This concept can also be found at traffic congested sites like airports and shopping malls.

Will autonomous vehicles make transport greener?

Autonomous vehicles, often referred to as 'driverless', are a key feature of future mobility and transportation. Whereas in current vehicle design, more and more support technology is being introduced to help drivers with parking manoeuvres, automatic distance keeping, speed control and emergency braking, completely autonomous vehicles are seen as the next logical step and are expected to be the mainstream way of driving by 2040.

Internationally, governments, vehicle manufacturers and technology companies are investing heavily in the research and development of future driverless solutions. But how may this advancement of technology impact the sustainability performance of transport?

It is widely expected that autonomous vehicles will reduce the number of accidents. And although most drivers are worried about losing control to an automated system, these systems are capable of responding faster to sudden situations than humans and they are certainly less prone to speeding and road rage than human drivers.

Autonomous vehicles can also be expected to drive more fuel efficiently, particularly if traffic and other vehicles in the system were coordinated with each other to avoid congestion. A major sustainability improvement is also expected from an anticipated shift from individual car ownership to a shared use of vehicles, meaning the number of cars that are being manufactured could be reduced on a per person measure (overall the number of cars will probably still increase due to population growth).

There is, however, also a worry that autonomous vehicles may increase urban sprawl as people will be more willing to accept longer travels because they will be able to use the journey time productively when they don't have to pay any attention to driving anymore. The disappearing cost for lorry drivers may also lead to more and longer journeys as the cost savings make it then more economically attractive to use a supplier further afield or to place an extra delivery order. Another aspect to worry about will be the loss of employment opportunity for vehicle drivers. The UK on its own employs around 300,000 lorry drivers, with many more drivers being employed in delivery services, as couriers, and driving buses and taxis. The social impact of autonomous vehicles will need to be prepared for and addressed as technology advances and replaces some of these employment opportunities.

SOURCES Institute of Electrical and Electronics Engineers; *Guardian*; GreenBiz.

Wider aspects of sustainability in freight transport

At the early stages of sustainability in freight transport, the discussion was mainly limited to the reduction of greenhouse gases and often narrowed down to CO_2 only. This perspective, however, was replaced over the years with a more holistic view including more aspects of sustainability. Consequently, the discussion became more complex through the consideration of other environmental issues like biodiversity, but also through the addition of social and economic issues.

We have already discussed the production of biofuels, where an early-stage enthusiasm changed into a more critical debate over its effects on the environment and where ethical questions of food versus fuel are raised.

Public interest in the sustainability of global sourcing and freight transport was stimulated in the food miles debate. It also came with a trend for consuming more locally produced food products and generally a consciousness of eating healthier. Environmentally aware consumers started considering 'food miles' – the distance a food product has travelled from the place where it's harvested to the place of consumption – in their shopping decisions. The perception was that the longer the journey of a food product, the more harmful it was for the environment. This perception, however, turned into more complex lifecycle assessments. Food miles came up as a form of criticism towards a lifestyle where consumers in northern countries expect fresh fruits and vegetables to be available all year round, ignoring seasons and locally available alternatives. However, a sole focus on food miles did not consider different modes of transport or greenhouse gas emissions from the transport. Food miles also completely ignore the emissions coming from the food's production, as well as the fact that many fruits and vegetables can hardly be grown in northern countries and the income of many farmers in developing countries depends on the export of their produce to Europe (Rama and Lawrence, 2008).

In a lifecycle assessment comparing dairy, lamb, apples and onions produced in New Zealand and sold in the UK with the same products produced in the UK and sold in New Zealand, a more complex picture emerged. Despite the additional transport, lamb and dairy products from New Zealand showed much lower greenhouse gas emissions than those from the UK. The lower emissions for the imported products were explained by the lower consumption of energy and fertilizers in the production of fodder in New Zealand, as agricultural and pasture space is more easily available. They also showed much fewer emissions from buildings, as the climate in New Zealand allows farmers to keep animals outdoors (Saunders *et al*, 2006).

Summary

Freight transport activities contribute to global greenhouse gas emissions. Although their share is much smaller than manufacturing, there is significant pressure to reduce transport emissions. With a still-increasing trend for globalization, more and more complex supply chains, specialized actors along the supply chain and higher customer expectations in developing markets, the growth of transportation is going to increase emissions further. Although mainly focusing on greenhouse gas emissions, transport also has sustainability impacts as it emits noise and causes accidents. On the positive side, it also makes goods available to people, enables us to travel and explore other cultures, and allows participation in society; or, more generally, transport makes our modern lifestyles possible.

The available transport modes vary significantly in their emissions, with the slower transport modes generally emitting less CO_2e than the faster ones. A reduction of emissions from transport can be achieved by avoiding transportation altogether, for example through local sourcing, a reduction of the emissions from transport by using cleaner engines and fuels or applying concepts like slow steaming, and through operational improvements achieved through technological support and collaboration.

Much of the shift towards greener transportation will come from public pressure and government initiatives to increase the costs for greenhouse gas emissions. The provision of infrastructure and support for the development and application of green technology are governmental incentives that help to reduce the impact of transport.

Which applications and technologies will become the mainstream solutions and standards of a more sustainable future in transportation will be the challenge of the next decade. With many green technologies moving from their infant stage to becoming feasible options, many may not be economically viable or lose out to the hen–egg dilemma of insufficient infrastructure coverage or may need reconsideration after some time. Most likely they will also create issues in other aspects of sustainability by using certain resources and replacing human workers through automation.

References

A P Møller Maersk Group (2011) Slow steaming – the full story [online] www.maersk.com [accessed 27 July 2012]

BBC (2012) US biofuel production should be suspended, UN says [online] www.bbc.co.uk/news/business-19206199 [accessed 16 July 2012]

BCG (2011) *Made in America, Again,* The Boston Consulting Group, Chicago

C E Delft (2012) Regulated slow steaming in maritime transport [online] http://www.cedelft.eu/publicatie/regulated_slow_steaming_in_maritime_transport/1224, 8 February

Chow, G (2010) Near shoring, off shore sourcing and global sourcing, *Inside Supply Management*, October

Cullinane, S and Edwards, J (2010) Assessing the environmental impacts of freight transport, Chapter 2 in McKinnon *et al* (eds) *Green Logistics*, Kogan Page, London

Defra (2011) Guidelines to Defra's GHG emission conversion factors for company reporting [online] http://www.defra.gov.uk/publications/files/pb13625-emission-factor-methodology-paper-110905.pdf [accessed 16 August 2012]

den Boer, L C and Schroten, A (2007) 'Traffic Noise Reduction in Europe', *CE Delft* [online] available at: https://www.transportenvironment.org/sites/te/files/media/2008-02_traffic_noise_ce_delft_report.pdf [accessed 28 December 2016]

Department for Transport (2011) *Road Freight Statistics*, October 2011

Department of Energy and Climate Change (2009) *UK Energy Sector Indicators 2009*, National Statistics Office, London

Eurostat (2016) Freight transport statistics [online] available at: http://ec.europa.eu/eurostat/statistics-explained/index.php?title=Freight_transport_statistics&oldid=222336#Modal_split [accessed 01 August 2016]

FEHRL (2006) *Tyre/road noise*, Brussels, TUV Nord, BAST, TRL, VTI

Freight Transport Association UK (2015) *Logistics Report 2015* [online] available at: http://www.fta.co.uk/export/sites/fta/_galleries/downloads/logistics_report/Web_files/LR15_WEB_270415.pdf [accessed 01 August 2016]

Germanischer Lloyd (2012) LNG heralds a new era in ship propulsion, *Germanischer Lloyd Navigator*, Special Issue LNG, Hamburg, February

Handelsblatt (2012) Linde plant flüssiggas-tankstellen für schiffe, 6 August

Heywood, M (2016) Life as a Hermes driver: 'They offload all the risk on to the courier', *Guardian* [online] available at: https://www.theguardian.com/money/2016/jul/18/life-as-a-hermes-driver-they-offload-all-the-risk-on-to-the-courier [accessed 01 August 2016]

IGD (2009) Nestlé and United Biscuits – taking a unique approach to collaboration [online] available at: http://www.igd.com/index.asp?id=1&fid=1&sid=5&tid=49&folid=0&cid=1384 [accessed 16 July 2012]

Lambert, J and Philipps-Bertin, C (2008) Perception and attitudes to transportation noise in France: a national survey, *9th International Congress on Noise as a Public Health Problem* (ICBEN), Foxwoods

Leopoldina – German National Academy of Sciences (2012) Bioenergy – chances and limits [online] available at: www.leopoldina.org [accessed 10 July 2012]

MAN (2012) Slow steaming practices in the global shipping industry, *MAN* [online] available at: https://www.swedishclub.com/upload/Loss_Prev_Docs/Machinery/MAN%20PrimeServ%20-%20Slow%20Steaming%20Rapport%202012[1].pdf [accessed 30 December 2016]

OECD International Transport Forum (2015) ITF transport outlook 2015 [online] available at: http://2015.internationaltransportforum.org/sites/files/itf2013/files/documents/en/ITF-model_0.pdf [accessed 01 August 2016]

Park, J, Sarkis, J and Wu, Z (2012) China's green challenges, *Inside Supply Management*, June/July, pp 38f

PE International (2010) *Energiebedarfs- und Emissionsvergleich von LKW, bahn und schiff im güterfernverkehr*, Leinfelden-Echterdingen

Peters, G P, Minx, J C, Weber, C L and Edenhofer, O (2011) Growth in emission transfers via international trade from 1990 to 2008, *PNAS*, 108 (21), pp 8903–08

Rama, I and Lawrence, P (2008) *Food Miles – A Critical Evaluation*, Economics and Policy Research Branch, Victorian Department of Primary Industries

Roland Berger (2011) *The End of the China Cycle?* Roland Berger Strategy Consultants, Detroit

Rushton, A, Croucher, P and Baker, P (2006) *The Handbook of Logistics and Distribution Management*, 3rd edn, Kogan Page, London

Saunders, C, Barber, A and Taylor, G (2006) *Food Miles: Comparative energy/ emissions performance of New Zealand's agriculture industry*, Lincoln University, Research Report No 285, July

Süddeutsche Zeitung (2015) Groß, größer, Gigaliner, 23 July

SWOV Institute for Road Safety Research (2011) *Electric Vehicles: What are the effects on road safety?* SWOV Article, July/August

Tankstellenmarkt (2012) Umweltauflagen für schiffe bringen flüssiges erdgas nach vorn [online] available at: http://www.tankstellenmarkt.com/ lng-umweltauflagen-fuer-schiffe-bringen-fluessiges-erdgas-nach-vorn-1131869. html [accessed at 16 July 2012]

US Department of Transportation (2016) Freight facts and figures 2015 [online] available at: http://www.rita.dot.gov/bts/sites/rita.dot.gov.bts/files/data_and_ statistics/by_subject/freight/freight_facts_2015 [accessed 01 August 2016]

Wenner, K and Trautrims, A (2012) Applications of telematics in fleet management, Conference Proceedings of the Logistics Research Network, Cranfield

World Economic Forum (2009) *Supply Chain Decarbonization: The role of logistics and transport in reducing supply chain carbon emissions*, World Economic Forum, Geneva

WPCI (2016) LNG fuelled vessels [online] available at: http://www.lngbunkering. org/lng/vessels/existing-fleet-orderbooks [accessed 03 January 2017]

Sustainable warehousing 04

Despite initiatives like 'just-in-time' and other inventory reduction approaches in modern supply chains, warehouses can usually still be found at almost all stages along the supply chain. Not only do they buffer imbalances in the supply chain, they fulfil various functional activities and roles alongside the mere storing of goods. This chapter starts with looking at the environmental impact of warehousing and how warehouses can be categorized. We will then portray the different functions of warehouses and their design before we investigate opportunities to reduce the impact of warehouses on the environment and to improve their wider environmental and social sustainability.

The environmental impact of warehouses

The World Economic Forum (2009) estimates that about 13 per cent of all supply chain emissions stem from logistics buildings and the UK Warehousing Association (UKWA, 2010) quantifies the emissions coming from warehouses to about 3 per cent of the UK's total greenhouse gas emissions. Understandably, the environmental issues of warehouses receive considerably less attention than transport operations which account for the remaining 87 per cent of emissions. Nevertheless, next to the improvement of environmental issues there is also a large potential for cost savings by running warehouses more efficiently (UKWA, 2010). Regulatory pressure on the construction industry to reduce the carbon footprint (RICS, 2010) and the cost of land usage in densely populated areas together with a reluctance of residents to have a warehouse close to their neighbourhood make it worthwhile to consider environmental issues in the design and operation of warehouses.

The impact of warehouses goes beyond their greenhouse gas emissions. Warehouses add to the traffic of heavy and lighter goods vehicles. They cause noise and cover large areas of land, interfering with wildlife and rain water trickling into the ground. They are also workplaces that offer employment, and are essential for making products available to consumers and keeping factories and other businesses running.

The roles and functions of warehouses

Warehouses are an important operational part of supporting a company's supply chain strategy. They are usually the nodes in a supply chain network and they greatly influence service levels and the costs of the network. Failures in holding and effectively dispatching the right stock at the right time in the right quantities and quality will result in unhappy customers. But warehouses and the inventory that is kept inside them also create costs. The costs for a warehouse consist of fixed costs for the erection of the building and equipment, and operational costs, which depend strongly on the initial design of the warehouse. Similarly, the environmental 'costs' also stem from the construction phase and from the operations.

The design of the warehouse – and the design of its operational processes – are supposed to support the overall business and supply chain strategy. At that stage, consideration must be given to what market the warehouse is located in – is it growing or stable or even declining? Where is the demand for the products and where does the supply come from? Take for example a fast fashion online retailer. The opportunity to provide a 24-hour delivery service may be an essential feature of the business model. Or look at aircraft spare parts; such warehouses are usually located right next to an airport with a dense flight network so that parts can be distributed to aircraft around the globe quickly. How much flexibility do operations require? Is cost more important than agility? What is the expected duration of the investment and who owns and runs the warehouse? In well-developed logistics markets there will be a range of service providers available to operate a warehouse. Nevertheless, they will offer a range of options and the selection depends on the underlying business imperatives of the client (Baker, 2010).

Warehouses have very different roles in the supply chain. The most prominent differentiator is whether they actually store stock. Cross-docking happens when goods are received, processed and dispatched without actually being stored. It is often used for goods that need to be moved rapidly, for example perishables, and in warehouses further away from centralized stockholding points. Besides the increased speed, cross-docking is also popular to centralize inventory and save inventory costs. Cross-docking is gaining further importance in future supply chains (BNP, 2010). With a reduction of warehouses holding the same inventory, the required safety stock can be reduced through the 'square root law'. This is based on the rule of thumb that when centralizing inventory the ratio of inventory held in a decentralized system to the inventory held in a centralized system equals the square root of the number of initial locations. As an example, by the reduction from 10 inventory-holding warehouses to only one centralized site, overall safety stock inventory can be reduced by 68 per cent (Maister, 1975). The number of inventory-holding warehouses is therefore, in extreme simplification, a trade-off between transport costs (for longer journeys) and the costs of holding inventory. As mentioned, the decision is usually more complex, with many more considerations.

Fulfilment centres are another role of warehouses, where many operational activities occur in the warehouse. Orders are picked either by workers or by automated systems, and items are put together in orders, packed and sent out to the customer. Online retailers who use these fulfilment centres also experience sometimes very high return rates. This led to improved and specialized facilities for processing returned items in fulfilment centres as returns require a high level of manual processing. The reduction of returns will reduce unnecessary extra journeys and handling.

Warehouses can also cover value-added activities in the final processing and customization of products. This can be part of assembly and packaging operations. In distribution centres for the retail trade, we can also see the preparation of goods for retail stores (for example putting items on hangers or adding price tags). But warehouses may also have a much stronger inbound focus. Consolidation centres bundle smaller deliveries into larger shipments. This can often be found in export-oriented places to ensure shipping containers are filled up with loads from multiple suppliers, and work warehouses in port-centric logistics concepts, where goods are received and consolidated in the warehouse at the port of arrival.

In just-in-time supply chains, warehouses at the customer end of the supply chain are avoided. Stock is stored at the suppliers (or ideally only produced as needed) and transported to the assembly line when it is needed. This concept is particularly widespread in car manufacturing. Due to the high levels of customization, just-in-time concepts developed into just-in-sequence, whereby the delivered products are arranged to suit the production schedule. These concepts are very complex and vulnerable and require a high level of logistics competence and sophisticated operations in all parts of the supply chain, including the warehouse nodes. Warehouses in these supply chains are mainly buffering supplier and customer production schedules and preparing goods for their delivery directly to the assembly line.

Despite all these trends and changes in warehouse design, most warehouses still fulfil the classic warehouse function of receiving goods, storing them and dispatching them at a later point. Most warehouses also combine several roles and operational aspects and would for example have a cross-docking area despite holding some stock of other products.

Many logistics activities are outsourced to external logistics service providers. In Europe, a bit more than a third of the warehousing market is outsourced, as well as a similar proportion of the contract logistics market, which is the outsourcing of the entire distribution function to a third party, usually including warehousing, fulfilment and delivery operations in one contract (Fraunhofer SCS, 2014). The outsourcing of warehouse and fulfilment operations can have many facets, usually categorized by who owns the assets and manages the operations. Important for sustainability issues is therefore whether the owner of the warehouse has a long-term perspective for a site, which impacts the decision of investing in sustainability measures that have a longer payback period (Rushton and Walker, 2007). Using external service providers also makes it easier to collaborate with other customers or to use shared facilities, which can result in better utilization and economies of scale. Logistics property developers also construct sites speculatively without knowing the eventual specifications, making it more difficult to estimate whether future clients are willing to pay for the sustainability features of a new site.

Warehouse location

The number and locations of warehouses in a logistics network determine to a large extent the amount of transportation that is required within the network. Ideally a warehouse is located at the so-called 'centre of gravity' of the transport journeys in the area that it serves. The number of warehouses in the overall network and the areas they serve are ideally the optimal trade-off between the costs for transport and the costs for the warehouses (and the inventory, etc).

As outlined, the reduction of inventory holding points leads to a reduction of safety stock and consequently a cost reduction in inventory. In this trade-off between inventory holding and transport journeys, a general trend towards more centralization of inventory could be observed over recent decades. This can mean that a central distribution site may be run more efficiently, but it may also mean more journeys and transport kilometres (Kohn and Brodin, 2008). The centralization of inventory is encouraged by low transportation costs. Additionally, the elimination of border controls (and the resulting reduction of waiting times at border crossings) in Europe encouraged companies to centralize their distribution into fewer sites and often a single European site (Ferrari *et al*, 2006). Furthermore, logistics approaches like just-in-time (JIT) in manufacturing and efficient consumer response (ECR) in retailing led to more frequent deliveries of smaller batches.

The decision for a warehouse's location is more complex than a pure optimization of the transport network in the centre of gravity. Planning permission for a greenfield development may be difficult to obtain and land use can be restricted by legislation. If an already existing site is used, it can be likely that available sites are not in the preferred location and a suitable warehouse at a less favourable location is the next best option.

Another criterion can be access to particular transport modes. BNP (2010) reports that the majority of logistics real estate customers consider multi-modal transport as being increasingly important. The access to rail and water transport may be an essential feature for particular products and sustainability strategies. With increasing cross-border trade, port-centric logistics is also becoming more popular. Locations like ports can also be chosen if the warehouse needs to be in a free-trade zone or access to service providers specialized around sea transport is required.

The proximity to the customers or to supply sources is a strategic decision that can be an essential feature of a warehouse to support a business's market strategy and may be even a requirement in the contract with a large single customer. The access to labour is another aspect of the location decision. Fulfilment centres provide opportunities for employment. In the case of online retailers, for example, demand during the Christmas period peaks and the fulfilment centre therefore needs large numbers of temporary staff. The availability of sufficiently skilled staff gains even more importance the more value-added services are performed at the site and the more complex the logistics processes and handling equipment are.

Handling equipment

The operational processes in a warehouse are supported by the use of handling equipment, which is also a consumer of operational energy. The selection of handling equipment is usually determined by the purpose and design of the warehouse and the goods that are processed at a site. The level of automation varies considerably between warehouses. Unmanned automated warehouse equipment, often referred to AS/RS (Automated Storage/Retrieval System), usually leads to higher throughputs but also decreases flexibility enormously. Using humans also allows for the covering of peaks more easily, particularly in retail fulfilment centres which rely on human labour, as the packing of boxes is difficult to handle using automated equipment and returned goods rely on human judgement as to whether they are in a re-sellable condition. Automation might be a preferable option in harsh environments, for example in refrigerated warehouses or in low-oxygen environments. Conveyor belts, cranes and dredgers are used to handle bulk cargo. Other typical handling equipment includes fork-lift trucks, which are commonly found in palletized goods environments and come in many varieties and engines, using batteries, diesel or even hydrogen.

All these types of handling equipment have different characteristics. After strategic considerations of longevity of investments, flexibility and operational aspects of throughput capacity, item characteristics and the warehouse site need to be looked at. If a warehouse is expected to have a high throughput, goods need to be stored more densely, otherwise the journeys between receiving, storage, order picking and dispatching become too long. In addition, the site and cost aspects may restrict the land use of the warehouse. Automated warehouse equipment can cope with a higher throughput, and also achieves a higher storage density as it can reach higher levels in the warehouse and needs less aisle space for manoeuvring than fork-lifts.

Assessing the impact

The environmental balance of a warehouse consists of two levels: the emissions from the construction and the operational emissions. Before we look into how the impacts from those can be reduced, we need to learn about the current standards for assessing the environmental performance of warehouses. The most widely used standards for assessing the sustainability of warehouse design are LEED, the Leadership in Energy and Environmental Design framework by the US Green Building Council, and BREEAM, the Building Research Establishment Environmental Assessment Method by the Building Research Establishment (BRE) based in the UK.

Both schemes measure the sustainability of warehouses by awarding point scores in several weighted categories. Depending on the overall score, the warehouse is accredited a certain sustainability class: BREEAM statuses range from 'Pass' to 'Outstanding'; LEED's categorize warehouse sustainability from mere 'Certified' up to 'Platinum'. The assessment categories and the weighting factors for the individual categories within the two schemes can be compared in the following figures. Additionally, both schemes add a weighting factor of 10 per cent for innovation.

Figure 4.1   BREEAM weighting factors for new constructions

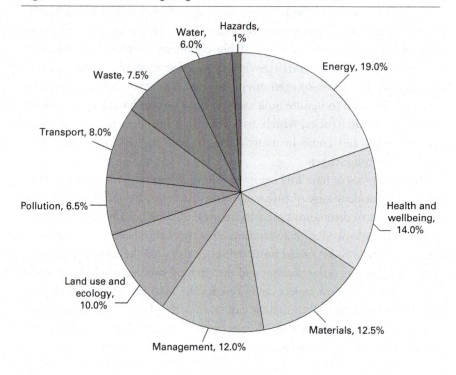

Figure 4.2   LEED weighting factors for new constructions

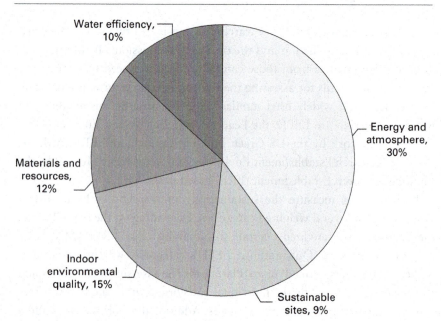

Within each category points are awarded according to a warehouse's performance against the scheme's benchmark standards. The awarded points are multiplied with the category's weighting. The scoring and weighting are adjusted to local circumstances when the scheme is firstly applied in a country (BRE Group, 2016). Under the BREEAM scheme, for example, a score of 85 per cent must be obtained to be classified as 'Outstanding' and 70 per cent for 'Excellent'. Minimum scores in some subcategories must also be obtained; for example, 10 out of the 15 available credits for reducing CO_2 emissions are needed to achieve 'Outstanding' compared to 6 credits for being rated as 'Excellent' (BRE Group, 2012).

The first warehouse to achieve 'Outstanding' status under the BREEAM scheme was the G. Park Blue Planet distribution centre in Chatterley Valley, UK. The developer, Gazeley, projected the savings in operational costs due to the environmental features in its design to be £300,000 per annum (BRE, 2012). It features non-stick, self-cleaning roof lights, solar photovoltaic laminates and the use of kinetic plates to recover energy from arriving vehicles (Baker, 2012).

Despite the proposed operational savings resulting from high environmental ratings, this does not necessarily lead to equivalently higher yields in terms of rent or value. A recent study found that energy savings expressed in better EPC (energy performance certificates) ratings did not result in a similarly equivalent increased rent and there was only a little evidence indicating that better EPC ratings had an impact on yields (Fuerst and McAllister, 2011). Although tenant surveys express willingness to pay a premium for operational savings, tenants also identify a tendency towards shorter-term leaseholds, which reduces the attractiveness of longer-term investments into sustainability measures (BNP, 2010; ProLogis and Capgemini, 2006).

The gap between environmental performance and rents may be explained by the different interests of the many stakeholders involved in a building over its lifetime. Real estate developers are mainly interested in the return on investments and short-term risks, and only indirectly in the functional quality of the warehouse. Financial investors also have their main interest in the return on investment, the expected development of the property value and the anticipated risks. If the warehouse is going to be owned by the user, future rents are not part of the consideration, but more focus is on functionality, risks and lifecycle costs. Tenants, in contrast, are mainly focused on the rent and functional quality. On the other hand, the public and public authorities are mainly interested in the external costs and total costs of the warehouse and the risks anticipated with the construction (Gregori and Wimmer, 2011).

The accreditation schemes initially focused very much on the design stage of warehouses. However, lately they also developed guidelines for assessing sustainability improvements at already-existing sites. Embodied energy in existing buildings is an often-unconsidered aspect of the sustainability of a construction. An assessment of the whole lifecycle of a building, considering the already-embedded energy, carbon and other emissions in the building, is therefore a more complete approach. This also applies to considerations of end-of-life issues, such as the disposal of materials and the energy consumed in the deconstruction. Overall, the lifecycle analysis should consider inputs and outputs from raw material extraction, manufacturing, construction, use, and disposal (Menzies, 2011).

The overall environmental balance depends on the sum of emissions from all stages of the warehouse lifecycle. It may therefore be less environmentally damaging to use an existing site despite poor operational performance, since the embedded energy and emissions have already occurred (Menzies, 2011).

Only a complete lifecycle assessment of the warehouse can give clarification on the best option for achieving sustainability. The proportion of operational impact to embodied impact differs significantly between warehouses and also strongly depends on the life span of the warehouse. In a comparison of various roof light ratios and insulation options, Rai *et al* (2011) identified that the combined impact of embodied and operational CO_2 emissions of a warehouse over a 25-year life span did not show huge differences in the total CO_2 impact. The study compared scenarios of decisions around roof lights and insulation at the design stage of a conventional distribution centre of 8,000 m^2 and the effects they had on the heating during the operational phase of the warehouse. Due to the higher carbon embedded in the insulation material and the roof lights, an increased level of insulation had only a very marginal positive effect on the environmental balance of the warehouse over its whole life. However, the proportion of operational impact to embedded impact is crucial in the lifecycle assessment. Gregori and Wimmer (2011) assume that 80 per cent of costs are caused during the operational phase of a logistics building, which gives sustainability considerations in the design stage more emphasis. They also point out that over the 25-year life span of a warehouse, one needs to assume rising costs for energy. An assessment is becoming even harder to make when looking at the often high turnover of tenants of logistics sites. A warehouse may therefore often not be fully utilized, leading to inefficiencies. It can also mean that additional emissions from construction activities occur at a later point to adjust the warehouse to a new tenant's needs.

Reduction of environmental impact

Following the lifecycle concept, for buildings we can generally differentiate between operational carbon (or carbon equivalent) emissions and embedded emissions. Investments into the operational improvement of the sustainability of a warehouse may often occur at the construction stage and it is therefore important to understand the purpose and the anticipated lifecycle of the building. RICS (2010) considers the share of embodied carbon-equivalent emissions to be 60 per cent of a warehouse's overall CO_2e emissions. However, if assuming a lifecycle of only 10 years, the share of embodied CO_2e rockets to 95 per cent, shifting the focus of emission savings from the operational phase to the construction itself. In comparison, a supermarket over its lifetime would usually have a ratio of 10 per cent embodied energy to 90 per cent operational energy, as a supermarket typically uses a lot more energy than a warehouse.

The differentiation becomes crucial when discussing what emission reduction levels are supposed to be achieved (RICS, 2010). For the erection of a short-term warehouse, operational emissions can almost be neglected, and more emphasis needs to be placed on avoiding CO_2e in the construction operations and material. For long-term use of a warehouse, operational savings become more worthwhile even if they cause emissions (for example for additional insulation) in the construction phase.

In the construction phase, emissions are caused by the construction materials and the construction processes. The emissions embodied in the construction materials vary, but so does their lifespan. An aluminium curtain wall contains around 1,000 MJ/m^2 of embodied energy and has a life expectancy of less than 40 years. The lifespan of a timber frame with aluminium cladding is of similar length, but the embodied energy is only 400 MJ/m^2. When comparing the aluminium curtain wall with a concrete panel the importance of lifespans becomes apparent. The concrete wall does contain a bit more than 800 MJ/m^2 energy – not even 20 per cent less than the aluminium curtain wall – but its life expectancy is almost double that of the aluminium curtain wall. If a structure was really used for more than 40 years, the energy savings become extremely significant, as the aluminium curtain wall needs to be fully renewed (RICS, 2010). When looking at timber, the importance of local sourcing becomes obvious. Whilst imported timber typically embodies 7,540 kWh/m^3 (significantly more than the 800 kWh/m^3 for concrete even), the local timber alternative contains only 110 kWh/m^3 (Harris, 1999).

For warehouses, however, one can be doubtful whether constructions will really be usable for the full 40-year lifetime. Storage and logistics requirements change over time and the layout of a multi-client site in particular needs to be flexible to allow for adjustments in the number of doors, more height, additional floor strength for heavy goods or special storage arrangements like clean rooms or refrigerators (ProLogis and Capgemini, 2006).

Many logistics sites cluster in areas that are close to the aforementioned centres of gravity of transportation for the markets they are serving, or else they cluster around ports and airports. Availability of the right warehouse space in the right areas therefore becomes an issue, and the most popular locations are most often found in relatively densely populated areas, where space is scarce and expensive anyway. Additionally, traffic congestion and local restrictions on traffic and operating hours are limiting to warehouse operations. The limitation to areas where space is expensive may also lead to the construction of higher buildings and the installation of handling equipment that uses up less space. In areas of limited available space for warehouse construction, real estate developers will naturally also look into brownfield developments and the (re-)development of already established sites. Although this incurs demolition costs, it may benefit sustainability, as upgrading existing structures avoids the addition of embodied carbon from construction material that would be used for building a new warehouse (ProLogis and Capgemini, 2006).

The use of land itself is an emission and newly built warehouses interfere with the environment. This can refer to rainwater not running into the ground anymore, interference with local wildlife and destruction of green areas, and optical impact on the landscape. The area also becomes unable to absorb any carbon which, in the case of the site being vegetated or used agriculturally beforehand, has a permanent effect. The land used for warehousing space in the UK has been increasing significantly over the last decade and is now greater than the land covered by offices or retail stores.

Emissions also stem from the construction operations, since construction processes rely on heavy machinery and engines to move building materials, earth and rubble. Lane (2012) assesses the carbon created in the construction process of a 10-storey office building in inner London to be 13 per cent and estimates the demolition process to clear the building site to be 2 per cent of the lifetime carbon footprint. Although warehouses are usually of a lighter structure than office buildings, it shows that the construction processes add significantly to the carbon footprint of any building, including warehouses. However, supply chains in the construction industry are influenced by many stakeholders who have different interests. Involving all stakeholders of a building's lifetime is complex and must look beyond the client-contractor-supplier relationship. The shift towards sustainability in construction must come through the purchasing power of influential buyers and their demand for specified performance criteria (Ofori, 2000). In the transport operations during the construction phase, much of the building material is delivered directly from manufacturers to the site and very little communication exists across the network of manufacturers, contractors and hauliers. Transport efficiency is also negatively affected by the geographical location, accessibility and a lack of infrastructure at greenfield sites (Sternberg *et al*, 2012).

Besides the embedded emissions in the building stemming from the construction materials and processes, the operational emissions need to be considered. Although the discussion is mainly focused on reducing the energy consumption of a site, the warehouse's operational sustainability also consists of other aspects like using all resources more efficiently and reducing the waste generated by a site.

Benchmarking and comparison of energy performances of warehouses are difficult, as they are built in different environments, contexts and for different lifespans, products and purposes. In addition, the boundaries of environmental auditing vary between schemes and may work in favour of particular solutions. For example, the PAS 2050 carbon auditing guidelines exclude employees' commuting journeys from the audit – thereby giving an advantage to a warehouse that's operated with more human labour and less technology and also ignoring the additional emissions from commuting journeys if a warehouse is poorly connected to public transport and far away from the employees' residences.

Temperature control is estimated to contribute up to 20 per cent of a frozen goods warehouse's operating cost (Marchant, 2010). Refrigeration units are using electricity; the way that electricity is produced therefore determines much of the carbon footprint. Heating systems are usually based on burning fossil fuels or materials from renewable sources. The loss of heat depends on the temperature difference between the inside and the outside of the warehouse, insulation and building fabric, and controlled and uncontrolled air ventilation (Carbon Trust, 2012).

Warehouses may require a wider storage environment control of humidity or even the oxygen content. For example, fresh fruits are usually stored in a CO_2-filled environment to decelerate the ripening process. However, temperature control also needs to consider the comfort of warehouse employees. Although the storage area might be refrigerated, the common room right next to it will be heated at the same time. Health and safety regulations limiting employees' time in the low-temperature environment and work safety clothing limits the operations in such warehouses. The heat from handling equipment, lighting and machines adds to the required refrigeration effort. Temperature controlled warehouses therefore not only depend on the ability to achieve the required temperatures, but also to hold that temperature.

Regardless whether the warehouse requires heating or cooling, thermal insulation and heat/cold loss barriers are reducing the consumed operational energy (although they might increase the embedded emissions as discussed earlier). Some ventilation is needed to exchange air and maintain an environment that is safe for humans to operate in; however, controlled and uncontrolled air ventilation need to be considered separately. The exchange of air means constant temperature adjustment. A warehouse with high rates of uncontrolled ventilation (also called air infiltration) wastes energy for heating/cooling. Air leakage causes about 25 per cent of heat loss in a typical industrial building (Carbon Trust, 2012). Unnecessary losses of temperature-controlled air from air exchange can be prevented through separating temperature zones effectively, installing fast-acting gates, closely fitting doors, the use of thermostats and opening doors and gates only when necessary (Marchant, 2010). Warehouses are usually built with very high ceilings. Naturally hot air rises, which can lead to temperature differences between ground level and close to the ceiling of up to 10 degrees Celsius. Ceiling circulation fans redistribute the heat back to the ground floor where the operators are working. Usually the savings from the value of heat exceed the energy consumed by the fans (Carbon Trust, 2012).

The thickness of insulation reduces the temperature loss and therefore also reduces the required energy for constant temperature adjustment. However, the thicker the insulation, the larger the embodied energy in the insulation material and there is consequently a maximum point to which insulation makes sense (Harris, 1999). Warehouses can also be separated into zones, with barriers between them to limit the air exchange to smaller units and to adjust temperatures more precisely. The lower the temperatures required, the higher the refrigeration effort and the electricity consumption. Therefore, products can be separated into groups of the same temperature storage requirement levels, avoiding the storage of products at temperatures lower than necessary.

An ambient warehouse of an average size uses about two-thirds of its electricity consumption for lighting (UKWA, 2010). Installing more efficient lighting technology, rooflights, and switching off unneeded lights can reduce the electricity used for lighting.

New energy-efficient lights, like LEDs or fluorescent lights, convert a higher proportion of the input energy into light and less into heat than conventional lights. They are also lower in maintenance and have a short payback period of only a few years (Long, 2010). The overall number of installed lights can also be reduced by about 30 per cent through the installation of reflectors above the light source (Gregori and Wimmer, 2011). Generally, however, the lighting requirements are determined by the tasks performed in a particular part of the warehouse; for example, lighting at the storage area depends on aisle width and height. Solutions therefore need to be applied to individual warehouse designs and purposes (Marchant, 2010).

Allowing the sunlight to shine into the building, for example through the installation of roof lights, can be a way to reduce the need for artificial light (Marchant, 2010). Natural sunlight is also perceived as more comfortable than electric light (Gregori and Wimmer, 2011). However, roof lights need to be considered in their overall effect, as they may have a negative impact on insulation (Baker, 2012). Both roof lights and electric lights need cleaning periodically, as the dust of two years' operating time can reduce the light levels by up to 50 per cent, increasing energy consumption by 15 per cent (Marchant, 2010).

Arranging for light only in the areas where it is needed, and turning off lights manually or through the installation of movement sensors or time-controlled light switches saves significant amounts of electricity (Gregori and Wimmer, 2011). Changes in the warehouse lighting usually show rather short payback periods, therefore also making it an attractive sustainability improvement for rented warehouse sites and shorter lease times (UKWA, 2010).

Another area of energy consumption in the warehouse is the use of handling equipment. These can be automated storage systems, which consume electricity for moving goods around, but also for computer systems controlling the movements and storage. Forklifts at a warehouse site can come in many varieties depending on the characteristics of the goods and the site. They run on various types of fuels or electricity (see the paragraphs on alternative fuels in Chapter 3). Similar to lighting installations, material handling equipment emits heat besides the pure energy consumption, increasing the energy consumed in temperature-controlled warehouses. Fumes from fuel-based handling equipment also increase the need for ventilation, reducing the thermal efficiency of the building.

A shift to lower-emission fuels and electric forklifts reduces the CO_2 emissions from warehouse operations, but no clear general statement of what energy type for forklifts causes the least emissions can be made from prior studies. Evaluation boundaries differ between 'well-to-pump', 'well-to-wheel', 'outlet-to-battery', 'battery-to-wheel' and 'wheel-to-exhaust', making the alternatives hard to compare. A full lifecycle assessment including maintenance, lifespan, disposal and energy consumption would have to be considered to fully compare the options. The complexity of such an assessment and the difficulty of comparing the alternatives tends to lead to a cost-of-ownership approach rather than a total emissions assessment (Marchant, 2010).

Improvements in battery technology and battery energy efficiency may increase the sustainability and attractiveness of electric forklifts. As they are charged from the electric mains, the source for the electricity can be determined by the warehouse user. Modern electric forklifts can also regain energy when the forks are lowered with a load or when the machine brakes (Marchant, 2010). The re-gaining of energy, together with improved battery endurance, faster charging modes and better energy efficiency, results in longer operating times, reducing the overall number of required batteries or forklifts. Through the advance of technology, electric forklifts have become the main mode for indoor use (Long, 2010).

As with the optimization of any other transport network, journeys within the warehouse made by forklifts or other mechanical handling systems can be optimized by application of information technology and the use of warehouse management systems (WMS). Forklifts enabled to communicate with the WMS can also reduce the number of journeys, for example by avoiding detours to input data into a computer station (Long, 2010). Other electricity-consuming technology applications in the warehouse are picking systems, such as pick-to-voice or pick-to-light (Marchant, 2010).

A warehouse's overall emissions can also be reduced by consideration of the wider operational issues. Operating hours and delivery can be scheduled to avoid peak traffic times; avoiding congested areas for the warehouse site also means fewer lorries are sitting in traffic (Thuermer, 2009).

Warehouses also consume water. Water is consumed for the human needs of workers, but also in the cleaning of the warehouse, lorries (Gregori and Wimmer, 2011) and in the processing of goods (if value-added activities are happening at the warehouse site). Refrigeration units may also consume water. Due to their usually large roof surface, many warehouses are also ideal for harvesting rainwater and re-using it in greywater areas in the warehouse.

Depending on the level of value-adding activities and packaging processes, warehouses also create waste like any other industrial site. Incoming deliveries may need to be split up, unpacked or re-packed before they are stored. Outgoing products need wrapping, may be put on disposable pallets or packaged in other ways. Reducing and avoiding packaging and recycling packaging materials reduce the environmental impact from the warehouse's waste.

Green energy

Since many of the operational emissions are related to energy consumption, the harnessing of green energy at warehouse sites can be used to improve the overall operational sustainability of the warehouse. Warehouses are often situated away from residential areas or in industrial estates, close to ports, motorways and other transport infrastructure. The often-experienced opposition from local resident groups against green energy-harnessing installations in residential neighbourhoods can therefore often be avoided, making warehouse sites most suitable for the generation of green energy. Solutions towards the sustainability of new non-domestic buildings are categorized into 'on-site rich' (63 per cent of regulated reductions to comply with targets coming from on-site improvements), 'off-site rich' (44 per cent of reductions from on-site), and 'balanced' (54 per cent of reductions from on-site). On-site reductions mainly come from higher building energy efficiency and the use of low- and zero-carbon energy generation. The ability to generate low-carbon energy on-site and therefore the reduction of emissions on-site will depend hugely on a site's context and environment; the installation of wind turbines, for example, may be politically much easier at a rural site close to a motorway than in an urban location (UK GBC, 2010).

Green energy produced on-site can either be consumed directly, fed into the electric grid or a combination of both, whereby green energy produced is consumed by the site but a connection to the electric grid is used for balancing out the site's power supply and demand. Nevertheless, electricity bought in from energy suppliers can also be sourced from 'green' forms of electricity generation.

Energy at a warehouse site can be generated from biomass or low-carbon fuels (which are not totally carbon neutral, but nevertheless might be of lower emissions impact than a previously used fuel), wind turbines, solar panels, recovered waste energy, kinetic energy and thermal exchange units (Marchant, 2010).

The way energy is generated and sourced for a warehouse site is individual to the site's requirements, settings and context. The decision of which types of electricity and energy are to be used depends on operational, regulatory, environmental and market factors. The general issues in this decision are operational patterns of energy consumption against the generation of energy at the site; the costs of the energy-generation technology and at what scale the energy can be produced at a reasonable cost (and whether there is enough demand to build a power-generating facility of the necessary scale);

the availability and maturity of technology; and regulations and market conditions (Marchant, 2010).

The generation of energy on-site increases the complexity of energy management. Balancing energy demand with supply, the fluctuation of energy market prices and at the same time the fluctuation of production depending on local geographical circumstances and weather, and the proximity of other energy consumers nearby and infrastructural access to the national grid, all make energy management and the investment decision making a more complex task. Despite energy generation on-site, warehouses need to be connected to the electricity grid to transfer electricity into the wider network and to source from it. Around 44 per cent of the on-site-generated electricity will be fed into the national grid. Governments worldwide are currently implementing different ways of encouraging or even enforcing an increase of low- and zero-carbon energy generation. Feed-in tariffs (a regulated price for renewable energy that is fed into the national grid) financially encourage the installation of renewable energy-generating infrastructure (Marchant, 2010). Other regulations impose minimum energy efficiency levels for sites, the purchase and trade of renewable obligation certificates or emission allowances, the sourcing of a certain percentage of the consumed energy from renewable energy sources, or the inclusion of on-site energy generation in planning permissions for new buildings (UK GBC, 2007).

The costs for sourcing and generating 'green' energy vary strongly across the available options. Comparing the costs for on- and off-site-generated energy from renewables, the on-site solutions appear more costly in many cases. The annual cost per kilogramme CO_2 avoided for small-scale wind is more than tenfold the cost of large-scale wind. The cost for solar photovoltaic installations is even higher, whereas the usually off-site installation of a biomass CHP (combined heat and power) plant is not much more expensive than the large-scale wind option (UK GBC, 2007). Large-scale wind and biomass CHP are more likely to be off-site, as they often require more than one user. Off-site solutions in most cases use an external supplier, so that the warehouse operator is not tied to a long-term commitment. Solar panels, for example, only make sense if the warehouse user owns the facility or if the owner considers the solar panels as a worthwhile investment as the payback period for example in the United States is around 15 years (Long, 2010). Sourcing 'green' energy from an external supplier might therefore in most cases be cheaper and less of an investment risk than small-scale, on-site generation. It may often be governmental regulation and incentives that make on-site energy generation a considerable option.

Looking at the large investments and long payback periods for 'green' energy generation on-site, it is probably unsurprising that managers prefer to invest in energy saving and waste-avoidance solutions like improved lighting, recycling and air circulation fans than in solar panels or wind technology (Material Handling Industry of America, 2011).

Sustainable distribution centre – Alnatura

Alnatura was founded in 1984 and is today Germany's largest supermarket chain specializing entirely in organic and sustainable products. The chain runs 70 stores of usually around 550 m^2 in size in 39 cities across the country, each store listing around 6,000 organic SKUs, including around 1,000 lines of its own-label-branded products. The company also sells organic products through a network of other retailers, and is owned and run by its original founder.

Besides its achievements in the area of environmental sustainability and organic agriculture, the company uses a multi-bottom-line approach, adding for example a spiritual/cultural dimension to the usual social, economic and environmental of the triple-bottom-line approach.

In 2009, the company built a new distribution site for dry goods in Lorsch in central Germany to serve its stores and retail customers; this was extended in 2014 with the world's largest wood-built, high-bay shelf racking. The site comprises 32,000 pallet places and office space of 1,400 m^2. The building blends in with the surrounding area and much green space is left around it to provide a pleasant environment for employees and passers-by. The space around the building is also used to transfer rainwater from the roofs into the ground, thereby maintaining ground water levels. The building achieved the highest outcome – gold – in the ranking of the German Council for Sustainable Building.

The new site also saves emissions in the transport network. Previously the distribution network was run in a decentralized fashion and suppliers delivered into multiple locations. Perishable produce is delivered by local suppliers directly to the stores and nationwide supplies are distributed centrally, saving transport kilometres.

The outer shell of the buildings consists of larch wood which is sourced locally from a nearby forest and the wood for the extension came from entirely PEFC-certified sources. Similarly, most other construction materials were sourced locally to save emissions embedded in the materials. Even the spades used in the traditional German ceremony starting the construction works were manufactured locally.

The building's rooftop is covered by a photovoltaic installation of 7,821 m², producing 1,100 kW at peak – enough to provide energy for approximately 260 households and saving 918 tonnes of CO_2 annually. Heating and cooling of the warehouse area is achieved through the use of an air-warmth pump; energy for the office building is generated through the use of a geothermal station. Energy bought in from outside to cover times when the on-site energy sources are low is generated from water power.

Going beyond the sustainability of the distribution warehouse, the organic products stored in the warehouse are all produced under a sustainability approach, for example using natural fertilizers to avoid the emissions that come from chemical fertilizers usually used in growing non-organic food.

SOURCES Alnatura, Deutsche Gesellschaft für Nachhaltiges Bauen.

Social dimension of sustainability in warehousing

The social dimension of sustainability also needs consideration in warehousing. With tasks and processes being increasingly shifted to logistics service providers, warehouses and distribution centres employ more people with a wider set of skills. Technology and the increasing complexity of supply chains mean that warehouse operators require new skill sets and knowledge.

Issues of health and safety need to be considered in the warehouse and workplace design. With the demographic change to older societies in many developed countries, ergonomic workplace design and wellbeing are gaining more importance. The use of handling equipment and supportive technological applications needs to be considered differently in the light of an ageing workforce. Additionally, the overall number of workers is shrinking, making it more important to keep staff and to provide an attractive workplace.

Sports Direct

Since its foundation in 1982, Sports Direct became the largest sports goods retailer in the UK. It is still today managed by its founder Mike Ashley, who became not only one of the wealthiest Britons but is also famous for owning the football club Newcastle United.

The backbone of Sports Direct's retail operations is its National Distribution Centre in Shirebook in Derbyshire. It was seen as a welcome source of employment in the area after the last colliery in this ex-coal-mining area closed. It is the size of 13 Olympic swimming pools, operating 24 hours, 365 days a year, with about 2,000 workers; one can believe that it contributes greatly to employment opportunities in the area.

In 2015, the distribution centre received sudden intense media interest after an undercover investigation by the *Guardian* – a UK national newspaper – referred to work conditions at the Sports Direct distribution centre as a 'gulag' – a historical term for inhumane Soviet hard labour camps.

Workers – the vast majority of them recent immigrants – were employed through so-called zero-hours contracts which allow the employer to access workers at very short notice without any commitments, and were put under huge pressure to pick orders fast enough or face humiliation and sacking. Being made to clock out and then continue to work and not being paid for waiting time for security searches were also among the reported practices. News organizations further reported that 110 ambulances and paramedic vehicles were called out to the warehouse site in less than four years, with 50 cases classified as life-threatening, as well as cases of pregnancy difficulties.

After public outrage about the labour conditions at the retailer, a parliamentary select committee examined the case. The founder and head of the company Mike Ashley initially refused to follow parliament's orders but did eventually give witness to the committee, explaining that as the captain of the ship he couldn't possibly know what was going on in the engine room. He further explained that Sports Direct had policies that protected workers' dignity, that external labour providers caused some of the problems and that he was unaware of the practices used.

The parliamentary select committee labelled the labour conditions as 'Victorian workhouse' and described the situation as unacceptable. It further accused Mike Ashley of 'turning a blind eye to conditions at Sports

Direct in the interests of maximizing profits' and violating the national minimum wage legislation. The company kept a high level of control over the external labour agencies who were using appalling and unlawful practices and were actually found to give misleading evidence in their statements to the select committee. Sports Direct promised to improve conditions and practices and the distribution centre will be visited by the select committee, which also ordered the Gangmasters Licensing Authority to investigate the practices used by Sports Direct and its labour agencies.

SOURCES *Financial Times* (2016); *Guardian* (2015); BBC (2015); Commons Select Committee (2016).

Risks and vulnerability in warehousing

In the economic dimension of sustainability the aspect of risks and supply chain disruptions has gained importance. Globalization, extremely lean supply chains with low inventory levels and a trend for centralization of inventory has increased the vulnerability of supply chains and increased the impact if a warehouse fails to operate properly (Christopher, 2011). Warehouses are essential nodes in supply chains and the damage or loss of a warehouse can cause significant disruptions to a business and threaten its economic wellbeing. Preparing for supply chain disruptions does not always necessarily come with higher inventory levels, but depends more on risk profiling, visibility and the right supply chain design (Eltantawy and Giunipero, 2012).

Natural and man-made disasters can disrupt companies' supply chains. Warehouses form a sort of buffer for such cases and can be set up to mitigate supply chain risks; however, they are also vulnerable themselves even if they are located in otherwise safe locations. The outbreak of a fire in a distribution centre or warehouse will most likely have an immediate and significant impact on business operations. The Buncefield oil depot fire in the UK is a good example of supply chain disruption. The depot burst into flames shortly before Christmas 2005, which had a serious impact on oil distribution in England. Furthermore, distribution centres on a commercial estate nearby could not be accessed for several days due to heavy smoke and the damage to the building's structure caused by the explosion of the oil depot. Most of the stock was damaged not only by the explosion but also by the water from sprinklers. It took fire brigades several days to stop the fire. During that time, ASOS, one of the fastest-growing online fashion retailers, could not use its central warehouse and distribution site and couldn't send goods out. The company had only moved into its single global distribution site months before. The potential effect on the business in the run-up to Christmas was so significant that its shares were initially suspended from trading (Sturcke, 2005; Daley, 2006). Although ASOS recovered from the disruption, it shows the significance of warehousing on the economic dimension of a business's sustainability.

Data centres

With the advent and rapid development of computer and internet technology, a new form of warehousing emerged: the storage of electronic data. Whereas physical documents and files used to be stored in archive buildings (which are essentially warehouses), the introduction of electronic documents did by no means eliminate the need for storage. Although the storage of paper documents may be reduced, data storage nevertheless has an impact on the environment too. Storage facilities for electronic data are usually called data centres. Within a data centre, an often large number of servers perform computing operations to store and process data. Although only little physical traffic goes in and out of the site after the construction phase is finished, a lot of data traffic emerges and is 'transported' in and out by communication technology.

The amount of data that needs processing and storing is continuously increasing. The energy consumed by US data centres alone in 2014 is estimated at 70 billion kWh, the equivalent to 2 per cent of the country's overall energy consumption, or that of 6.4 million average homes. The growth of energy use for data centres has been extreme in the past and is still growing, although energy efficiency is improving as well. If energy efficiency levels had not been improved, and had remained at 2010 levels, the energy use in 2014 would have been an additional 40 billion kWh (DataCenterKnowledge, 2016).

Data centres are a worthwhile target for energy savings. The typical annual energy costs per square metre are 15 times that of a typical office building (Greenberg *et al*, 2006). In extreme cases, data centres consume up to 100 times more energy than a standard office building (US Department of Energy, 2006). Data centres also operate continuously with peaks following office working hours and therefore have to source much of their electricity when it is the most expensive in time-dependent tariffs (Greenberg *et al*, 2006).

Opportunities for energy efficiency improvements in data centres exist at four major points: cooling, server load and computing equipment, power conversion and distribution, and alternative power generation.

The electricity consumption in a data centre can be differentiated into supply (support systems like cooling, lighting, etc) and demand (computing equipment such as server power supply, processors, and communication equipment). More energy-efficient server components therefore have a leverage effect on the overall data centre's energy consumption, as not only the energy in the 'production' is saved but additionally the energy required by the support systems is reduced (Emerson, 2008).

Energy required for cooling can be reduced through improved air management. Optimized distribution of cool air and the collection of waste heat for energy production can be addressed in design and operations at the data centre. On average, cooling takes around 38 per cent of a data centre's energy consumption (Emerson, 2008). Cooling is one reason why Facebook built its own 30,000-square-metre data centre in northern Sweden, where temperatures are low most of the year and even in summer do not rise over 20 degrees Celsius. For 10 months per year, outside air can be used for cooling. Furthermore, Facebook can source its energy for the site primarily from a nearby hydropower plant, reducing its carbon emissions even further (BBC, 2011).

A major performance figure for benchmarking data centres is the power usage effectiveness (PUE), which is the total power used by the data centre divided by the energy used for IT systems. The lower the consumption of auxiliary systems, the lower the PUE score becomes. A state-of-the-art data centre like Facebook's in northern Sweden achieves a PUE score of 1.07 and Google claims to reach a PUE of 1.12 across all its data centres (BBC, 2011; Google, 2016). Apple, on the other hand, has built up its own green energy supply by building a large solar array park in North Carolina to supply its nearby data centre and powers all its data centres with 100 per cent renewable energy (Apple, 2012).

Summary

Warehouses are the nodes in logistics networks. Within the network design, their number and locations influence the need for transportation. But they also have a footprint from their building and the activities in and around the warehouse. The environmental impact is usually classed into two main parts: construction and operations.

The emissions in the construction phase are often in a trade-off with the operational emissions. More insulation in the construction means more energy is embedded in the building but less is consumed during its everyday operations. As a consequence, the anticipated lifetime of a warehouse building is a crucial component in this trade-off between embodied energy and operational energy.

Whereas much of the energy consumption is determined at the design stage of the warehouse, the warehouse's energy consumption and its environmental impact can also be reduced to some extent later through the installation of energy- and water-saving technology, for example in updating temperature control or lighting systems.

Warehouses are not necessarily built or run by a single company that owns the stored products inside them. Logistics service providers or real estate investors may own the building and use it for more than one client. Different interests and priorities between these stakeholders may lead to less than optimal solutions.

Warehouses also fall into the social dimension of the triple bottom line, as they are places of employment. The wellbeing of the workforce therefore also must be part of sustainability considerations.

References

Apple (2012) Data centers and renewable energy [online] available at: http://www.apple.com/environment/renewable-energy/ [accessed 24 October 2012]

Baker, P (2010) *The Principles of Warehouse Design*, 3rd edn, The Chartered Institute of Logistics and Transport in the UK, Corby

Baker, P (2012) The environmental impact of warehouses, Proceedings of the Logistics Research Network Conference, Cranfield University

BBC News (2011) Facebook sets up data centre in Lapland – Sweden, 27 October [online] available at: www.bbc.co.uk/news/technology-15477194

BBC News (2015) Sports Direct called ambulances 'dozens of times' [online] available at: http://www.bbc.co.uk/news/uk-england-34178412 [accessed 31 December 2016]

BNP Paribas Real Estate (2010) *The Warehouse of the Future*, BNP Paribas Real Estate in association with Gazeley and The UK Logistics Fund, London

BRE Group (2012) First design-stage BREEAM outstanding [online] available at: http://www.bre.co.uk/page.jsp?id=1808 [accessed 26 September 2012]

BRE Group (2016) BREEAM International new construction 2016 [online] available at: http://www.breeam.com/new-construction [accessed 31 December 2016]

Carbon Trust (2012), Building fabric [online] available at: https://www.carbontrust.com/media/19457/ctv014_building_fabric.pdf [accessed 31 December 2016]

Christopher, M (2011) *Logistics and Supply Chain Management* (4th edn), FT Prentice Hall, London

Commons Select Committee (2016) Mike Ashley must be accountable for Sports Direct working practices, 22 July, *Parliament.uk* [online] available at: https://www.parliament.uk/business/committees/committees-a-z/commons-select/business-innovation-and-skills/news-parliament-2015/working-practices-at-sports-direct-report-published-16-17/ [accessed 31 December 2016]

Daley, J (2006) ASOS back in fashion after Buncefield fire, *Independent*, 11 May

DataCenterKnowledge (2016) Here's How Much Energy All US Data Centers Consume [online] available at: www.datacenterknowledge.com/archives/2016/06/27/heres-how-much-energy-all-us-data-centers-consume [accessed 04 August 2016]

Eltantawy, R and Giunipero, L C (2012) Strategic supply management: the litmus test for risk management in a three-echelon supply chain, Chapter 17 in Khan, O and Zsidisin, G (eds) *Handbook for Supply Chain Risk Management: Case studies, effective practices and emerging trends*, ISCRIM and J. Ross Publications, Fort Lauderdale

Emerson Network Power (2008) *Energy Logic: Reducing data center energy consumption by creating savings that cascade across systems*, White Paper

Ferrari, C, Parola, F and Morchio, E (2006) Southern European ports and the spatial distribution of EDCs, *Maritime Economics and Logistics*, 8 (1), pp 60–81

Financial Times (2016) Mike Ashley refuses again to face MPs on Sports Direct, 3 June [online] available at: https://www.ft.com/content/ec0803ee-296c-11e6-8ba3-cdd781d02d89 [accessed 31 December 2016]

Fraunhofer SCS (2014) Top 100 der Logistik 2015/16 [online] available at: https://www.scs.fraunhofer.de/de/studien/logistikmarkt/top100.html [accessed 28 December 2016]

Fuerst, F and McAllister, P (2011) The impact of Energy Performance Certificates on the rental and capital values of commercial property assets, *Energy Policy*, 39, pp 6608–14

Google (2016) Efficiency: How we do it [online] available at: www.google.com/about/datacenters/efficiency/internal [accessed 04 August 2016]

Greenberg, S, Mills, E, Tschudi, B, Rumsey, P and Myatt, B (2006) Best practices for data centers: lessons learned from benchmarking 22 data centers, *ACEEE Summer Study on Energy Efficiency in Buildings*, pp 76–87

Gregori, G and Wimmer, T (2011) *Grünbuch der Nachhaltigen Logistik: Handbuch für die ressourcenschonende gestaltung logistischer prozesse,* Bundesvereinigung Logistik, Vienna and Bremen

Guardian (2015) A day at 'the gulag': what it's like to work at Sports Direct's warehouse, 9 December [online] available at: https://www.theguardian.com/business/2015/dec/09/sports-direct-warehouse-work-conditions [accessed 28 December 2016]

Harris, D J (1999) A quantitative approach to the assessment of the environmental impact of building materials, *Building and Environment*, 34, pp 751–58

Kohn, C and Brodin, M H (2008) Centralized distribution systems and the environment: how increased transport work can decrease the environmental impact of logistics, *International Journal of Logistics Research and Applications,* 11 (3), pp 229–45

Long, M (2010) Tech cuts warehousing energy bills, *Light & Medium Truck*, 23 (2), p 29

Maister, D H (1975) Centralisation of inventories and the 'Square Root Law', *International Journal of Physical Distribution and Logistics Management*, 6 (3), pp 124–34

Marchant, C (2010), Reducing the impact of warehousing, Chapter 8 in McKinnon *et al* (eds) *Green Logistics: Improving the environmental sustainability of logistics*, Kogan Page, London, pp 167–92

Material Handling Industry of America (2011) *Sustainability in warehousing, distribution and manufacturing*, presented at ProMat, Chicago

Menzies, G F (2011*) Embodied Energy Considerations for Existing Buildings,* Historic Scotland, Heriot Watt University, Technical Paper 13, September

Ofori, G (2000) Greening the construction supply chain in Singapore, *European Journal of Purchasing and Supply Management*, 6, pp 195–206

ProLogis and Capgemini (2006) *Warehousing space in Europe: Meeting tomorrow's demand: A pan-European warehousing trends study*, Utrecht

Rai, D, Sodagar, B, Fieldson, R and Hu, X (2011) Assessment of CO_2 emissions reduction in a distribution warehouse', *Energy*, 36, pp 2271–77

RICS UK (Royal Institute of Chartered Surveyors) (2010) *Redefining Zero: Carbon profiling as a solution to whole life carbon emission measurement in buildings*, RICS Research, May

Rushton, A and Walker, S (2007) *International Logistics and Supply Chain Outsourcing: From local to global*, Kogan Page, London

Sternberg, H, Germann, T and Klaas-Wissing, T (2012) Who controls the fleet? Initial insights into the efficiency of road freight transport planning and the control from an industrial network perspective, Proceedings of the 17th Annual Logistics Research Network Conference, Cranfield University

Sturcke, J (2005) Fuel blasts close neighbouring firms, *Guardian*, 12 December

Thuermer, K E (2009) DC site selection: time to scrutinize the details, *Modern Materials Handling*, **64** (4), p 36

UK GBC – United Kingdom Green Building Council (2007) *Report on carbon reductions in new non-domestic buildings*, Queen's Printer, London

UKWA – United Kingdom Warehousing Association (2010) *Save Energy Cut Costs: Energy efficient warehouse operation*, UKWA, London

US Department of Energy – Energy Efficiency and Renewable Energy (2006) Federal energy management program: data center energy consumption trends [online] available at: http://www1.eere.energy.gov/femp/program/dc_energy_consumption.html [accessed 28 December 2016]

World Economic Forum (2009) *Supply Chain Decarbonization: The role of logistics and transport in reducing supply chain carbon emissions*, World Economic Forum, Geneva

Product design, 05
cleaner production
and packaging

Background

Traditionally, the main objectives of product design, production and packaging are to reduce cost while at the same time meeting product pricing strategies, specifications and customer needs, as well as maintaining compliance with health, safety and environmental legislation. In the past, there was very little awareness about the amount of natural resources, energy and chemicals used, the adverse health effects to workers, or the amount of pollution being discharged during the production and usage of a product. Limited efforts were put into creating systems that recycled and reused products, components and materials after use. There is now growing evidence indicating that the ways supply chains manage product design, production and packaging are among the major contributors to various environmental sustainability, health, safety and social responsibility problems.

Let's take the production of a pair of jeans as an example. According to WWF research, it takes an average of 8,500 litres of water to grow one kilogram of cotton lint, which is required to make one pair of jeans (WWF, 2012). In comparison, a person only needs to consume about two to three litres of water a day. Water is also required to produce food, industrial crops, livestock and fish, as well as to generate electricity. Furthermore, the printing and dyeing of jeans involves hazardous substances such as cadmium, chromium, lead and mercury, which are found to be illegally discharged into rivers, affecting the health of many workers in China and other developing countries (IPE, 2009; Greenpeace, 2011). In some countries, the enforcement of regulation on the discharge of industrial waste or effluent is rather difficult. As a result, hazardous substances are released into the water systems in large volume. Not only do such pollutions kill aquatic lives and other food sources, they also destroy the water systems which provide the main sources of water for the production of food and agricultural products in many countries. Globally, 70 per cent of the freshwater withdrawals from rivers and groundwater are used for growing agricultural products (FAO, 2011). Many of these water systems are in danger of being heavily polluted, while there is a shortage of water supply in many countries. Water scarcity is affecting around 1.2 billion people in all continents, which is almost one-fifth of the world's population (UNESCO, 2012). In addition, the production of goods and packaging materials also emits Greenhouse Gases (GHGs) and contributes to global warming and climate change.

Based on the natural resource-based view, Hart (1995; 1997) laid down a framework toward sustainable development. This framework can be used to guide transformation in the ways we manage product design, production and packaging processes. Accordingly, the first step is to achieve pollution prevention by shifting away from pollution control. While the control of pollution in factories in developing countries is still a problem, the time taken for these countries to truly enforce regulations up to the developed world's standards would be too long. Pressures from non-government organizations (NGOs), regulators and buyers from the developed countries could make some differences but is still inadequate. Instead of focusing on the end-of-pipe solutions to control pollution, some companies have begun to look into the design of products and adoption of cleaner production processes that minimize pollution and consume less energy and fewer materials. However, investment in the prevention of pollution could mean loss of cost competitiveness and therefore jobs in some countries. New forms of financing sustainable development are required to address the question of who is paying for the pollution prevention solutions.

In the next stage, the focus is product stewardship. In addition to minimizing pollution from manufacturing processes in the factories, more efforts are made to minimize the environmental impacts during the full lifecycle of a product. This stage extends the efforts in pollution prevention by reducing the use of natural resources and energy all the way from the extraction of raw materials to the end-of-life management of the product. That means there is a need to go back to the drawing board – greener product design. During the product design stage, companies can review key decisions related to product design so that more environmentally friendlier raw materials and packaging materials can be utilized, and product designs for recycling or recovery are adopted. The design of products may be modified to make disassembling and segregation easier so that it is possible to facilitate the reverse flows or circulation or restoration of products, components and raw materials. This also means companies need to extend their environmental management efforts to collaborate with suppliers, customers, governments and NGOs. In this stage, companies can take the opportunity to set new environmental standards in the industry and take this as a sustainable advantage.

In the third stage, companies are encouraged to invest in the planning and development of clean technologies which make the entire supply chain sustainable. This is because the ways we produce food and goods today are still environmentally damaging and consume a great deal of energy and natural resources. In many sectors and producing nations we rely heavily on non-renewable sources of energy and materials. A lot of water and chemicals are consumed by power plants, farms and factories. New technologies such as biotechnology, cleaner chemical engineering, agricultural technologies, and renewable energy are required. For example, a lot of research has been conducted to develop clothing and washing machines that do not require water for cleaning. According to the natural resource-based view, companies that excel in the above stages can finally develop a shared corporate vision moving towards solving social and environmental problems, and achieving sustainable development.

Product design for environmental and sustainable logistics

Traditionally, industrial designers have concerned themselves with improving products by reducing cost, enhancing ease of use, and making products that are beautiful and distinctive in the market place (Walker and Dorsa, 2001). Nowadays, design for environment (DfE) or eco-design is becoming the main concern among industrial designers and original equipment manufacturers (OEMs), who are realizing that more than 80 per cent of the environmental impact of a product is determined at the design stage. DfE is guided by the principle of sustainable development and the aim is to simultaneously reconcile environmental sustainability, economic security and social wellbeing. Circular economy is another concept that can be used to guide DfE. As defined by the Ellen MacArthur Foundation, circular economy emphasizes restoration (technical) and regeneration (biological) by design; it aims to keep products, components and materials at their highest utilization and value at all times (Ellen MacArthur Foundation, 2015). Guided by these principles, industrial designers have started to modify their practices to address ecological damage caused by materials and resource acquisition, manufacturing processes, product packaging and product disposal.

Design for environment (eco-design or circular economy design) can be achieved by looking into the selection of materials, minimizing water and carbon footprints, design for cleaner production, design for sustainable consumption, and design for circular economy (sustainable logistics). Figure 5.1 illustrates how these key principles can be applied to address sustainability issues in five major phases of a value chain or product lifecycle: raw materials, manufacturing (factory), transport (distribution), use, and end-of-life management. The two sets of half circles represent regeneration and restoration; the former represent techniques to transform end-of-life products into useful biochemical or biofuel, and the latter represent methods to prolong, reuse, refurbish, remanufacturer and recycle end-of-life products, their components and materials.

Figure 5.1 Design for environment

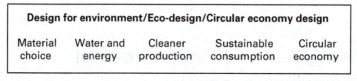

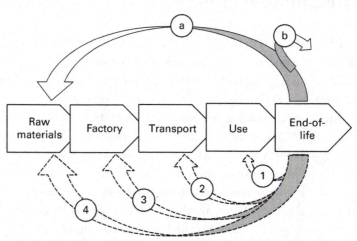

NOTES Restoration cycles (lower dotted arrows): 1 – share, maintain, prolong;
2 – reuse/redistribute; 3 – refurbish/remanufacturing; 4 – recycle. Regeneration cycles (upper arrows):
a – biochemical feedstocks; b – biogas.

Selection of materials

Selection of materials for product design is a challenging task. Most of the essential raw materials we use are infinite resources. Materials such as anthracite, bauxite, beryllium, caoutchouc, chrome, coal, cobalt, diamonds, gold, indium, iron, manganese, nickel, platinum, silicon, silver, titanium, vanadium, water, crude oil, and natural gas are crucial for human life. Some of them are still abundant but others are not. They will all one day become rare if they cannot be reused and recycled. Thus, the use of recycled materials helps reduce environmental damage. Moreover, the mining of minerals such as tantalite (coltan), cassiterite (tin), gold and wolframite (tungsten) in the Democratic Republic of the Congo or adjoining countries is known to be used to finance conflicts. That's why they are called Conflict Minerals. Similarly, in diamond supply chains there are Conflict Diamonds or Blood Diamonds.

Materials such as arsenic, mercury, lead and phthalates that are used for making electronic devices are now being phased out by many manufacturers because they are hazardous to human beings and the environment during the production or disposal processes. Manufacturing technologies used to process different raw materials may consume large amounts of water and energy, and also produce large amounts of air, liquid and solid emissions. Somehow, the selection of materials depends on the available manufacturing technologies. In various industries, managers ought to know that the applications of some substances help to meet product specifications but they are also hazardous. There are many types of hazardous substances:

- explosives;
- flammable substances;
- oxidizing agents and peroxide;
- toxic substances;
- substances causing diseases;
- radioactive substances;
- mutant-causing substances;
- corrosive substances;
- irritating substances;
- other substances, chemical or otherwise, which may cause injury to human beings, animals, plants, property, or environments.

Table 5.1 List of common hazardous materials

Materials	Common usage	Environmental and social impacts
Acid and alkalis	They are used for various cleaning processes and the production of chemicals.	Highly corrosive liquids used in industry that can corrode metals and destroy tissues of living organisms.
Arsenic	It is used as an alloy in lead shot and electrical circuits, as a pesticide, and as a preservative for wood. It is used in the microchip industry and copper production industry.	It is highly toxic and carcinogenic. People who work with pesticide and wood preservative can be exposed to arsenic. It may cause infertility, miscarriages, skin problems and brain damage.
Asbestos	It was once widely employed in construction primarily for insulation. It is still used to make gaskets, brakes, roofing and other materials.	When inhaled it can cause lung cancer and mesothelioma.
Cadmium	It is used in batteries, pigments, metal coatings, and plastics. It is also used in nuclear power plants. It is produced from the smelting of zinc.	Exposure risks are from metal refinery factories, cigarette smoke and contaminated foods. Breathing cadmium can damage lungs and kidneys, and cause infertility and cancer. It can pollute surface water and poison earthworms and soil organisms.
Chromium	It is used as a rust-resistant coating on other metals, a pigment in paint, and in wood preservatives and liquids for tanning hides. It is also used for leather and textile production.	People who smoke or work in the steel and textile industries can be exposed to chromium compounds. They may experience skin and respiratory problems, kidney and liver damage and lung cancer. Chromium can be toxic to organisms.
Clinical wastes	Hospitals must dispose of large quantities of syringes, medication baffles and other materials.	Can be infectious and spread pathogens and harmful micro-organisms.

Substance	Use	Health effects
Cyanide	Compressed hydrogen cyanide gas is used to exterminate rodents and insects on ships and to kill insects on trees.	In large doses can cause paralysis, convulsions and respiratory arrest. Chronic exposure to low doses can cause fatigue and weakness.
Dimethyl fumarate (DMFu)	Used as a biocide in furniture and shoes to prevent the growth of mould during transport.	Skin allergies.
Lead	Used in the production of batteries, ammunition, paints, metal products such as solder and pipes, and devices to shield X-rays.	If ingested or inhaled can harm the nervous system, kidneys, and reproductive system.
Mercury	Used to produce chlorine gas, caustic soda, thermometers, dental fillings, and batteries.	Exposure occurs through contaminated air, water and food and through dental and medical treatments. High levels may damage the brain, kidneys, and developing foetuses.
PCBs	Compounds used in industry as heat exchange fluids, in electric transformers and capacitors, and as additives in paint, carbonless copy paper, sealants and plastics.	Poses risks to nervous systems, reproductive systems, immune systems and livers.
POPs	Persistent organic pollutants include aldrin, chlordane, chlordecone, dieldrin, dichlorodiphenyl-trichloroethane (DDT), endrin, heptachlor, hexachlorobenzene, hexachlorocyclohexane, lindane, mirex and toxaphene are commonly used in agriculture to control pests.	POPs are a class of chemicals and pesticides that persist for many years in the environment, are transported great distances from their point of release, bioaccumulate (thus threatening humans and animals at the top of the food chain), and cause a range of health effects.
PBB and PBDE	Polybrominated biphenyls (PBB) were used to make products such as computer monitors, televisions, textile, plastic foams, etc. to make them difficult to burn. Polybrominated biphenyls ether (PBDE) is used for the same function.	Causes nausea, abdominal pain, loss of appetite, joint pain, fatigue and weakness, also possibly skin problems.

Table 5.1 provides a list of selected hazardous substances, most of which are identified by the essential directives and regulations on hazardous substances. Some of them are highly hazardous materials, which should be avoided. Some of them are banned in some countries but could be allowed in others.

Driven by regulations and/or sustainable development ambitions, most manufacturers have now established a list of banned and restricted materials, and another list of preferred materials. Proactive manufacturers such as HP and Dell have been updating a hazardous material watch list and assessing materials for future phase-out beyond the mandatory regulations. These lists have to be integrated into the procedures and protocols of environmental management within the companies and supply chains. Standards such as ISO/IEC 17050-1:2004 can be used as it specifies general requirements for a supplier's declaration of conformity in cases when it is desirable or necessary (ISO, 2014). Many manufacturers nowadays specify their own supplier codes of conduct. There is also a need for an effective and integrated information system which facilitates the application and compliance of the material list so that the companies can design out hazardous and environmentally damaging substances as well as reducing the consumption of energy and other natural resources. Below is a case study illustrating how all these can be achieved.

Towards an integrated product design for environment

Motorola, Inc was an American telecommunications company. They designed and sold network infrastructure equipment, mobile phones, and many other telecommunication components and products. In January 2011, the company was divided into two independent public companies – Motorola Mobility and Motorola Solutions. Motorola Mobility was later purchased by Google, Inc. Even though the company has been divided and partly sold, the ways in which they integrated the environment into their business deserve some attention. In 2011, Motorola was ranked 6th place in Greenpeace's *Guide to Greener Electronics* (www.greenpeace.org), and the company attempts to develop an integrated environmental management system (EMS) within its factories and subsidiaries as well as its supply chains. Environmentally Preferred Products (EPPs) is a programme aiming to achieve the following set of environmental product goals:

- designing products to increase recyclability;
- reducing the use of hazardous materials;
- reducing energy use in production and consumption of a product;
- increasing the use of recycled material in products;
- minimizing the ratio of packaging material to product volume;
- labelling all plastic parts weighing more than 4 grams to increase future recycling.

Motorola maintained specific internal protocols and reporting requirements for its factories worldwide. Each factory was required to report on a standard set of environmental metrics consistent with its corporate environmental goals. Some of the main environmental metrics were:

- volatile organic materials emissions (metric tonnes per billion dollars of sales);
- hazardous air emissions (metric tonnes per billion dollars of sales);
- hazardous wastes (thousands of metric tonnes per billion dollars of sales) and water use (million cubic meters per billion dollars of sales);
- electricity use (billions of kilowatt hours per billion dollars of sales) (Motorola, 2002, p 32);
- annual Environment, Health and Safety (EHS) compliance record (number of noncompliance notices and fines and penalties).

This case study focuses on the way Motorola integrated product design for the environment. Motorola divided its product design process into three tiers. Tier 1 involved concept development and product systems design; Tier 2 covered detailed product design and manufacture of a prototype; and Tier 3 covered actual mass production (Hoffman, 1997). During each design stage, some protocols and tools were developed to integrate environmental considerations. A list of banned substances (called W18 Specifications) detailed concentration levels of specific substances allowed (measured in parts per million). Motorola also developed and used specific software tools to assist its environmental improvement programmes. An environmental assessment tool called the Product Environmental Template (PET) was developed to support the identification, limitation or elimination of hazardous substances during the pre-design or concept development stages (referring to the W18 Specifications).

PET also helped the design team to identify the energy efficiency of the products, as well as meeting the various regulations.

The Motorola Toxicity Index was used to identify and weigh chemicals used in a product in terms of their toxicity. This allowed product designers to sum up the aggregate measure of the toxicity of a product. Green Design Advisor (GDA) was used in the detailed product design stage in order to improve the recyclability of products while designing out toxicity (Feldmann *et al*, 1999). GDA was also involved in the prototyping and production stage. During the prototyping stage, the environmental impacts of a new product were further assessed by the Environmental Product Assessment or REAL (Rapid Environmental Assessment Lab).

During the mass-production stage, the Parts Information Management System (PIMS) was used to track supply and production of parts. The Environmental Data Management Team (EDMT) was responsible for updating and recording the environmental data of the parts and products. Chemicals and substances embedded in each part were tracked and recorded, together with supplier details. Compliance Connect was used to ensure compliance of the environmental policies in the factories and supply chains. This is a tool which integrates electronically to identify each part in each Motorola product by part number, by preferred global supplier with contact information, by technical specifications (including the W18 specifications), and by toxic substance and toxicity.

The design of products which favour cleaner, reusable and recyclable materials requires knowledge about a lot of materials and regulations. For example, there are 58 families and over a thousand different grades of plastic used for different applications. Due to advancements in science and technology, the list of raw material is growing. Some of the more recent raw materials being considered are, for example, metal matrix, advanced composites, nano-materials, speciality polymers, flexible ceramics, and memory metal. In the textile industry, it is desirable to use materials for making fabrics that are free of carcinogens, mutagens, persistent toxins, heavy metals, endocrine disrupters and bioaccumulatives. Such fabrics are compostable and can be safely return to the earth at the end of their useful life. However, there is a need to consider the cost and feasibility of obtaining a constant supply of such fabrics. It can be difficult for non-technical logisticians and supply chain professionals to comprehend such scientific knowledge. In terms of the selection of material for designing sustainable products, there are several useful guidelines for logistics and supply chain professionals. One may refer to databanks for hazardous substances, for example:

- Hazardous Substances Data bank, United States National Library of Medicine (http://toxnet.nlm.nih.gov/).

- Priority list of hazardous substances, Agency for Toxic Substances and Disease Registry, (ATSDR) (http://www.atsdr.cdc.gov/).

- List of materials from Lenneth (http://www.lenntech.com/periodic/elements/f.htm).

- List of material subjected to several regulations in the United States, Environmental Protection Agency (http://www3.epa.gov/).

- Other material selection criteria and tools such as Okala Ecodesign, Cambridge Materials Selector Software, etc.

Even though manufacturers may try to choose environmentally friendlier materials and manufacturing technologies, they need to consider other factors such as supply availability, supply reliability, material and process quality, lead time and cost. The supply of raw materials, especially from agriculture activities, can be rather unpredictable due to the effects of climate change, over-finishing, pollution and natural disasters. Sourcing of raw materials from low-cost producing countries could reduce the cost of material input but increase lead times and supply uncertainty. In some cases, low-cost sourcing also increases the chances of suppliers using unacceptable labour practices and techniques that damage the environment.

Cleaner production

The terms cleaner production and pollution prevention often mean the same thing. Pollution prevention is generally used in North America, while cleaner production is the preferred term in other parts of the world. One of the most commonly used definitions of cleaner production is that of the United Nations Environment Programme (UNEP):

> Cleaner production is the continuous application of an integrated preventive environmental strategy applied to processes, products, and services to increase eco-efficiency and reduce risks to humans and the environment.

Figure 5.2 illustrates the main principles of cleaner production and explains how cleaner production contributes to cost efficiency, revenue and better

Figure 5.2 Cleaner production

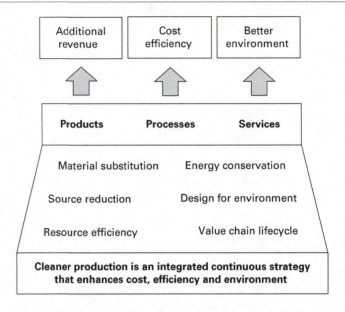

environmental performance. Cleaner production attempts to improve the efficient use of energy and water consumption and raw materials, and prevent undesirable pollution during the production processes and the delivery of the product and services to customers. Cleaner production also seeks to optimize the reuse and recycling of hazardous and non-hazardous materials by embracing a value-chain lifecycle approach. Cleaner production is an integrated strategy that continuously protects the environment, consumers and workers while improving the industrial efficiency, profitability and competitiveness of enterprises. The fundamental principles of cleaner production are supported by the natural resource-based theory by Hart (1995), which argues that the sustainable production of products and services for human consumption is the basis for the sustainable competitiveness of businesses.

Cleaner production requires a shift in the mindsets of industries. Industries have to shift away from ignoring pollution, diluting or dispersing pollution, or focusing on end-of-pipe or pollution control solutions simply to comply with regulations. There is a need to recognize that the use of end-of-pipe technology simply shifts waste or pollutants from one environmental medium to another. Governmental environment agencies have to realize the disadvantages of command and control methods, which may increase the cost of compliance and encourage companies to explore other cheaper and yet polluting solutions. To implement cleaner production there is a need to understand the following concepts:

- *Eco-efficiency*. Coined by the World Business Council for Sustainable Development in 1992, the term 'eco-efficiency' is defined as: 'the delivery of competitively priced goods and services that satisfy human needs and bring quality of life, while progressively reducing ecological impacts and resource intensity throughout the lifecycle, to a level at least in line with the earth's estimated carrying capacity.' Eco-efficiency means producing more goods and services with less energy and fewer natural resources. Eco-efficient businesses get greater value out of their raw materials as well as producing less waste and less pollution.

- *Waste minimization*. Introduced by the United States Environmental Protection Agency (EPA) in 1988, waste minimization means the use of a waste-prevention approach focusing on on-site reduction of waste at source by changes in the input of raw materials, technology, operating practices and product design, and off-site recycling by direct reuse after reclamation.

- *Zero waste*. Zero waste is a way to set targets for waste minimization. It means no waste is sent to the landfill. It is a philosophy that encourages the redesign of product/resource lifecycles so that their production processes produce no waste, or new techniques are used to transform all waste into recycled materials, energy or something useful.

- *Pollution prevention*. According to the United States Environmental Protection Agency (EPA), pollution prevention is about source reduction. It is about preventing or reducing waste where it originates, at source. This also includes conservation of natural resources through increased efficiency in the use of raw materials, energy, water and land. Pollution prevention is part of the national environmental policy of the United States (EPA, 1990).

- *Green productivity*. Similar to cleaner production, green productivity is a strategy for enhancing productivity and environmental performance in order to improve overall socio-economic development. Green productivity is used by the Asian Productivity Organization (APO) to address the challenge of achieving sustainable production. Resource efficiency is another term of similar meaning used for example by the European Commission.

- *Industrial symbiosis*. Industrial symbiosis is a form of eco-industrial development which applies the concept of industrial ecology to allow by-product resources (eg waste, heat and water) produced by one industry to be used by other industries. It focuses on energy and material exchange. It promotes the sharing of information, services, utility and by-products among one or more industries in order to add value, reduce cost and improve environmental performance. Kalundborg Symbiosis (http://www.symbiosis.dk/en) is the world's first functioning industrial symbiosis where private and public companies buy and sell waste from each other in a closed cycle of industrial production. The system helps save millions of cubic metres of water through recycling and reuse.

Cleaner production emphasizes the application of 'integrated' and 'preventive' systems instead of the typical end-of-pipe solutions. Based on the above concepts of cleaner productions, the following general principles of cleaner production can be applied to the entire production cycle:

- reduce the consumption of raw materials and energy used in the production of one unit of product;
- increase productivity by ensuring a more efficient use of raw materials, energy and water;
- promote better environmental performance through reduction at source of waste and emissions;
- reduce the environmental impact of products throughout their lifecycle by the design of environmentally friendly but cost-effective products;
- reduce at source the quantity and toxicity of all emissions and wastes generated and released;
- eliminate as far as possible the use of toxic and dangerous materials.

Taking the above fundamental principles to a practical level, companies can establish principles of cleaner production themselves. For example, the following are the typical principles for cleaner agricultural production:

- minimize the harmful impact of crop protection practices;
- minimize the harmful impact of crop growth stimulating practices;
- use water efficiently and care for the long-term availability of water;
- care about the health of the soil;
- conserve natural habitats;
- care for and preserve the quality and health effects of the produce;
- reuse and recycle packaging materials;
- promote decent work and fair labour practices.

In order to make the above principles work, companies need to identify opportunities for implementing cleaner production. Many such opportunities are related to lean production efforts. Evidence shows that the adoption of ISO 9001 provides a foundation for the effective adoption of ISO 14001 and waste reduction efforts. The use of the 5Ss (sort, straighten, shine, standardize and sustain) or good housekeeping routines can make sure materials for production are clearly labelled and located at the right place and therefore allow for more efficient use. Good housekeeping helps prevent leaks and spills of hazardous materials. It also forms the basis for the effective implementation of standardized operation and maintenance procedures and practices through the implementation of total preventive maintenance (TPM). The application of better process control using statistical process control (SPC) techniques helps to reduce process variations and subsequently less rejection and rework. The use of useful by-products for production helps to reduce consumption of raw materials while saving costs. Other by-products can be collected for on-site recycling and some can even be sold as another source of revenue. By-products and energy can be exchanged using a concept called industrial symbiosis. Workers are reminded to switch off lighting and air conditioning when they are not required. Some of these opportunities require minimum financial investment; other opportunities which may require some initial investment include material substitution and product modification. This requires a change in the product design and manufacturing process. Product equipment can be modified by incorporating the latest technologies such as sensors to enable preventive and predictive maintenance. In addition, production experts may consider equipment modification and technology change.

Cleaner production can be achieved through technology innovation. The following are some examples of innovation solutions for cleaner production in the textile dyeing process:

- To improve the techniques of purifying waste water discharged by the textile dyeing process, a Swedish researcher named Maria Jonstrup experimented with both fungal enzymes and bacteria from the drains at textile and municipal wastewater-treatment plants. She combined both biological and chemical purification techniques and collaborated with a Swedish clothing company, Indiska Magasinet, and its suppliers to test the new technique on a large scale.

- In 2012, A Dutch Company called DyeCoo commercialized a machine to use carbon dioxide instead of water on an industrial scale to dye polyester. The fabrics dyed in this process, called Drydye fabrics, have the same quality as those conventionally dyed, but use no water. The process halves the consumption of energy and chemicals. Global brands such as Nike and Adidas have forged a partnership with the company; a Taiwanese contract manufacturer for Nike started using DyeCoo technology in 2013.

- In 2012, a Company called ColorZen developed a treatment which changes cotton's molecular composition, making it more receptive to dye without creating toxic discharge. They tested this formula on about 400 pounds of cotton fibre, successfully dyeing it with 95 per cent fewer chemicals, 90 per cent less water, 75 per cent less energy, and 50 per cent less dye in less than one-third of the standard eight hours.

- A company called Novozymes, which specializes in developing enzymes for making products such as food, laundry detergents, bio-energy products, agri-food products and pharmaceutical products, received an innovation award by the Society of Dyers and Colourists (SDC) in 2014 for their patented Combi process, which uses neutral cellulases rather than acidic cellulasas to make it possible for textile manufacturers to combine biopolishing and bleach clean-up processes in the dying step. These new processes save time, water, energy and ultimately costs.

Towards a cleaner production of textiles

The textile industry is one of the many contributors of jobs and economic growth in many developing economies. The industry is also known as one of the dirtiest industries because it requires a great amount of chemicals and water during wet processing. Thousands of different chemicals, including heavy metals (mercury, cadmium, lead, chromium), bleaches, detergents, brighteners and others are used in the textile industry – some of them are used when making yarn from natural fibres such as cotton but a lot of them are used to dye and wash fabric. Textile workers, especially those involved in wet processing, are exposed to hazardous chemicals which may cause respiratory problems, asthma, and even carcinogenic problems (Zhang, 2009). A great amount of clean water is used together with the chemicals and discharged as wastewater which damages the natural environment. Some chemicals harmful to the environment are even found in finished textile products.

The above problems are among the reasons for the establishment of a restricted substance list (RSL) by textile and clothing retail and trading companies who generally trade under certain brand names. An RSL is a list of chemical substances that a company wishes to eliminate or to keep below a required concentration in their products. The effectiveness of the list depends on how suppliers are selected, monitored and managed. However, this effort has not been able to stop factories from using hazardous substances and discharging them into the natural environment. This is a reactive approach, so suppliers will only provide information when they are strictly required to by a customer. To control the selection and use of chemicals, some companies adopt eco-labels or standards such as EU Flower and Oeko-Tex Standard 100. Oeko-Tex requires suppliers to declare raw materials used in the production process and detailed information about each chemical used in every production stage, and they are verified by third-party tests and certification.

The challenge is that not all chemicals are sourced from established chemical manufacturers (eg Dyestar, BASF, Clariant, etc) which often already have products certified by the Oeko-Tex system. Many factories source chemicals from trading agents or local chemical producers and therefore information regarding the contents and certification can be rather inaccurate. As discovered by the study of Chinese textile factories by Zhang (2009), the main problems are the lack of proper records of chemical usage and the passive attitudes of the suppliers toward customer demands for compliance to documentation requirements. Another problem is that new textile factories are built in countries requiring less transparency in terms of waste water discharge. For example, the West Java region of Indonesia has been described as 'Pollution Paradise' by Greenpeace after they discovered some irresponsible factories which supply clothing to many global brands. Until the day when voluntary Environmental Product Declarations (EPDs) become common, the textile supply chain will still be using the reactive environmental information system.

Following the release of two Dirty Laundry Reports by Greenpeace in 2011, top clothing brands including Nike, Puma, Adidas and H&M have agreed to eliminate discharges of all hazardous chemicals across their entire supply chain and product lifecycle by 2020. For example, H&M has defined seven ambitious commitments on sustainability:

1 provide fashion for conscious customers;

2 choose and reward responsible partners;

3 be ethical;

4 be climate smart;

5 reduce, reuse, recycle;

6 use natural resources responsibly;

7 strengthen communities.

H&M is committed to conserving water, soil, air and species. In terms of raw materials, H&M aims to use only cotton from sustainable sources by 2020 by switching to certified organic cotton and other raw materials made from recycled materials including fabric. The use of organic cotton grown without chemical pesticides or fertilizers is good for the health of the farmers as well as the environment. H&M has been actively involved in the Better Cotton Initiative (BCI), and also continues to increase the use of conscious materials such as recycled polyester, polyamide and wool which receive third-party certification following the Global Recycling Standard (GRS). In terms of water and chemicals, H&M needs to work with the factories to improve the way water is used and treated from cotton to customer, to ensure the use of chemicals safely and to eliminate discharges into water, soil and air. The company does not own factories and therefore develops environmental requirements for suppliers according to the above commitments. Suppliers are audited by external auditors according to the Textile Exchange Standards or Organic Content Standards (OCS) and transactional certificate (TC). The OCS verifies the presence and amount of a given raw material in a final product. It is a voluntary standard that tracks the flow of a raw material from the source to the final product and is certified by an accredited third party. The certification of the raw materials itself is verified independently by another production process certification.

For those who own factories which use a lot of water and chemicals, cleaner production becomes the main strategic objective. Esquel Group is a producer of premium cotton shirts, and has production facilities in China, Malaysia, Vietnam, Mauritius, and Sri Lanka, with a network of branches servicing key markets worldwide. Esquel manufactures for the world's best-known and most highly respected brands, including Ralph Lauren, Tommy Hilfiger, Nike, Brooks Brothers, Hugo Boss, Lacoste, Bestseller and Muji. Esquel chooses to vertically integrate its supply chain operations to retain control of its product quality in every step of the production process. Cotton is grown in its own facilities in Xinjiang province in north-western China. The company takes care of the remaining value chain activities including spinning, weaving, dyeing, manufacturing, packaging and retailing.

Esquel uses a pollution database developed by Institute of Public and Environmental Affairs from China to identify environmental problems with suppliers and its own factories. External auditors are sent to the factories whenever a problem is reported. Strict instructions are given to suppliers to make corrections and offer explanations whenever an environmental problem or offence is discovered. In some cases, suppliers do not have the financial capability to install water treatment facilities, and customer orders are not large enough to support investment in such facilities. In such instances, the company helps suppliers to identify chemicals that are less polluting and use less water. As a result, suppliers save energy and water, and some of them even receive ISO14000 certification and rewards from the Chinese government. The company also uses Oeko-Tex Standard 100 to require suppliers to declare raw material use in the production process and detailed information about each chemical used in every production stage. These are verified by third-party tests and certification. The drivers for adopting cleaner production appear to come from Esquel's 'E-culture'. E-culture comprises Ethics, Environment, Exploration, Excellence and Education. Since ethics and environment are the main corporate culture, corporate and environmental responsibility is at the heart of the whole organization.

The journey towards toxic-free textiles has been tough. Some global fashion companies believe that it is not possible to make their supply chains fully transparent and ban all toxic chemicals from all steps of production. The 'Detox Campaign' launched by Greenpeace has helped companies identifying and eliminating the use of major hazardous, persistent and hormone-disrupting chemicals in the textile industry (http://www.greenpeace.org/). Under pressure from various stakeholders including Greenpeace, fashion companies such as Adidas, Puma and Nike have promised to go toxic-free by 2020, while many others are still resisting. With these pioneers leading the change and demonstrating the payoffs of such audacious ambitions, there will be followers.

The textiles case above illustrates the role of standards and certifications. To make cleaner production an integrated part of environmental management efforts, it is desirable to make it a part of the environmental management system (EMS). EMS is a 'formal system and database which integrates procedures and processes for the training of personnel, monitoring, summarizing, and reporting of specialized environmental performance information to internal and external stakeholders of the firm' (Melnyk *et al*, 2003, p 332). EMS generally provides formal structures of rules and resources for managers to establish organizational routines that help achieve corporate environmental goals and innovate. EMS is also the main mechanism for creating awareness and providing training to workers. A number of well-known international manufacturers (eg Shape, 3M and Xerox) have decided to manufacture their products according to (or beyond) the highest environmental standards (Thierry *et al*, 1995), and they are achieved through the establishment of an integrated environmental management system.

ISO 14001 is the international standard for EMS and among the most widely used in the world. Eco-management and Audit Scheme (EMAS) is the second most popular EMS standard in Europe. These two standards have very similar structures but there are some fundamental differences. EMAS firms must be compliant to relevant environmental rules and regulations to guarantee their certification. However, ISO 14001:2004 emphasizes only the commitment to compliance but such compliance is not essential to keep their certification. In addition, the evaluation of the EMAS standard is guaranteed by obligatory audits every three years where all requirements are checked and a statement is made public. ISO 14001:2004 audits check for environmental system performance against internal benchmarks; somehow there are no penalties for lack of improvement and the frequency of audits is left to the discretion of the individual firm. The revised 2015 version of ISO 14001 has increased the onus on the organization's strategic planning processes leadership roles to promote environmental management. Organizations are expected to commit to proactive initiatives to protect the environment. This is a shift away from simply improving management systems to improving environmental performance, and an increase in control and influence over environmental impacts associated with product design and development to address each stage of the lifecycle, communication and documentation practices.

In the literature, other than zero emission, some novel concepts such as Factor 4 and Factor 10 have been established. These concepts can be used to guide companies when they set cost and environmental improvement targets. Factor 4 (http://www.wupperinst.org/) means being twice as productive with half the resources (Weizsacker *et al*, 1998). That also means the same functions of a product can be achieved by using only a quarter of the resources. To achieve factor 4, a seven-step toward resource productivity has been proposed (Weizsacker *et al*, 1998) based on the idea of using material input per service (MIPS). This method is very similar to the concept of value engineering, whereby fewer components or lower quantities of materials are used to create the same value for the customers (functions or perceived benefits). Another concept, Factor 10, means 10 times more productive with the same input; this is a more ambitious target. The main motif is to drive environmental ambition. These concepts have been applied by governments as well as commercial firms. Similarly, zero emission cannot be practically possible but it is a goal which could drive serious efforts. Zero emission is now becoming a benchmark among industries. In some industries, some companies are competing to become the first to achieve zero emission.

Packaging for the environment

Globally, the packaging industry has a turnover of around US $5000 billion (World Packaging Organization, 2012). Packaging is required for practically all goods such as food, beverages, healthcare, cosmetics, electronics, clothing, etc. For some beverage products, packaging is actually the most expensive part. The packaging of goods is typically made of materials such as glass, plastic, paper, cardboard, metal and wood. Glass is used typically for beverages and liquids, papers are used for light goods, and corrugated cardboards can be used for heavier goods. Woods are typically used to make crates and pallets, and metal cases and tanks are suitable for containing and transporting bulk products. Packaging is very important for supporting production, logistics, supply chain and marketing activities because it protects goods, allows goods to be contained and transported in a standard unit of loading (eg cartons, pallets and containers), and it also allows marketers to provide essential information about the goods to customers.

Paper and cardboard are among the most popular packaging materials, but there is an increasing trend to use plastic as a packaging material. Since plastic is light in weight it reduces both the weight of transported goods and the amount of packaged goods that go to waste, both of which reduce CO_2 emissions. Without plastic packaging, it is estimated that the tonnage of alternative packaging materials would increase by a factor of four, Greenhouse Gas (GHS) emissions by a factor of two, costs by a factor of 1.9, energy use by a factor of 1.5 and waste by a factor of 1.9 in volume (PlasticEurope, 2009). That means the abandonment of plastics in packaging would result in a significant increase in weight of waste, energy consumption in making the alternatives, and subsequent increase in the cost of packaging. From the supermarket perspective, whether to give customers paper over plastic bags is still an ongoing debate. For example, Americans use 100 billion plastic bags a year, made from about 12 million barrels of oil. Instead, the use of

10 billion paper bags each year means cutting down 14 million trees (Science World, 2008). According to Science World, the production of every tonne of paper bags consumes four times more energy and more air and waterborne pollution than the production of plastic bags, and furthermore, the recycling of paper consumes 85 times more energy than the recycling of plastic bags.

Using innovative technology and appropriate materials, packaging also helps to conserve resources, reduce carbon emissions and make a supply chain more cost efficient. For example, it protects food as it travels from farm to supermarket and into our kitchens so less waste is produced along the supply chain. The same principle is applied to extend the lives of prepared sandwiches and meals. At the supermarket, loosely packed fruits and vegetables create more waste than pre-packed produce. Plastic film extends the shelf life of vegetables from a few days to about two weeks. Multilayer films in a MAP (modified atmospheric packaging) used to pack meat extends shelf life from a few days to over a week. Based on a lifecycle perspective, the amount of CO_2 used to produce a single portion of meat is almost 100 times more than that used to produce the multilayer film.

Technically, all packaging materials can be reused, recycled or recovered. However, packaging is also one of the main waste streams which could harm the environment, if not properly managed. This is because not all packaging materials (eg plastic) are biodegradable and there are scientific studies which prove that such materials could affect biodiversity. According to PlasticEurope (2009), 265 million tonnes of plastic are produced globally each year; 38 per cent of that is for packaging. Since plastic waste is relatively more difficult to collect and recycle, millions of tonnes of packaging materials made of plastic are being landfilled globally. Since there is a lack of efficient recycling systems and participation in many countries, packaging industries are under pressure to develop more biodegradable packaging materials or materials which can be used for energy recovery without side effects on human health and the environment. Some packaging manufacturers develop food-grade recyclable packaging materials, such as r-HDPE for milk containers. Such milk containers can be recycled into plastic pellets for producing milk containers again.

The following principles for environmentally friendlier packaging design, production and commercialization are particularly aimed at manufacturers. These principles form part of the EU directive for packaging and packaging waste (94/62/EC).

- Use minimum packaging volume and weight as long as it meets minimum adequate amount to maintain the necessary levels of safety and hygiene acceptable for the packaged product and for the consumer.

- Packaging shall be designed, produced and commercialized for reuse, recovery, recycling and to minimize its impact on the environment when being disposed of.

- Packaging shall be produced so that the presence of noxious and other hazardous substances as constitute the packaging material be minimized when they are being incinerated or landfilled.

- Packaging designed for the energy recovery option shall have a minimum inferior calorific value to allow optimization of energy recovery.

- Packaging designed for composting shall be biodegradable so that it should not hinder the separation collection and the composting process.

- Biodegradable packaging shall be capable of undergoing physical, chemical, thermal or biological decomposition so that the finished compost ultimately decomposes into carbon dioxide, biomass and water.

In order to make the packaging materials lighter and yet strong enough to contain goods (being functional), research and technology developments are used to strengthen existing packaging materials. Lighter corrugated cardboard is an example. Others look into issues related to over-packaging for online business. Another very important development is the use of recycled packaging materials and labelling to facilitate recycling.

Towards sustainable packaging for grocery supply chains

Grocery retailers in the UK are facing increasing pressure from regulations and NGOs. In September 2010, several companies were prosecuted for using excessive packaging. Sainsbury's was prosecuted for using 'excess' wrapping on its 'Taste the Difference Slow Matured Ultimate Beef Roasting Joint' (*Daily Mail*, 2010). The joints were packed in plastic shrink wrap, placed inside a plastic tray, topped with a transparent plastic lid and surrounded with a cardboard sleeve. The law on excess packaging introduced in 1999 in the UK says packaging should be limited to 'the minimum adequate amount' to ensure safety and hygiene. The fines for excessive packaging according to the law were relatively low and some activists are trying to lobby the government to increase them. The company later redesigned the packaging and reduced the total amount of packaging by 53 per cent.

Sainsbury's was founded in 1869 and in 2016 operates over 1,300 stores in the UK. It employs over 150,000 employees, and is a major grocery retailer in the UK. It's main businesses are supermarkets, convenience stores and internet-based home delivery shopping services. Its vision is to be the most trusted retailer where people love to work and shop. One of its main purposes is to provide great (healthy, safe, fresh and tasty) food to its customers. The ways the retailer operates its business is largely guided by five values: (1) best for food and health, (2) sourcing with integrity, (3) respect for environment, (4) make a positive difference to the community, and (5) a great place to work.

Sainsbury's has been one of the first supermarkets in the UK to adopt sustainable initiatives to reduce environmental management. Sainsbury's joined a voluntary agreement with WRAP called Courtauld Commitment to improve resource efficiency and reduce carbon and the wider environmental impact of grocery retail. The supermarket has been continuing to actively participate in Courtauld II and III. In November 2012, Sainsbury published a document called *20x20 Commitments* to declare its 20 commitments to help people to live well for less. Sainsbury's is committed to making sure that its own packaging has been reduced by half compared to 2005. The following examples demonstrate how redesign of packaging materials can help to reduce environmental impacts as well as fuel consumption:

- glass used in peanut butter jars replaced with plastic, cutting packaging by 83 per cent or 882,000 kilograms;
- the size of the outer sleeves for ready-meals packaging reduced by 45 per cent, leading to a saving of 5,500,000 kilograms of cardboard each year;
- heat-seal lids on soft fruit lines introduced to reduce 440 tonnes of packaging each year;
- reducing Easter egg packaging by 57 per cent since 2008;
- removing the cartons from canned tuna fillets in order to reduce packaging by 20 per cent;
- reducing the cardboard on pizza base mix to save 87 per cent of packaging;
- reducing the diameter of the inner cardboard tube of toilet rolls by 24 per cent, which cut down 500 delivery lorries, saved 140 tonnes of CO_2 as well as saving 335 tonnes in packaging a year;
- promoting the use of refill instead of the original bottles and boxes in order to reduce the use of heavier packaging materials.

The use of biodegradable packaging materials is another great opportunity. Sainsbury's has looked into the use of home-compostable packaging. Instead of plastic, Sainsbury's replaced it with packaging made of maize, sugar cane or starch. Such packaging materials can naturally break down in a garden compost heap, and eliminate the need to landfill or recycle. Sainsbury's first tested the use of such home-compostable packaging in 2001 on a small range of food, plans to use its scale to make home-compostable packaging mainstream. In 2007, Sainsbury's made an announcement that it would replace 150 million plastic trays and bags on ready meals and organic food with home-compostable packaging every year. The use of compostable packaging also means saving of the fossil fuel required to make plastic for packaging and reduces the amount of plastic waste reaching landfill sites. The launch of the home-compostable packaging received a lot of publicity in the media.

Sustainable consumption and logistics

The concept of sustainable consumption and production was recognized in the Johannesburg Plan for Implementation and adopted at the World Summit on Sustainable Development (WSSD) in 2012. Sustainable consumption was defined by the 1999 Oslo Symposium on Sustainable Consumption as:

> the use of services and related products which respond to basic needs and bring a better quality of life while minimizing the use of natural resources and toxic materials as well as emissions of waste and pollutants over the lifecycle of the service or product so as not to jeopardize the needs of future generations.

It calls for increasing efficiency in consumption, a change in consumption patterns and the reduction of consumption.

At a global level, the Organization for Economic Co-operation (OECD) has contributed to the UN Marrakech Process on Sustainable Consumption and Production by working with different governments and companies to encourage the adoption of sustainable consumption. There are mandatory government actions to promote sustainable consumption and standards for verifying energy efficiency as well as voluntary sustainability-related standards such as those that limit energy use for manufacturers. Manufacturers of household products such as refrigerators, air conditioners, washers and dryers, heating, ovens and lighting are nowadays required to conform to energy efficiency standards and labels. Additional labels are added to guide consumers in terms of their recycling obligations and to encourage greater participation in the collection and recycling of products. Governments are also encouraged to use taxes and charges to raise the prices of less sustainable products.

However, very often taxes and charges are not set at a level high enough to change consumer decision behaviours. Taxes and charges can be used to limit car emissions (eg congestion charges, road tax), household energy use, water use, and household waste as well as to reduce the consumption of tobacco and alcohol. Alternatively, subsidies and incentives have been used to encourage the purchase and use of more energy-efficient vehicles, solar panels, solar and thermal water heaters and even separation and recycling of waste.

Some manufacturers have put more investment in R&D to develop new products that consume less energy and water during use. This initiative can be explained by the natural resource-based view (Hart, 1995). When a company develops new and greener products it also develops new standards that can be used as a competitive weapon. For example, the Energy Star voluntary energy efficiency programme sponsored by the US Environmental Protection Agency (EPA) was created by pioneering companies such as Xerox and HP. While such innovations create new revenue streams, some companies successfully transform their product portfolios such that more revenues are generated by sustainable products, allowing consumers to achieve energy, water and cost savings.

Another approach some companies apply is to produce durable products to prolong their lives and avoid wastage. For most companies, this is a rather controversial business or product strategy. Producing and selling more durable products could mean the reduction of sales volume even though the products can be sold at higher prices. Price premium owing to durability does not always appeal to consumers. For example, fast fashion is a business model that relies on selling large quantities of cheap and less-durable clothing in a way that opposes to the idea of sustainable consumption. Patagonia, a company that sells clothing, aims to build the best products that cause no unnecessary harm, and uses such a business model to inspire and implement solutions to the environmental crisis. Some of its clothing is produced by incorporating recycled materials whenever possible and some clothing is made more durable. Their famous 2011 advert, 'Don't buy this jacket', explains the possibility of 'environmental bankruptcy' owing to the shortage of water, topsoil, fisheries and wetlands as the natural systems that are fundamentally the main supports of businesses. The advertisement explains that one of Patagonia's best-selling jackets consumed 135 litres of water, enough to meet the daily needs of 45 people. Even though the jackets were made of 60 per cent recycled polyester there are still significant environment impacts, where two-third of its weight ended up in waste. The advertisement explains that the jackets were made exceptionally durable and therefore do not need replacing as often. The advertisement was part of the launch of an initiative called the Common Threads Initiative, which promotes reduce, repair, reuse and recycle. By promoting 'buy less, buy used', the initiative also allows consumers to sell used Patagonia products through eBay.

However, there are still products where durability or prolonged use do not appeal, as they may seem unaffordable, or consumers are unaware. High-tech devices such as mobile phones are phased out frequently by the introduction of new technologies in order for manufacturers to compete with each other for market share. This means that while the devices can be designed for recycling, refurbishment, remanufacturing and reuse, there is a need for effective collection schemes that encourage collection by offering lease, buy-back and deposit options.

Washing machines represent another product that could be more resource efficient if they were made to last longer. Due to the different sizes of households there will be those single-person households who run their washing machines for 110 cycles per year while the laundromats machines need 1,500 to 3,000 cycles per year. Consumers may choose to buy an entry-level washing machine that lasts 2,000 washing cycles instead of a high-end machine that runs 10,000 cycles. Due to a short period of warranty (one or two years), average consumers are incentivized to buy lower-quality machines, even though there are nowadays more energy- and water-efficient ones. This causes frequent replacement and therefore large numbers of used washing machines end up as waste. To address this issue, manufacturers have redesigned machines to enable replacement of components that frequently break down such as the pump, motor and plumbing. By using more durable components and energy-enhancing features such as a wide range of programmes, sensor technologies and automatic dosing systems, new generations of washing machines can be upgraded to prolong their use. New ways of thinking mean washing machines can be upgraded by simply uploading new software.

However, issues facing the low-cost segment of the washing machine market cannot be resolved by technologies that make the machines more expensive. Alternatively, companies may design product service systems that encourage prolonged use and reuse of products. For example, consumers may be attracted to leasing washing machines and returned washing machines can be repaired and refurbished for reuse over up to 20 years. Consumers contribute to part of the long-term cash flow, resulting in a win-win situation that promotes business sustainability (the leasing companies, maintenance and repair companies and manufacturers) and overall positive material and energy implications. There are even experiments that use smart meters to enable the 'pay-by-wash' scheme. Other companies sell refurbished industrial washing machines to domestic markets.

Traditionally, the proponents of sustainable or reverse logistics have been focusing on the effective management of physical flows of end-of-life products. One may design components so that they can be easily identified and dissembled for recycling, and reduce time of disassembly. Others look into ways that minimize space and weight to reduce the need for fuel and transportation costs or reduce the need for materials and packaging materials. The different product service systems discussed earlier essentially create different closed-loop reverse logistics processes to manage end-of-life products. In the circular economy dictionary these are called technical (restoration) cycles. There is still a need to consider nature's biological metabolism as a way to develop a technical metabolism flow of industrial materials. There is therefore a need to consider cradle-to-cradle design concepts that eliminate waste altogether. Waste equals food and energy. That means industrial leaders should create and participate in systems to collect and recover the value of all materials following their use.

Regulatory frameworks

There has been an ongoing debate about the value of regulations. Some companies view regulations as additional costs, while others argue they are necessary. Alternatively, there is a famous hypothesis that challenges the notion that tough environmental regulations imply additional costs that harm competition. It is called the Porter Hypothesis. This hypothesis suggests that stricter environmental regulations in the form of economic incentives can create a win-win situation that drives innovation that may create competitiveness in the market. Such competitiveness may outweigh the initial or short-run costs of the regulations. By moving managerial attention from trading off between environmental costs and other economic factors to compliance with strict regulations, companies will eventually develop breakthrough technologies that significantly improve environmental performance while creating new competitive advantages in the products. While there is still no widespread evidence supporting the Porter Hypothesis, the UN and many governments are developing and imposing new and stricter regulations following their commitments to various environmental improvement targets.

Therefore, logistics and supply chain professionals need to understand the legislation frameworks related to product design, production and packaging. At a global level, the Basel Convention, Rotterdam Convention, Stockholm Convention, Kyoto Protocol and Marrakesh Accords are highly instrumental in setting up legislation frameworks for the application and trans-boundary movements and environmental sound management of hazardous and other waste. Some of the earlier legislations established during the 1980s focus mostly on the controlled use of those highly hazardous substances and the control of pollution. Nowadays there are also regulations or certifications that can be adopted voluntarily. The following are some of the essential regulations.

Voluntary regulations

Organizations may choose to adopt standards or certifications voluntarily, for example, EU Ecolabel, certifications of treatment facilities for electronic waste and recyclate streams, recycling schemes, Product Environmental Footprint (PEF) and Organizational Environmental Footprint (OEF). In 2011, the European Commission (EC) recommended the use of PEF and OEF. These are based on common and harmonized methods to measure and communicate the lifecycle environmental performance of products and organizations. They can be used to evaluate environmental footprints based on a multi-criterion, supply-chain-wide, lifecycle assessment paradigm (ISO 14040/44) covering raw materials, manufacturing, repair and eventually disposal. The PEF/OEF methodologies have been tested during 2013–2016 to develop category rules suitable for different industrial sectors.

Eco-design directive

Eco-design means taking into account the environmental impacts of a product right at the early stage of design. It helps coordinate product design and planning so that the attempt to eliminate a toxic substance does not compromise energy consumptions during material extraction, production and recycling. The Eco-design of Energy Related Products Directive 2009/125/EC is a framework directive which primarily focuses on energy in use (http://ec.europa.eu/). It does this by setting minimum requirements for certain energy-consuming products. It applies to all energy-using products

(EUPs), including many domestic electrical and electronic appliances such as washing machines, TVs or computers and energy-related products (ERPs) such as windows, insulation and bathroom devices. While the aim is to minimize energy consumption, the directive does not mean to lower the functionality of a product, its safety, or have a negative impact on its affordability or consumer health. It means the need to meet requirements while remain cost effective. In Europe, only products that comply to the Eco-design Directive with a CE marking can be sold, leading to considerable energy saving. However, it only applies to companies trading in the EU with significant sales (more than 200,000 units) and therefore a significant environmental impact and potential for improvement. The Eco-design Directive is used together with other policy tools, such as the Energy Labelling Directive, EU Eco-label and Green Public Procurement (GPP).

Restriction of the use of certain hazardous substances (RoHS)

Computers, laptops, monitors, mobile phones, tablets, and other electronics contain certain amounts of lead, cadmium, chromium, PBB and PBDE. Owing to the increasing speed of new product introduction there are also more obsolete products being discarded, ending up in landfills, or in countries like China, Pakistan, and other third-world countries for recycling. People (both adults and children) collecting and recycling such e-waste have been found to be poisoned by the above heavy metals. These problems become the main drivers for the need for the RoHS and WEEE directives.

RoHS (Directive 2011/65/EU of the European Parliament and of the Council of 8 June 2011) is an EU directive on the restriction of the use of certain hazardous substances in electrical and electronic equipment. RoHS was adopted in February 2003 by the European Union and took effect on 1 July 2006, and is required to be enforced, becoming law in each member state. This directive restricts the use of six hazardous materials (lead, mercury, cadmium, hexavalent chromium, polybrominated biphenyls, and polybrominated biphenyls ether) in the manufacture of various types of electronic and electrical equipment. The maximum permitted concentrations are 0.01 per cent for hexavalent chromium and 0.1 per cent or 1,000 ppm by weight of homogeneous material for the other five materials. RoHS goes hand in hand with the Waste Electrical and Electronic Equipment Directive (WEEE) 2002/96/EC which sets collection, recycling and recovery targets for electrical goods. These two legislations attempt to solve the problem of toxic e-waste. There are other standards or legislation similar or equivalent to RoHS. Two examples are the Final Measures for the Administration of the Control and Electronic Information Products, also known as RoHS China (or China Order No 39), and the Electronic Waste Recycling Act of 2003 (EWRA) passed by California state. New revision of RoHS (RoHS2) is expected to cover other equipment such as medical devices, control and monitoring instruments, and industrial control and monitoring instruments, in phases.

Products affect by RoHS are, for example, paints, pigments, PVC (vinyl) cables, solders, printed circuit boards, leads, glass in television, CRT and camera lenses, metal parts, lamps and bulbs. Batteries are not included within the scope of RoHS. RoHS has been criticized for causing high cost of compliance. Some complained that RoHS is not fair for some electronics which use less of the above restricted materials. Others complained about the adverse effects of limiting the concentration of the above substances on the reliability of the electronics products. Some companies managed to innovate such that they could comply with RoHS without incurring too much additional cost while at the same time maintaining the reliability and quality of their products.

Registration, Evaluation, Authorization and Restriction of Chemicals (REACH)

REACH is the European Community regulation on chemicals and their safe use. REACH aims to improve the protection of human health and the environment through the better and earlier identification of the intrinsic properties of chemical substances. REACH also aims to enhance the innovation and competitiveness of the EU chemicals industry. Under this regulation, the industry is given greater responsibility for managing the risks from chemicals and for providing safety information on the substances. Manufacturers and importers of chemicals in volumes of more than one tonne are required to gather information on the quantities and properties of their chemical substances and register the information with the European Chemicals Agency (ECHA) in Helsinki. The Agency acts as the central registrar. ECHA manages the databases of chemical registration, and coordinates the evaluation of suspicious chemicals. Its aim is to build up a public database in which consumers and professionals can find hazard information and therefore help to ensure the safe handling of the chemicals in Europe.

Under the regulation, the manufacturers and importers will also have to pass the safety information on to downstream users. They have to ensure that the use of the chemicals in their production processes does not create risks for their workers, the end consumers or the environment. Chemicals that cause cancer require authorization. Similar to RoHS, there is also a list of restricted substances – there are about 59 categories involving 1,000 such substances. For example, the amounts of benzene in toys and PBB in textiles are restricted. REACH becomes one of the drivers that make manufacturers and importers begin asking their suppliers to disclose the use of chemicals in their production and products. REACH also calls for the progressive substitution of the most dangerous chemicals with suitable alternatives. Just as with any new legislation, there are complaints about the high cost involved in collecting and maintaining the information required by the manufacturers and importers. The European Union argues that at a macro level overall there are more benefits to society and commercial firms in the long term. REACH in Europe has also some influence in other countries. In 2010, the Ministry of Environmental Protection (MEP) in China released a revised version (Order No 7) of the Provisions on Environmental Administration of New Chemical Substances. Since this regulation is similar to EU REACH it is also known as the 'China REACH', and means the importation of chemicals into China also requires registration.

Regulations on packaging and packaging waste

The 94/62/EC Directive on packaging and packaging waste is a single-market measure with environmental goals. The Directive applies to all packaging placed on the market within the EU, and all packaging waste – whether disposed of at industrial or commercial sites, or from private homes. 'Packaging' means all products made of any materials of any nature to be used for the containment, protection, handling, delivery and presentation of goods, from raw materials to processed goods, from the producer to the user or the consumer. 'Non-returnable' items used for the same purposes shall also be considered to constitute packaging. In principle, the directive promotes:

- packaging to be minimized;
- packaging to be designed for recovery and re-use;
- recovery targets to be met by the UK for waste packaging;
- heavy metals in packaging to be restricted.

There are three essential requirements of the directive:

- packaging volume and weight must be the minimum amount needed to maintain the necessary levels of safety, hygiene and acceptance for the packed product and for the consumer;

- packaging must be manufactured so as to permit reuse or recovery in accordance with specific requirements;
- noxious or hazardous substances in packaging must be minimized in emissions, ash or leachate from incineration or landfill.

In addition, there are aggregate heavy metal limits applicable to cadmium, mercury, lead, and hexavalent chromium in packaging or packaging components. While the directive promotes the prevention of packaging waste and sets recovery and recycling targets for EU member states, it is the responsibility of involved governments to take appropriate measures, including national programmes and the introduction of producer responsibilities. The UK, for example, has established the Producer Responsibility Obligations (Packaging Waste) Regulations 2007, which basically specifies 'collective producer responsibility'. It requires producers of packaging to take responsibility for their environmental impact by paying a proportion of the cost of the recovery and recycling of their packaging. Under this legislation, the 'packaging supply chain' is divided into four activities, each with a different percentage responsibility:

- 6 per cent for manufacturers of raw material for packaging;
- 9 per cent for converters, eg manufacturers of the packaging can, bottle, etc;
- 37 per cent for packers/fillers or those who put a product into packaging or apply packaging to a product;
- 48 per cent for sellers or those who supply the packaging to the end user of that packaging, eg the supermarkets or wholesalers.

Importers may have to pay the rolled-up obligation, meaning all of the above costs. The above producers or importers pay the obligations by buying a Packaging Waste Recovery Note (PRN) issued by reprocessors who are licensed to issue PRNs. For the export of packaging waste, the export version (PERN) is used. This legislation applies to those with a turnover of more than £2 million and who have handled more than 50 tonnes of packaging in the previous calendar year.

Summary

There has been growing recognition that the ways we design products and their production and delivery processes have to change. In addition, to make sure that the product is making money, there is a need to reduce the natural resources and chemicals used, while making sure that there are no adverse health effects to workers and minimizing environmental damage. It is not just about carbon footprint; one has to consider water footprint, energy consumption and biological metabolism. The design of cleaner products and the use of cleaner production technologies and packaging are essential for preventing pollution, conserving natural resources and recycling. Many innovative solutions and methods are now developed such that design of a product should consider reducing energy and material consumption during production and use. One important starting point is the selection and discovery of environmentally friendlier materials. In this respect, many regulations have already been developed to control the use of the most hazardous substances and to track the production and use of chemicals.

In addition, it is also possible to design cleaner production and logistics processes. It is not just about pollution prevention; a more comprehensive cleaner production programme should take into account waste minimization, greener packaging, green productivity, energy and eco-efficiency. Those who invest in developing new and cleaner technology for production can lead the industry and even make this a new business opportunity. Others who develop new packaging materials or work with suppliers to reduce packaging weights are becoming environmental leaders in the industries, gaining more business and better reputations. It is also evident that success in implementing eco-design, cleaner production and packaging requires an integrated environmental management system and the ability to extend the environmental improvement efforts to the supply chains. Companies at the forefront are taking challenges such as Factor 4, Factor 10 and zero emissions. Even though companies are investing in many efforts, they rely on the consumers to drive the demand for environmentally friendly products; ultimately it is the end consumers who pay for the products. Companies should consider working more with consumers and making them realize the environmental implications of their consumption of the products they purchase so that they share responsibility just as much as anyone else in the supply chain.

References

Daily Mail (2010) It's war on store waste: Landmark case will force supermarkets to end needless packaging, 17 September [online] available at: http://www.dailymail.co.uk/news/article-1312599/Sainsburys-landmark-case-force-supermarkets-end-needless-packaging.html#ixzz2EC9P94d2

Ellen MacArthur Foundation (2015) Towards a circular economy: business rationale for an accelerated transition, *Ellen MacArthur Foundation*, December, [online] available at: https://www.ellenmacarthurfoundation.org/publications/ towards-a-circular-economy-business-rationale-for-an-accelerated-transition

EPA (1990) Pollution Prevention Act of 1990 [online] available at: https://www. epa.gov/p2/pollution-prevention-act-1990 [accessed 31 December 2016]

FAO (2011) Water for food water for life: a comprehensive assessment of water management in agriculture, *International Water Management Institute* [online], available at: http://www.fao.org/nr/water/docs/summary_synthesisbook.pdf, pp 1–40

Feldmann, K, Meedt, O Trautner, S, Scheller, H and Hoffman, W (1999) The 'Green Design Advisor': a tool for design for the environment, *Journal of Electronics Manufacturing*, 9 (1), pp 17–28

Greenpeace (2011) *Dirty Laundry: Unravelling the corporate connections to toxic water pollution in China*, Greenpeace.org [online] available at: http://www. greenpeace.org/international/en/publications/reports/Dirty-Laundry/

Hart, S L (1995) A natural-resource-based view of the firm, *The Academy of Management Review*, 20 (4), pp 986–1014

Hart, S L (1997) Beyond greening: strategies for sustainable world, *Harvard Business Review*, Jan–Feb, pp 67–76

Hoffman, W (1997) Recent advances in design for the environment at Motorola, *Journal of Industrial Ecology*, 1 (1), pp 131–47

IPE (2009) *Sustainable Apparel's Critical Blind Spot*, Friends of Nature, Institute of Public and Environmental Affairs (IPE), Green Beagle, Envirofriends, Nanjing Green Stone

ISO (2014) *ISO/IEC 17050-1:2004* Conformity assessment – supplier's declaration of conformity – Part 1: general requirements, *International Standards Organization* [online] available at http://www.iso.org/iso/catalogue_ detail?csnumber=29373 [accessed 31 December 2016]

Melnyk, S A, Sroufe, R P and Calantone, R (2003) Assessing the impact of environmental management systems on corporate and environmental performance, *Journal of Operations Management*, 21, pp 329–51

Motorola, Inc (2002) *Motorola: 2002 global corporate citizenship report*, Motorola, Inc, Schaumburg, IL

PlasticEurope (2009) The compelling facts about plastics 2009: an analysis of European plastics production, demand and recovery for 2008, *PlasticEurope* [online] available at: http://www.plasticseurope.org/Documents/ Document/20100225141556-Brochure_UK_FactsFigures_2009_22sept_6_Final-20090930-001-EN-v1.pdf [accessed 31 December 2016]

Science World (2008) 'Paper or plastic?' *Science World*, 64 (13), pp 14–15

Thierry, M, Salomon, M, Van Nunen, J and Van Wassehove, L (1995) Strategic issues in product recovery management, *California Management Review*, 37 (2), pp 114–35

UNESCO (2012) *Managing Water under Uncertainty and Risk*, United Nations World Water Development Report 4, Vol 1, United Nations Educational, Scientific and Cultural Organization

Walker, S and Dorsa, E (2001) Making design work: sustainability, product design and social equity, *The Journal of Sustainable Product Design*, 1, pp 41–48

Weizsacker, E V, Lovins, A B and Lovins, L H (1998) *Factor Four: Doubling wealth, halving resource use*, Earthscan, London

World Packaging Organization (2012) *Position Paper, Market Trends and Development*, World Packaging Organization

WWF (2012) *The Hidden Cost of Water*, report, World Wildlife Fund

Zhang, U, (2009) *Chemical Information in Two Textile Supply Chains: A case study of producers in China*, MSc Thesis, Chalmers University of Technology, Gothenburg, Report no 2009:10

Sustainable purchasing and procurement 06

The idea that it is not products competing with each other but supply chains directs the view on sustainability away from an intra-organizational perspective to the inclusion of suppliers, sub-suppliers, customers and service providers. Businesses do not exist in isolation and their sustainability performance is judged on the final overall impact of their supply chain. Consumers hold companies accountable for their wider supply chain, regardless of how peripheral a supplier might be to a brand. Much of the environmental and social impact often stems from earlier stages in the supply chain and the suppliers' and customers' operations add to the sum of the sustainability balance.

In an organization aiming for sustainability, the procurement activities are given a crucial role in reducing environmental and social footprint as they mainly control emissions stemming from the upstream supply chain by selecting suppliers, making wider sourcing decisions and determining collaboration and interaction with suppliers.

This chapter starts with a look at the development of the procurement function, what sustainable procurement is, why it is crucial to a company's sustainability efforts and what the main drivers and barriers for sustainable procurement are. We are looking at 'green' (or environmentally sustainable) procurement but also explicitly include the growing area of social responsibility. Initially, sustainability in businesses was mainly concerned about the environmental dimension, as social aspects are relatively well protected in Western countries. Increasingly, however, a more complete view on our modern global supply chains raises concerns about the social impact of what we buy from other parts of the world.

After covering green and socially responsible procurement, this chapter will go deeper into how they actually work and how they support sustainability improvements in the supply chain.

The role of procurement in the supply chain

The role of the procurement function changed significantly with the genesis of the idea of competing supply chains. From simple sourcing and buying, procurement developed into the boundary-spanning function that links the company to the downstream suppliers. Due to an increase in specialization, global competition and a focus on core competencies, supply chains started to involve larger numbers of international suppliers – resulting in an increase of complexity and the need to coordinate and manage suppliers in a structured way. Today's supply chains usually show a high proportion of third-party spending (the services and products that are bought in from outside) (Booth, 2010).

With the increase in outsourced activities, the selection and management of suppliers became much more important for a successful supply chain. When mapping supply chains, suppliers are structured into tiers. The first tier of suppliers consists of those closest to the focal organization. Their suppliers are then referred to as second-tier suppliers, etc. Picking the 'right' supplier for a particular product or service has a strategic dimension. Supply chain maturity, stages of the product lifecycle, sourcing risk, importance of the sourced good and plenty more considerations need to be made in strategy frameworks (Booth, 2010).

How green is your pint? Muntons Maltings

Malt is one of the key ingredients for beer brewing and is made from roasting barley. Like other grains, it is a food product grown on farmland. Farming itself is a major contributor to greenhouse gas emissions and the growing of cereals accounts for 5 per cent of land use globally. With a rapidly growing world population, the land occupied for farming will increase tremendously. At the same time, rising temperatures caused by global warming make crops more vulnerable to damaging organisms, meaning more pesticides need to be used or the agriculturally used land is expanded even further.

Although in the UK farming contributes only 1 per cent of overall CO_2 emissions, it causes 7 per cent of NOx (nitrous oxides) and CH_4 (methane), which have a much stronger effect on global warming. The atmospheric warming effect of a tonne of CH_4 equals the effect from 25 tonnes of CO_2 and one tonne of NOx emitted has the same effect as 295 tonnes of CO_2.

Another major emission from food production comes from the consumption of fresh water. The waste water stemming from malting could be treated to the standards for human consumption so that 70 per cent of the process water could be saved. But the water treatment creates a trade-off with CO_2 emissions, as 1.23 kg of CO_2e is required for the treatment of one tonne of water.

Muntons Maltings analysed their malt supply chain from the farm to the sold malt and discovered that almost two-thirds of the overall carbon footprint stemmed from the initial barley growing and therein nitrogen fertilizers are contributing almost half of the footprint and N_2O from soil nitrogen losses. The largest contributor within the malting operations is the consumption of energy (gas and electricity), mainly in a process called kilning, in which the malt is dried in an oven-type facility. The specifications from customers usually request a final moisture level of around 3 per cent. However, achieving a moisture level of 3 per cent uses 45 per cent more carbon emissions than a level of 3 per cent; and even a moisture level of 4 per cent needs 25 per cent more emissions than the 6 per cent level. Although that would require a bit more haulage overall to deliver the same amount of dry weight, the emission increase from haulage is negligible in comparison to the huge potential carbon savings in the kilning.

An essential part of becoming greener was then to talk to the farmers in the upstream supply chain to substitute previously used fertilizers with biofertilizers. At the downstream direction of the supply chain, Muntons' customers needed to be consulted on higher levels of moisture in the malt. Customers did not really require such a low moisture level for their operations and were willing to accept higher moisture levels (also because the energy saved meant that prices could be lowered too). A higher moisture level than 3 per cent was simply something nobody ever looked into before and customers had been using the standard 3 per cent level that they were accustomed to. The footprint analysis and collaboration with supply chain partners on either end enabled Muntons to reduce the carbon footprint of their malt significantly on their mission to be the greenest maltster in the world.

SOURCE www.muntons.co.uk.

With the number of tiers and the number of suppliers the complexity increases and monitoring the supply chain – including all subsuppliers – is a difficult task. Nevertheless, customers and consumers tend to hold companies responsible for what is happening further down their supply chain (Wilhelm *et al*, 2016). Furthermore, the large share of the activities in the supply chain being outside an organization's core boundaries also means that to improve sustainability, an organization must include all its suppliers and supply chain activities whether they are within direct control or not, as businesses are often being held accountable for unsustainable behaviour anywhere in their supply chains (Grimm *et al*, 2016).

What is sustainable procurement?

The aim of sustainable procurement practices is the inclusion of sustainability issues in the procurement strategy and in procurement decisions, for example in sourcing decisions or supplier selection. Similar to the development from a debate focused only on 'green' to a wider supply chain perspective, this chapter does not want to limit the discussion to the dimension of the natural environment but addresses all parts of the triple bottom line. Sustainable procurement has increasingly often an ethical perspective.

Social injustice (for example the situation of farmers in less developed countries) and the violation of basic human rights (for example in child labour or modern slavery) triggers consumer reactions in two ways: avoidance of particular brands and retailers or the support of 'good' products like Fairtrade-labelled coffee. Beyond consumers punishing or rewarding businesses for bad or good behaviour, businesses also face legislation that aims to make them behave responsibly.

Areas covered by legislation are, for example, bribery and corruption and modern slavery, but also embargoes against certain products and the conducting of business with certain countries and individuals. Such legislation can be issued by national governments, for example the trade restrictions against Russia and Russian individuals by the European Union and the United States after the invasion of Ukraine, or by international bodies like the United Nations, for example the trade sanctions against North Korea. As legislation is usually accompanied by punishment for its violation, which can be financial or sometimes even imprisonment of decision makers, it becomes a compliance topic for businesses.

Although the terms 'procurement' and 'purchasing' are often used interchangeably in the literature, they are distinctly different. Procurement has a more strategic positioning and covers all activities of acquiring goods or services (including the purchasing function), whilst purchasing is described more narrowly as the functions and activities of the buying process (Vitasek, 2010). Consequently, we have to differentiate between the more strategic picture of procurement and the more operational perspective of the purchasing activity.

The focus on procurement as a key function for making supply chains greener and more socially responsible is based on stakeholder theory and the idea that in many cases the customer has the more powerful position in the supply chain and can therefore lead a supply chain towards more sustainability. However, the idea that the buyer is always in a stronger power position in the supply chain relationship is a common misperception. In supply-side-dominated markets with little and fragmented buying power on the demand side, this theory will not hold. Businesses are also in a global competition over resources; if companies from one part of the world impose tough sustainability requirements on their suppliers, those suppliers may look into selling to customers in other parts of the world. Additionally, in-sourcing operations if no suitable external supplier is available may often be more of a theoretical option.

Nevertheless, on many occasions the push for a more sustainable supply chain needs to come from the customer or even consumer side. The pressure on the downstream supply chain to support sustainability initiatives often needs leadership from the larger and more powerful actors. Public procurement can play a crucial role in the leadership for green and sustainable procurement. Within the European Union, around a seventh of the overall GDP is spent through public procurement by authorities from all levels, whether it's spending through municipalities, state governments or the European Union's own budget. However, much public spending occurs in the construction and maintenance of buildings and physical infrastructure and the importance and impact of sustainability considerations in public procurement would be mainly in this area (Erdmenger, 2012). But even in areas where public spending is not the main buyer, the insistence on sustainable practices from public authorities can stimulate the creation of a market for more sustainable products and services. Public spending can hereby provide the base demand to enable the development of new products which can then also be acquired by commercial buyers (Crespin-Mazet and Dontenwill, 2012).

Sector-wide initiative against modern slavery in UK construction

UK construction and facilities management companies have for some time been under media and public scrutiny for the labour conditions in their supply chains. Media coverage about slave labour on overseas sites, particularly in the Gulf region and for the Qatar World Cup, is threatening the companies' reputations and investors' perception of the companies' risk profile. Although these companies do not sell to end consumers and hence have less to worry about in terms of brand damage cost, institutional stakeholders may be less willing to invest and cooperate, and potential staff less inclined to join if these companies are being seen as unethical in the public eye.

In 2015, the UK passed the Modern Slavery Act, effectively combining a number of previous acts and other measures into a targeted piece of legislation to combat modern slavery. Slavery was an unlawful criminal activity already, but the Modern Slavery Act went beyond slaveholding and also legislates aspects of victim protection and reporting duties for businesses on their measures against modern slavery in their operations and supply chains.

The passing of the Modern Slavery Act made a response to slavery and other ethical labour issues more urgent. Construction, facilities management and building supplies businesses decided to collaborate in a sector-wide response, led and coordinated by an industry-wide body called Action Sustainability, as they share many ethical issues in their supply chains. The market-leading large companies in the sector are all at the downstream end of the supply chain, using many much smaller contractors and suppliers in their activities.

Those smaller contractors often use further subcontractors and their own material suppliers, leading to a fragmented supply chain with usually little or no end-to-end visibility. The highest risk for slavery and unethical labour practices, however, lies towards the upstream end of the supply chain, making the larger downstream companies reliant on the support of their contractors and suppliers for any slavery eradication efforts.

The selection of and relationships with contractors and suppliers are naturally managed by procurement departments and it was hence their key task to introduce procurement guidelines that allow companies in the sector to identify modern slavery risks and to consider modern slavery in their selection process for contractors and suppliers. The collaboration also created information and education material for contractors and suppliers in the sectors' supply chains. Being aware that the much smaller contractors and suppliers cannot produce in-house capabilities, the larger companies realized there was a need and responsibility to educate the supply chain instead of 'pushing the problem down the chain' if they wanted to achieve real improvement beyond mere legal compliance box-ticking.

Drivers and barriers for sustainable procurement

Generally, the drivers and barriers for sustainable procurement can be divided into two groups: external drivers and internal drivers. Next to the above-mentioned pressure from customers, external drivers are also under pressure from the general public, governmental regulation and legislation, investors, and the desire for a competitive advantage by gaining a positive and sustainable image (Walker *et al*, 2008).

The main internal drivers are personal commitment of managers and investors, and the wish to reduce costs by a reduction of waste, pollution, brand damage or litigation costs. The drivers are somehow interlinked; for example, an internalization of costs for emissions through governmental regulation backs the internal driver to save costs through sustainable practices. Sustainability violations in the supply chain in essence became a commercial risk to business organizations and with procurement departments often being involved or in charge of selecting suppliers, sustainable procurement was driven by risk considerations.

The adoption of sustainable procurement practices is going hand in hand with an ever-increasing need to improve the visibility and transparency of supply chains. The need for transparency is not only required to monitor sustainability but also other risks and potential disruptions in the supply chain. Visibility is also required for formally conducted supply chain audits (Awaysheh and Klassen, 2010) and for operational improvements such as keeping inventory levels down.

Although sustainable procurement is considered a strategic decision needing top management support, at a purchasing level, sustainability is actually more connected with the personal and ethical values of a company founder filtering into the wider organization and related to middle-management support. The increase in sustainability requirements on the supply chain has certainly given the supplier selection process – and therefore procurement departments – more strategic and operational importance in business organizations.

The internal adaptation of sustainable practices in organizations can be categorized into four groups: resistant, reactive, receptive, and constructive adaptation (Walton *et al*, 1998).

Resistant adaptation of sustainable practices means that organizations only adapt such practices if there is no way around it. The attitude here is that sustainability issues are per se 'anti-business'. There is no intrinsic motivation to improve sustainability in the organization and sustainability-related laws are followed only by the letter but they do not feed into policies or strategy of the organization.

Reactive adaptation derives from the mere ambition to comply with environmental and social responsibility law and to avoid penalties. Solutions often focus on reducing the harm from emitted pollutants – for example by collecting and disposing of waste – and not on reducing emission levels in the first place. Environmental and social issues are appreciated but with no change of current processes and solutions are usually happening at the end of the supply chain with only incremental solutions.

Receptive adaptation starts considering possible competitive advantages coming from sustainability improvements, but the translation into operational processes and procedures is still minimal.

Constructive adaptation embraces the value of integrating product and process design into the sustainability planning. These companies also maximize the benefits from environmental initiatives as well as from the productivity of resources.

These four levels of internal adaptation of environmental and socially responsible practices, however, do not go beyond the organization's boundaries. To achieve truly environmentally and socially responsible practices, the involvement of more supply chain members is crucial. Achieving sustainable procurement may often start at an operational level, but needs to develop into an integration of sustainability considerations in the strategy. From its focus on the operational side of the supplier–customer relationship, it therefore started to include more and more supply chain stakeholders, developing the discussion further into the downstream and upstream supply chain and into making the entire supply chain management more sustainable.

Whilst the wish for cost reduction is a major internal driver for sustainable procurement, cost concerns are also a major barrier. Customers may aim for the lowest possible price and are not willing to pay a premium for more sustainable products. Costs associated with the implementation of sustainable practices are even more significant for small and medium-sized companies with fewer resources at their hands for investment. A managerial attitude of seeing ecology and social responsibility in a trade-off with economy increases the cost barrier even further.

Not knowing how to make procurement more sustainable can be an internal barrier too. Incorporating sustainability issues at a concrete, practical level appears to be difficult for many managers, even if they accept the necessity for more sustainability in their procurement. Managers are used to addressing issues of efficiency or governance in their interaction with suppliers and are often simply 'illiterate' in how to address sustainability. In such situations, the development of suppliers can be a way to improve the sustainability performance and development targets can be included in supply contracts.

A lack of legitimacy is another barrier. Paying only lip service to sustainability and working on sustainability purely from an advertisement perspective for 'greenwashing' purposes prevents individuals from buying into the agenda and committing to sustainability improvements.

We already mentioned the importance of including other supply chain actors in sustainability improvements in the supply chain. Before we look further into this, we discuss what external drivers and barriers determine whether organizations embark on the implementation of sustainable supply chain practices or not.

Regulation can be considered a major driver for organizations' environmental and social compliance efforts. Although compliance is not a guarantee of improved environmental and social performance, it is related to involvement in sustainable practices in purchasing. Improvement in sustainability performance is more likely to be seen in those companies who adapt and integrate sustainability into their supply chain rather than using a reactive adaptation strategy. Nevertheless, regulation is a motivator for new solutions for reducing environmental and social impact at a low cost. Regulation can be the initial trigger to start thinking about new ways of doing this and for reducing wasteful activities, therefore leading to improved production yields.

Customers are drivers for sustainability considerations in supply chains and procurement in many ways. This pressure can stem from the final consumer, and is then carried up the supply chain. Consumer-facing companies are particularly exposed to pressure groups and environmental campaigners. Large, high-profile corporations with much buying power are also often seen as being in the driving seat of demanding sustainability improvements in the upstream supply chain and therefore face most attention from campaigns and media and the most potential threat of negative publicity.

In a business environment, competitors also act as drivers for better supply chain practices. Competitors may become technology leaders or guide the industry to norms and legal frameworks, thereby driving other companies down the same route. Solution and innovation leadership amongst competitors can mean a competitive advantage since the pioneers often set the industry standards for future developments. When competitors gain a competitive advantage because of their supply chains' sustainability, companies have to respond to this challenge by implementing sustainability improvements themselves.

Increasing public awareness and the influence of non-governmental campaigning groups are among the societal drivers for sustainable supply chain practices. Pressure groups and campaigners often have the potential to publicly embarrass companies and thereby influence customers and lawmakers.

Suppliers as a possible driver for sustainable supply chains have received little attention in academic research. Some argue that suppliers are generally not the driving force behind sustainable supply chain practices but can support their implementation and provide valuable knowledge (Carter and Dresner, 2001). In addition, the ability for supply chain integration and collaboration with customers is an essential contributor to sustainability improvements. New products and services developed with other customers can also make the supplier the more knowledgeable partner for sustainability improvements.

Many of the external drivers can also act as external barriers. Regulation can reduce innovation or lead to changes that want to satisfy the law rather than achieving objective sustainability improvements. These can also be industry-specific. Regulatory priorities (for example to ensure a free market) might prevent organizations from sourcing the most environmentally friendly and socially responsible option.

Suppliers may not be willing to share more information in the supplier–customer relationship, preventing further integration necessary to make the supply chain more sustainable. Depending on the power balance in the relationship, customers may not be able to convince their suppliers about suggested changes and suppliers therefore become a barrier for improvements.

Drivers, barriers and practices vary across different industries. Sectors are adapting to sustainable supply chain practices at different speeds. Market structures, ownership, governance, industry-specific regulation, and the contextual situation put organizations into more or less individual situations.

Procurement frameworks

Knowing about the internal and external drivers and barriers leads us back to how companies can actually achieve sustainable procurement. As mentioned earlier, purchasing and procurement functions developed into the concept of managing supply chains. Consequently, sustainable purchasing and procurement must develop into sustainable management of supply chains (or supply networks). The main idea for the development from purchasing to supply management was published by Kraljic in 1983. His matrix framework categorizes supplied items into four sections according to their profit impact and their supply risk: strategic (high profit impact – high supply risk), bottleneck (low profit impact – high supply risk), leverage (high profit impact – low supply risk) and non-critical (low profit impact – low supply risk).

Whilst suppliers of strategic items are managed in a partnership with a lot of collaboration and innovation between the supply chain partners, bottleneck items are mainly about volume insurance and control. The supply of leverage items is focused on making the most use of purchasing power and short-term and spot buying. The supply of non-critical items is aiming at efficient ordering processes and standardization. Consequently, the supply chain relationships between customer and supplier vary between the item classifications, therefore requiring different approaches for integrating sustainability in the procurement activity.

For strategic items, sustainability as a performance criterion leads to new product development and innovation with the suppliers, benefiting from each other's knowledge to minimize the environmental and social impact of

Figure 6.1 Kraljic matrix

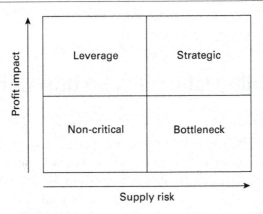

SOURCE Adapted from Kraljic (1983)

supply chains. Due to the close relationship, sustainability will also become a priority for the supplier and within the supplier's organization.

Bottleneck items are probably the most complicated ones for adding sustainability to procurement, as the buying company does not have much power to force the supplier into sustainability improvements or to change suppliers. Buying organizations can try to push for industry-wide standards and regulation to improve the sustainability of bottleneck items.

Improving the sustainability of leverage items, however, may be easier. Sharing best practices with suppliers enables sustainability improvements. Solutions consider a reduction of material intensity, using recyclables with a focus on leading into lower costs.

For non-critical items, sustainability needs to be included in the supplier selection criteria. To keep processes simple and efficient, certifications can be used for the achievement of the sustainability criteria. Since the number of potential suppliers is sufficient, suppliers who do not comply can be changed easily (Krause *et al*, 2009).

For all items the supply risk may increase as the number of potential suppliers is cut by those that do not satisfy the sustainability criteria or do not want to contribute to the sustainability agenda. Although the actions for achieving sustainability differ between the item categories, sustainability must be part of the agenda in all of them. Sustainability may become more and more a common performance criterion and therefore eventually develop into an order qualifier (Krause *et al*, 2009). Sustainability performance measures may also be raised as sustainability becomes common practice and buying organizations need to keep pace with the developments and sustainability performance level increases.

Understanding that sustainability must become a criterion in procurement decision making, we now need to understand how sustainability of an offered product or service can actually be judged, which is essential when suppliers are compared in a selection process.

Sustainability labels and certifications

To simplify the selection of supplier certifications and labels, external and most often independent organizations can be used. Certifications show that the supplier is following certain standards set by the awarding organization. The burden of monitoring and auditing the supplier is therefore shifted to an external auditor, usually paid for by the supplier, who is charged by the awarding organization for the use of the awarded label. Certifications are mainly used for suppliers of non-critical items and leverage items; nevertheless, they are also found in other supplier categories. Certifications and labels are also a way to avoid the pressure from campaigners as they provide evidence that the company fulfils the set standards. However, these standards are determined by the awarding organization and often only focus on a particular aspect rather than the overall sustainability of the product or service. In the following paragraphs, we are going to look at some of the more well-known environmental certifications.

Fairtrade

The Fairtrade label is awarded through national bodies that form part of the international Fairtrade organization. It focuses on ethical aspects and aims to help producers from developing countries out of poverty. Chocolate, coffee, cocoa, sugar, bananas and other agricultural commodities are the main products certified with the label. The retail value of Fairtrade-certified products in the UK exceeded £1.3 billion in 2011. It certifies that farmers are supplying in long-term contracts and are paid a stable and 'fair' price. The long-term engagement enables the farmers to invest into the development of their farms and provides them with a more predictable stream of income than the global spot prices for commodities. Farmers are also paid a premium for their products which can only be used for the social and economic benefit of their workers and communities. It also favours small-scale farmers and cooperatives to support rural communities and their development (Fairtrade, 2012).

Maritime Stewardship Council

The label of the Marine Stewardship Council (MSC) was founded by the environment protection organization WWF and the frozen fish producer Unilever (WWF, 2012). It focuses on setting standards for the sustainability of wild-captured fishing. It is not auditing any fishing businesses itself, but simply sets standards for fisheries and supply chain traceability. A product can apply the MSC label if the product can be traced back under MSC standards to an MSC-certified fishery. The MSC considers the fishing stock levels, the fishing operations and the managerial procedure towards sustainability (MSC, 2012). Despite the recognition of its achievements in environmental benefits, it has been criticized for setting its standards too laxly (Smith, 2011).

Rainforest Alliance

The Rainforest Alliance ecolabel does not focus on a single product category but on the protection of the rainforest in the production of a product. It also has wider considerations towards the empowerment of forest communities and the establishment of sustainable business opportunities for small- and medium-scale enterprises in these communities. The Rainforest Alliance is a nonprofit auditing organization for its own frog-themed ecolabels and the Forest Stewardship Council (FSC) ecolabel. The FSC itself is – similarly to the MSC – only a standard-setting organization, and does not get engaged in the auditing process. Accreditation is aimed at the producers and at the traceability through the supply chain to avoid the mixing of certified wood with others (FSC, 2012; Rainforest Alliance, 2012).

Carbon Trust

The Carbon Trust is an independent non-dividend-paying limited organization. Since its creation in 2001, it has helped clients to cut CO_2 emissions by 60 million metric tonnes ($MtCO_2$) and save £5.5 billion in energy costs. Any profits made are reinvested into the trust, whose aim is to 'accelerate the move to a global low-carbon economy' through work for and with business and public sector. The trust is engaged in advising decision makers, supporting the development of new technology and the assessment of carbon footprints. It measures and certifies the carbon footprint of organizations, products and supply chains. For the carbon label certification, clients have a choice of the two most widely accepted carbon footprint standards: the Publicly Accepted Standard (PAS) 2050 by the British Standards Institution (BSI) and the Department for Environment, Food and Rural Affairs; and the Greenhouse Gas Protocol of the World Business Council for Sustainable Development (WBCSD) and the World Resources Institute (WRI).

In contrast to other labels it does not only focus on one particular aspect or industry sector, but covers all areas of the supply chain (although it ignores the social and economic dimensions of the triple-bottom-line concept). It awards two labels: one merely shows that an organization is working with the Carbon Trust, while the other one requires active reduction of the measured carbon footprint, with such activities assessed every two years for recertification. Organizations applying the label to their products can decide whether they want to display the carbon footprint per unit within the label or not (Carbon Trust, 2017; Greenhouse Gas Protocol, 2012).

LEED

LEED (Leadership in Energy and Environmental Design) is the certification of the US Green Building Council (see also Chapter 4 on warehousing), which sets standards towards the sustainability of buildings. The standards vary in scope and requirements depending on the type and purpose of the building and differentiate between new constructions, existing buildings and refurbishments. Those applying for certification need to submit the details of their building and pay a charge for the review and certification of the building. Different to other environmental labels is the award of different achievement levels. The best-performing buildings gain platinum status, followed by gold, silver and certified (USGBC, 2012).

ISO 14001

Labels and certifications are not only applied in a consumer-facing environment. Manufacturers and other business customers also have a need to assess the environmental performance of their suppliers. In this setting, the International Standards Organization developed standards for environmental management systems. These are part of the ISO 14000 series. Most notable is ISO 14001, which sets standards for the establishment and improvement of environmental management and aims to engage organizations in a continuous improvement process of their environmental management. However, the ISO does not perform any audits or certifications itself, but simply develops standards at an international level, leaving the certification to independent auditors. Consequently, certifications in the 14000 series often go hand in hand with certifications of the ISO 9000 series on quality management and ISO 19000 series on auditing standards. The ecolabel image shows ISO 14001 certification by the British Standards Institution.

Beside the costs and time resources associated with ISO certification, the use of the ISO 14001 standards is also subject to other criticisms (Murphy, 2012). Adopting the ISO 14001 standards does not specify environmental targets, so achievements therefore depend solely on the organization's ambition, which makes comparison across sites, units and organizations difficult (Coglianese and Nash, 2001).

The adoption of ISO 14001 can also lead to a focus on establishing formal structures, procedures and policies rather than on increasing efficiency and improving sustainability. The formal set-up may also not always reflect the reality of activities in the organization (Meyer and Rowan, 1977).

Another criticism is that the comprehensiveness of the ISO 14001 standards varies widely from vague generalizations to detailed goals. Targets and their achievement can be seen as a rather mechanical process within a set regime of rules, limiting staff in choice and using their individual skills for improvements (Matthews, 2003). The ISO 14001 also does not include the supply chain and supplier selection; its scope is limited to the accredited unit and may in some cases ignore the main sources of a product's emissions (Krut and Gleckman, 1998).

Labels and certifications in general are subject to limitations and criticism. The focus on particular aspects of sustainability makes a comparison and sourcing decisions difficult. When comparing products and suppliers in a sourcing decision, the question becomes, what makes one product more sustainable than another? A widely applied and accepted way of evaluating the environmental balance of sourcing options is the use of lifecycle assessments. The manufacturing of one product may be causing more emissions than an alternative product but be more favourable in terms of maintenance and disposal, or a socially favourable option may cause more CO_2e emissions. Hence, the foundation of such a lifecycle assessment is to cover all emissions and impacts from cradle to grave (Schmidt and Frydendal, 2003).

Lifecycle assessment

A full lifecycle assessment (LCA) is the most comprehensive and also most commonly accepted way of determining the impact of a product or service. Depending on the complexity of the assessed product and its supply chain, the assessment can become an extensive activity. To reduce the resource intensity of an LCA, average values are often used, for example for the carbon emissions per kilometer from a 40-tonne diesel lorry or the use of a unit of main grid electricity. However, the more average values are used, the less exact and specific an LCA becomes.

An LCA consists of four steps. First, the scope of the assessment needs to be defined: what function, system or product is to be assessed; the definition of a functional unit; assumptions; and, importantly, the boundaries. The assessment is an iterative process and boundaries may be adjusted throughout the exercise. Nevertheless, standards like PAS 2050 now determine boundaries for the assessment. Although LCAs were initially developed for environmental emissions, and in particular greenhouse gases, the principle can be applied to any impact that a supply chain may cause.

Examples of a functional unit can be the emissions 'per visit' for a service, per kilogram of a product, the usual lifetime of product (for example energy savings from the improved energy efficiency of an electrical item), or per driven kilometer.

Second, within the boundaries, all input is recorded and assessed in an inventory analysis which forms the basis of the assessment. Collecting data hereby is often a more complicated task than initially anticipated and transferring input into functional units needs some consideration.

Third, following the analysis of the input side, all emissions are evaluated in an impact assessment. This is connected to the inventory data; all inventory data is put into impact categories and then processed within each category. As a result, the contributors to a particular impact can be grouped together. They can have different weightings, depending on their impact; for example, within the group of greenhouse gases that contribute to global warming, some have worse effects than others and therefore need to be factored differently.

In the last step, the interpretation, the results from inventory analysis and impact assessment are connected to gain knowledge about the environmental impact of the assessed product and to make recommendations on improvements (BSI, 2011).

As thorough LCAs have the potential to require significant resources, different levels of detail and sophistication have evolved. The most accurate investigation can be found in a detailed LCA, where all parts are evaluated in detail individually. This requires expert knowledge about the processes and emissions occurring at the individual stages of the supply chain. It also differentiates between global impact and regional impact. The major disadvantage of the detailed LCA is the effort that is needed to assess the supply chain to such a level of detail. Therefore, more simplified methods – conceptual LCA and simplified or streamlined LCA – evolved. The conceptual LCA is positioned at the opposite extreme to the detailed assessment. It qualitatively examines what factors and areas in the lifecycle need to be focused on and then only assesses those. This can, however, only be used as guidance for management, as the limited scope does not comply with the ISO standards for an LCA.

The streamlined LCA is placed in between these two approaches. It allows a comprehensive assessment, but rather uses generic data and does not measure each aspect individually. Therefore, it contains all relevant aspects but does not require the effort of a detailed LCA. Using generic data, however, means the assessment loses accuracy. Simplification can also be achieved through a screening stage in which insignificant emission contributors are identified and then do not need to be assessed in the analysis. Through this process, the LCA focuses on the key contributors, where the most environmental improvement potential lies (BSI, 2011).

The definition of the boundaries for an LCA crucially influences the overall result and environmental performance of a product. The most comprehensive guidelines and definitions for boundaries of LCAs exist in the area of greenhouse gases and carbon footprints. Standardized guidelines limit deviation in the assessment activity and simplify carbon footprint evaluations. PAS 2050 is currently the most commonly applied standard for carbon footprinting. For example, it provides a threshold so that inputs in the inventory analysis can only be deemed insignificant if they contribute less than 1 per cent of the lifecycle greenhouse gas emissions of a product.

When assessing greenhouse gas emissions, the time dimension of the greenhouse gases' impact influences the results. A range of greenhouse gases exists and their impact can be more short term or long term after they are released. Depending on the chosen time horizon, the impact of greenhouse gases such as CO_2 equivalents changes. The PAS 2050 standard sets 100 years as the time horizon for the impact of emitted greenhouse gases, which needs to be included in the lifecycle assessment. It also specifies how carbon storage is allowed to be considered and that land use changes are included for the first 20 years (Sinden, 2009).

The significance of system boundaries is shown in a study on the carbon footprint of office paper. The study applies three approaches: ISO 14040/14044, PAS 2050 and the framework by the Confederation of European Paper Industries (CEPI). Unsurprisingly, the industry's framework considers the least number of materials in its system boundary and the PAS 2050 standard still included significantly more materials than the ISO standards. In the assessment using the CEPI framework, only 90 per cent of greenhouse gas emissions were accounted for. Cut-off rules were comparatively narrow; for example, in transportation using the CEPI framework only the journey to the distribution platform is taken into consideration. The ISO 14040/14044 standards considered 98 per cent of greenhouse gas emissions compared to the assessment using the PAS 2050 standard. However, they also required significantly less effort in the data collection. The study allocated carbon footprints per tonne of office paper of 860 (CEPI), 930 (ISO 14040/14044) and 950 $kgCO_2e$ (PAS 2050). However, when it comes to labelling products with a carbon footprint, the functional unit of a 'sheet of A4 paper' might be more accurate, as produced sheets can be of different weight categories depending on their thickness and density (Dias and Arroja, 2012).

Charcoal BBQ versus LPG grilling

Having a barbeque is a popular way of preparing food on a sunny day. Over the years several fuel options developed, the most commonly used probably being the more traditional charcoal and LPG (liquefied petroleum gas) from gas cylinders. Maybe most consumers simply chose the option that they perceive as more convenient or they are used to, but even in such a sourcing decision environmental performance can be compared.

Johnson (2009) compares the carbon footprint of these two barbeque methods in an LCA. Considered in the system boundaries are the production of the fuel, use and disposal (for charcoal) of the fuel, and production, use and disposal of the grill and cylinder.

Charcoal is made of wood heated under a deficit of oxygen. Sometimes it is argued that the wood used is waste wood, but nevertheless it needs to be included in the inventory analysis as the wood could otherwise be used for energy generation or other forms of use. Charcoal in the UK is mainly imported from outside the European Union.

LPG is liquefied and filled into cylinders in which it is transported to retailers and final customers.

The consumption of charcoal or LPG in a barbecue session was estimated through a test programme of grill sessions by experienced amateur grillers. Although the consumption of fuel varies a lot between users depending on the amount of meat, the design of the grill, cooking style and personal preferences towards the amount of charcoal, these variations have much larger amplitude for charcoal than for LPG. For LPG, most grillers stayed within a range of 25 to 45 per cent of the food's weight, whereas charcoal consumption varied from 30 to 140 per cent. The consumption of firelighters was fairly consistent across charcoal barbecue sessions. Charcoal ashes are disposed of via municipal waste services. The calculations assumed 150 grill sessions over the barbecue's lifetime, with 1.5 kg of meat, 525 g of LPG or 733 g of charcoal and 115 g of firelighters per session.

The production of the LPG grill causes more CO_2e emissions than the charcoal alternative. Additionally, LPG is transported in cylinders, which need to be manufactured and can only be reused for a certain time and number of refills. On the other side, the firelighters consumed over the lifetime of a charcoal barbecue add up to 74 kgCO_2e.

The biggest difference is the fuel. The production and combustion of LPG emits so much less CO_2e than the charcoal that the emissions from the cylinder system are more than compensated for. Only if waste wood was used to produce charcoal do the two fuel alternatives almost draw even.

Assuming a lifetime of 150 grill sessions for both types, in total each LPG barbecue session causes 2.3 $kgCO_2e$, the equivalent of driving an average European car for 13km. In comparison, each charcoal barbecue session emits 6.7 $kgCO_2e$, almost half of it stemming from the charcoal combustion.

LPG grilling appears to be the more environmentally friendly solution, mainly due to the greater efficiency in production and cooking.

SOURCE Johnson (2009).

For suppliers, their customers' requirements will matter the most when adopting an LCA standard. In particular, small and medium-sized enterprises may not have the resources to run a detailed LCA and need to fall back on standards that allow them some level of simplification. For suppliers, it is essential to understand what frameworks their target markets apply and how environmental performance feeds into the decision making.

Comparing purchasing options

One clearly needs to differentiate between the more strategic perspective of procurement, which includes market analysis, supplier portfolio management, etc, and the more operational dimension of purchasing.

We covered the strategic perspective in earlier parts of this chapter. Making use of LCAs and supplier portfolios become part of the operational perspective. Quantifying the sustainability advantage of one supplier over another is difficult and evaluating the value of improvements even more so.

The consideration of sustainability performance can be a knock-out criterion (for example only suppliers achieving a particular certification are considered in the first place); it can be measured in monetary values and compared, or form part of the decision in a multi-criteria analysis (all criteria are scored and, for example, 20 per cent of the decision may be allocated to the score in social responsibility performance).

Quantifying the monetary value of more sustainable products is a difficult task. Similar to the environmental LCA, the lifecycle costs need to be measured. The results of the lifecycle costs can then be used in cost–benefit analysis or cost-effectiveness analysis. The cost–benefit analysis looks at the positive and negative effects on the welfare of the environment. This approach considers environmental and other sustainability costs only if these external effects can be monetarized (for example health care cost savings due to fewer respiratory illnesses if exhausts from a factory are reduced). But it cannot capture the costs of unethical actions such as child labour other than through the damage to the brand or lost business. Hence, ethical expectations towards suppliers will be communicated and potential suppliers not matching these standards will not be considered.

The cost-effectiveness analysis limits its focus on the project. The cost-effectiveness approach can be used to investigate and compare solutions on the way towards a specific target. The target itself, however, is most times not measured in money but in a unit of environmental impact. If several impact categories are considered, each category can be weighted (Pierrard and Faßbender, 2003).

Organizations need to evaluate their own sustainable supply chain performance to benchmark themselves against their competition. Often managers in supply chains are confused about what to measure and why for sustainable supply chains. The confusion arises from being traditionally focusing on cost in relation to output (for example service performance like the proportion of on-time, in-full deliveries). Measures for environmental performance, however, are mostly looking at inputs and emissions, examples being the electricity consumed, fuel consumption, number of pallet movements and vehicle utilization. A monetary measure of environmental performance is often preferred by managers (Shaw *et al*, 2012). Ethical aspects, however, are usually binary in nature; either the company uses forced labour or it doesn't.

Summary

Procurement is a crucial lever to improving the sustainability of the overall supply chain, and becomes even more crucial if most of a supply chain's impact is caused outside the organization. Much pressure to improve sustainability performance usually comes from the customer end of the supply chain, which is why concentrations of buying power like public procurement and the procurement practices of industry leaders play an essential role in the development of more sustainable products and supply chain practices.

The individual drivers and barriers vary between sectors, market segments, countries and companies. However, regulation clearly plays a key role, especially for those companies that have little intrinsic motivation to improve their sustainability and the internalization of external costs makes it easier for companies to consider sustainability issues in their purchasing decisions. In a different way, labels and certifications simplify sustainability in procurement as they set standards and take auditing and monitoring burdens off the buying side.

Implementing sustainability into procurement becomes particularly difficult when more sustainable products are more expensive and when sustainability achievements are hard to measure in a monetary value. Performance targets and sustainability specifications are needed to direct purchasing managers in the execution of their tasks.

References

Awaysheh, A and Klassen, R D (2010) The impact of supply chain structure on the use of supplier socially responsible practices, *International Journal of Operations & Production Management*, 30 (12), pp 1246–68

Booth, C (2010) *Strategic Procurement: Organizing suppliers and supply chains for competitive advantage*, Kogan Page, London

BSI (2011) The guide to PAS 2050: grow to carbon footprint your products, identify hotspots and reduce emissions in your supply chain [online] available at www.bsigroup.com [accessed 03 January 2017]

Carbon Trust (2017) About us [online] available at: carbontrust.com/about-us/ [accessed 03 January 2017]

Carter, C R and Dresner, M (2001) Purchasing's role in environmental management: cross-functional development of grounded theory, *Supply Chain Management*, 37 (3), pp 12–26

Coglianese, C and Nash, J (2001) Environmental management systems and the new policy agenda, Chapter 1 in C Coglianese and J Nash (eds) *Regulating from the Inside: Can environmental management systems achieve policy goals?* Earthscan, London, pp 1–25

Crespin-Mazet, F and Dontenwill, E (2012) Sustainable procurement: building legitimacy in the supply network, *Journal of Purchasing and Supply Chain Management*, 18 (4), pp 207–17

Dias, A C and Arroja, L (2012) Comparison of methodologies for estimating the carbon footprint: case study of office paper, *Journal of Cleaner Production*, 24, pp 30–35

Erdmenger, C (2003) The financial power and environmental benefits of green purchasing, Chapter 7 in C Erdmenger (ed) *Buying into the Environment:*

Experiences, opportunities and potential for eco-procurement, Greenleaf Publishing, Saltaire

Fairtrade (2012) What is Fairtrade? [online] available at: www.fairtrade.org.uk [accessed 27 November 2012]

Forest Stewardship Council (2012) Certification [online] available at: fsc.org [accessed 27 November 2012]

Greenhouse Gas Protocol (2012) About WRI and WBCSD [online] available at: ghgprotocol.org/about-ghgp/about-wri-and-wbcsd [accessed 29 November 2012]

Grimm, J H, Hofstetter, J S and Sarkis, J (2016) Exploring sub-suppliers' compliance with corporate sustainability standards, *Journal of Cleaner Production*, **112** (3), pp 1971–84

Johnson, E (2009) Charcoal versus LPG grilling: A carbon-footprint comparison, *Environmental Impact Assessment Review*, **29**, (6), pp 370–78

Kraljic, P (1983) Purchasing must become supply management, *Harvard Business Review*, September–October, pp 109–17

Krause, D R, Vachon, S and Klassen, R D (2009) Special topic forum on sustainable supply chain management: introduction and reflections on the role of purchasing management, *Journal of Supply Chain Management*, **45**, (4) (October), pp 18–24

Krut, R and Gleckman, H (1998) *ISO 14001: A missed opportunity for sustainable global industrial development*, Earthscan, London

Marine Stewardship Council (2012) www.msc.org

Matthews, D H (2003) Environmental management systems for internal corporate environmental benchmarking, *Benchmarking: An International Journal*, **10** (2), pp 95–106

Meyer, J W and Rowan, B (1977) Institutionalized organizations: formal structure as myth and ceremony, *American Journal of Sociology*, **83** (2) (September), pp 340–63

Murphy, E (2012) Key success factors for achieving green supply chain performance: a study of UK ISO 14001 certified manufacturers, unpublished PhD Thesis submitted at the University of Hull

Pierrard, R and Faßbender, S (2003) Integrating environmental and economic costs and benefits, Chapter 11 in C Erdmenger (ed) *Buying into the Environment: Experiences, opportunities and potential for eco-procurement*, Greenleaf Publishing, Saltaire

Rainforest Alliance (2012) Sustainable Forestry [online] available at: rainforest-alliance.org.uk [accessed 27 November 2012]

Schmidt, A and Frydendal, J (2003) Methods for calculating the environmental benefits of 'green' products, Chapter 8 in C Erdmenger (ed) *Buying into the Environment: Experiences, opportunities and potential for eco-procurement*, Greenleaf Publishing, Saltaire

Shaw, S, Grant, D B and Mangan, J (2012) Selecting green supply chain performance measures, Proceedings of the Logistics Research Network Conference, Cranfield University

Sinden, G (2009) The contribution of PAS 2050 to the evolution of international greenhouse gas emission standards, *International Journal of Life Cycle Assessment*, 14, pp 195–203

Smith, L (2011) Sustainable fish customers 'duped' by Marine Stewardship Council, *Guardian*, 6 January [online] available at: https://www.theguardian.com/environment/2011/jan/06/fish-marine-stewardship-council

USGBC (US Green Building Council) (2012) LEED [online] available at: usgbc.org/leed [accessed 29 November 2012]

Vitasek, K (2010) Supply chain management terms and glossary [online] available at: https://cscmp.org/imis0/CSCMP/Educate/SCM_Definitions_and_Glossary_of_Terms/CSCMP/Educate/SCM_Definitions_and_Glossary_of_Terms.aspx?hkey=60879588-f65f-4ab5-8c4b-6878815ef921 [accessed 31 December 2016]

Walker, H, Di Sisto, L and McBain, D (2008) Drivers and barriers to environmental supply chain management practices: lessons from the public and private sectors, *Journal of Purchasing and Supply Management*, 14, pp 69–85

Walton, S V, Handfield, R B and Melnyk, S A (1998) The green supply chain: integrating suppliers into environmental management processes, *International Journal of Purchasing and Materials Management*, 34 (2) pp 2–11

Wilhelm, M, Blome, C and Wieck, E (2016) Implementing sustainability in multi-tier supply chains: strategies and contingencies in managing sub-suppliers, *International Journal of Production Economics*, 182, pp 196–212

WWF (2012) *The Hidden Cost of Water*, report, World Wildlife Fund

Reverse logistics 07
and recycling

Background

Research published in *Nature* in 2013 predicted that the rate of global solid-waste generation will exceed 11 million tonnes per day by 2100 if we continue to create waste following a 'business-as-usual' attitude (Hoornweg *et al*, 2013). This rate is more than three times the rate in 2013. Such gigantic amounts of waste can cause significant public health and environmental problems, and if our waste continues to end up being landfilled and incinerated this will speed up pollution, global warming and the depletion of natural resources. This is a complicated issue because waste is generated by a long line of supply chain members, from material extraction to consumer consumption and disposal of end-of-life products. This problem is created by a 'linear economy' model that relies on simply the 'taking, making and disposing' of natural materials. Instead, a 'circular economy' approach that produces no waste and no pollution is required. Circular economy aims to regenerate biological nutrients (biochemical feedstock and energy) and restore technical nutrients (products, parts, materials). Resource efficiency is the key. That means the emphasis in working hard to manage waste created by industries and people, so-called 'waste management', has to be replaced by a 'waste and resource management' perspective (UNEP, 2015). By embracing circular economy, some countries (eg Germany, Scotland and Sweden) and cities (eg Kamikatsu, Capannori and San Francisco) are at the forefront of achieving zero waste, creating the possibility of reaching 'peak waste' sooner; however, there is still a long way to go.

Few people have any idea how much waste we dispose of each year. In the United States, 250 million tonnes of municipal solid waste were generated by American households in 2010 (EPA, 2011). On a larger scale, each year in the European Union three billion tonnes of waste are thrown away, some 90 million tonnes of it hazardous. Even fewer people know how much pollution their waste or garbage creates. With a liner model, most municipal waste ends up at landfill sites or incinerators. Landfills, without proper containment, can pollute ground waters and create methane, which is a form of greenhouse gas (GHS). Incinerations, though, generate energy from waste, and produce lots of toxic gases and ashes. Throwing away products before they become unusable and buying new ones more frequently not only creates more air and waterborne pollution but also puts demands on industries to consume more energy, extract more materials and produce more pollution. Many more environmental problems will be generated due to the rapidly expanding world population living in urban areas. By 2020, the OECD estimates, the European Union could be generating 45 per cent more waste than it did in 1995 (EC Environment, 2012).

In addition, the earth has finite natural and energy resources. With an exponential increase in the consumption of these resources to meet human needs there is a need for reverse logistics systems to reduce the use of natural materials and to reuse the products we have produced and used. Due to a lack of such systems in many countries we are increasingly confronted with the consequences of our 'throw-away' society. Improper management of waste generated by human activities can lead to severe land degradation and exhaustion of natural resources. Dumping sites in developed and developing countries are getting congested, which not only damages the environment, but also our health. Large areas of land are no longer fit for habitation as a result of the enormous pollution of the ground by the waste produced by human activities. In many countries, water extracted from the rivers and grounds has to be filtered before consumption, fish from large economically important rivers are not consumable, and smog in urban areas caused by traffic and industry is creating severe health problems for elderly people and children. According to UN Water, more than 40 per cent of the world's population live without improved sanitation (United Nations, 2016). In 2007, World Health Organization data showed that 13 million deaths worldwide could be prevented every year by making environments healthier (World Health Organization, 2007).

Reverse logistics and recycling play important roles in contributing to waste and resource management. Previously, manufacturers or retailers believed that they were not responsible for recovering their products after they were delivered to the consumers. When a product is no longer functional, needed or fashionable, its owner might want to dispose of or discard it without being responsible for the consequences. This operating model leads to increases in (1) consumption of virgin materials; (2) pollution due to the disposal of waste; and (3) losses of biological nutrients that could be used for producing more products or generating energy. Instead, by switching to a 'circular economy' model, supply chain members such as manufacturers, retailers and even consumers will take more responsibility for a product's life after its 'death'. For example, if the product is still functional it can be reused or shared by someone else. If it is repairable or part of it can be reused or refurbished, it can be re-manufactured and even upcycled and finally become useful for another user. This is where reverse logistics and recycling play a significant role. From a circular economy perspective, the different reverse logistics and recycling systems that enable reuse, refurbishment, re-manufacturing and upcycling are crucial for keeping products, materials and components at highest utilization and value at all times.

Increasingly, both governments and commercial organizations have recognized the urgent need for effective reverse logistics and recycling systems to manage our waste or garbage. Legislation at both global and national levels are enforced to control the use of natural resources and the logistics of waste. In some countries, incentives are used to encourage the use of greener waste disposal methods. Many households nowadays have to pay for their waste disposal, with municipals in the United States implementing variable-rate pricing. Some commercial organizations have started to reduce the waste they produce. This development is not only stimulated by the growing regulatory pressures from governments, but also driven by the movement of corporate citizenship or corporate social responsibility, as well as the need to save disposal, material and energy costs. In addition, more and more companies are being created to reap the valuable commercial opportunities in collecting, recycling and reusing products and materials (Kroon and Vrijens, 1995). Other waste management and third-party logistics companies have turned this opportunity into profit-making businesses. In 2002, research revealed that over US $750 billion annually was being spent on reverse logistics processes in North America alone (RLA.org, 2013).

Circular economy and regulations

Circular economy promotes an economy that is restorative and regenerative by design, and relies on effective management of two cycles. For the technical cycle, the aim is to recover and restore technical materials without consumption. It aims to keep product, components and materials at their highest utility and value at all times. The biological cycle consists of flows of renewable materials; the aim is to regenerate biological nutrients. The energy required to fuel the circular economy should be renewable as well.

To embrace the circular economy, we need to 'design out' waste so that technical materials are designed to be recovered, refreshed and upgraded, and energy input is minimized while the retention of value is maximized. Anchored on systems thinking, circular economy is guided by three principles (Ellen MacArthur Foundation, 2015):

- preserve and enhance natural capital by controlling finite stocks and balancing renewable resource flow;
- optimize resource yields by circulating products, components and materials at the highest utility at all times in both technical and biological cycles;
- foster system effectiveness by revealing and designing out negative externalities.

The above principles drive biological nutrient regeneration by enabling a more effective utilization of natural bioenergy resources. The priority is dematerializing utility, or delivering utility virtually, whenever possible. It requires careful selection of production and logistics technologies and systems that use renewable or better-performing resources. In some countries, more natural gas is used compared to petrol and diesel. The use of renewable fuels has become a regulated affair, such as with the Renewable Transport Fuels Obligation in the UK. Products and their supply chains can be designed to allow extraction of biochemical feedstock that is re-circled back to the flow of biological nutrients. Some biochemical feedstock can be used to produce fertilizers and feeds for farming; others can be collected for generating energy through anaerobic digestion. The recovery of biochemical feedstock for generating biogas is another option. This is a crucial alternative to the technologies that generate biofuel from food crops (eg corn ethanol).

The restoration of technical nutrients has always been a core objective of reverse logistics and recycling. The circular economy approach provides a hierarchical framework to prioritize the management of reverse logistics and recycling. Reducing is the most environmentally friendly option because it reduces consumption of natural resources and energy. Next is reuse of products or their components. Recycling involves collecting used products, components or materials and transforming them into other products, components or materials. If none of these are feasible, then they may be recovered into energy through incineration. The last option, which should be avoided, is landfill. Figure 7.1 illustrates the level of environmental 'friendliness' that can be determined from the hierarchy of waste and resource management.

Figure 7.1   Hierarchy of waste management

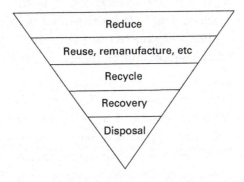

Reduce

Reuse, remanufacture, etc

Recycle

Recovery

Disposal

- *Reduce* involves use of fewer natural resources. It may also involve the use of fewer (hazardous) materials and less energy. Products can be designed to use alternative materials that are more resource efficient, or to use less packaging material. Cleaner production can help to reduce energy usage. Industrial production can be modified to reduce hazardous waste and other materials. This method is also called source reduction; it involves changes in manufacturing technology, raw material inputs, and product formulation. Consumer behaviour can also contribute to reducing. The fewer natural resources we consume the less waste is created.

- *Reuse* involves the use of a product or some parts of a used product if it can be shared, refurbished, repaired or remanufactured. Manufacturers are encouraged to produce reliable products with prolonged lifecycles and consumers can be provided with incentive and information about why such products are more beneficial. Reuse is a most resource-efficient and direct product recovery option. Products can be designed so that not all of them need to be discarded after being used by one user; they can be used again. Reverse logistics systems such as resource and tools sharing or hiring (eg openshed.com), upcycling, used-product exchange, car boot or garage sales, and secondhand sales for facilitating reuse can help to reduce landfill.

- *Recycle* helps to separate waste into materials that may be reprocessed and incorporated into new products. Recycling is a product recovery option which requires reprocessing. Activities such as composting and the reprocessing of used empty beverage containers or packaging materials are examples of recycling. Usually recycling consumes energy in order to change the physical properties of the material; however, recycling of metal, plastic, glass, wood and paper and biochemical feedstock helps to fuel a circular economy by reducing the use of natural or virgin resources.

- *Recovery* normally means the process of creating energy in the form of electricity or heat from the incineration of waste such as organic materials. Alternatively, it is called waste-to-energy or energy-from-waste. This is an option when the recovered materials cannot be reused or recycled, and they may contain bioenergy that would be wasted if landfilled.

- *Disposal* or *landfill* is the last option. There are strict regulations that restrict landfills in many countries but for many developing countries landfills have become the main destination of industrial and municipal waste. The problem of this option is that some materials will not be easily degradable and some of them contain toxic substances.

The effectiveness of reverse logistic and recycling systems is often driven by regulations. So far, the United States does not have a national recycling law. There is a national solid waste management law called Resource Conservation and Recovery Act (RCRA), but in reality, individual state legislation provides the main regulations for recycling in the United States. The European Commission (EC) has been instrumental in setting up regulations driving the reverse and recycling movements in Europe. For packaging materials, EU Directive 94/62/EC of 20 December 1994 on packaging and packaging waste suggested that member states return/collect 60 per cent of glass, paper and board, 50 per cent of metals, 22.5 per cent of plastic, and 15 per cent of wood from their municipal waste by 2008. New targets of 55–75 per cent have been proposed for 2025 and 2030. In addition to recycling, the incineration of waste for energy recovery is regarded as contributing to the realization of these objectives. Directive 2008/98/EC in 2008 further increased the targets. By 2020, the preparing for reuse and the recycling of waste materials such as at least paper, metal, plastic and glass from households and possibly from other origins as far as these waste streams are similar to waste from households, shall be increased to a minimum of 50 per cent by weight.

In addition, the EU Landfill Directive drives the reduction of the use of landfill (Defra, 2010). Each member state is required to reduce biodegradable municipal waste landfill to 35 per cent of that produced in 1995 by 2020. EU directives on both packaging waste and landfill are putting immense pressures on plastics recycling, as well as on local authorities and government. In June 2008, a compromised agreement was reached between the Council of Environment Ministers and the European Parliament on revisions to the Waste Framework Directive. The main changes include EU-wide targets for reuse and recycling 50 per cent of household waste by 2020, and for reuse, recycling and recovery of 70 per cent of construction and demolition waste by 2020. There has also been requirement for separate collection of paper, glass, metals and plastic since January 2015 where this is technically, environmentally and economically practicable. A new waste framework directive establishing a binding five-step waste hierarchy was implemented in 2008, bringing waste prevention, recycling and other recovery, with a view to achieving higher resource efficiency, more to the fore. The framework required European Union member States to develop national waste prevention programmes by December 2013, which will be reviewed every six years.

There are several directives or regulations that deal with recycling of specific materials or products. The WEEE (waste electrical and electronic equipment) Directive aims to reduce the amount of electrical and electronic equipment being produced and to encourage everyone to reuse, recycle and recover it. It also aims to improve the environmental performance of businesses that manufacture, supply, use, recycle and recover electrical and electronic equipment. Accordingly, a distributor may offer 'take back' on WEEE for a fee or free of charge. In the UK, a distributor will also be required to record the amount of WEEE returned in accordance with Regulation 34. A distributor may join the Distributor Take-Back Scheme (DTS). While distributors are responsible for providing information directing customers to their nearest recycling facility, producers are required to join an approved WEEE Producer Compliance Scheme, provide arrangements for the management of WEEE and provide their registration number to distributors. For equipment bought after August 2005, the producer is required to finance the collection, treatment, recycling and recovery of WEEE that the purchase replaces, on a one-for-one, like-for-like basis. In addition, the Energy-using Product directive (EuP) considers energy consumption from the mining of the raw material right through to recycling at end-of-life. On the other hand, the Batteries Directive specifies substance restrictions and labelling requirements with a focus on reducing the number of batteries that finish up in landfill.

Increasingly, commercial companies (producers) are expected to become responsible for the lifecycle impacts of the products they produce. In the past, producers were only required to provide wholesalers and distributors with information about methods to recycle their products, under the scheme called collective producer responsibility. Some OEMs have already established voluntary product recovery schemes, ahead of the new regulation. The new Extended Producer Responsibility (EPR) programmes typically hold the producer – a single actor defined by the regulator – to be responsible for the environmental impacts of end-of-life products (Jacobs and Subramanian, 2009). Producers will be required to provide and pay for take-back schemes for their products (take-back obligation); these are set by the government and have started to place more responsibility onto producers.

Product recovery options

Based on a detailed understanding of their products, companies can learn to manage the recovery and distribution of end-of-life products, planning of production and inventory, and supply chain management issues in reverse logistics (Rubio *et al*, 2008). Recovered products can be civil objects, consumer goods, industrial goods, minerals and chemical compounds, raw materials, distribution items and spare parts. The next step is to understand suitable product recovery options for each type of recovered product. Product recovery management (PRM) involves the management of all used and discarded products, components and materials that fall under the responsibility of a manufacturing company (Thierry *et al*, 1995). PRM aims to recover as much of the economic (and ecological) value as is reasonably possible, thereby reducing the ultimate quantities of waste. Due to the belief that the cost of PRM should not outweigh its benefits, most manufacturers focus on the forward logistic flows from the factories to the end customers but not the reverse flows of the used products. Therefore, the traditional approach of many manufacturers towards used products has been to ignore them or let other parties dispose of them. Recently, manufacturers are being pressured by both consumers and governments to reduce waste generated by their products. In general, there are six major product recovery options (Thierry *et al*, 1995).

Repair:

- The aim of repair is to return used products to working order.
- Used products are normally not disassembled. Used products are fixed and some parts may be replaced while some parts can be reused.
- The quality of the repaired products is usually lower than the quality of new products.
- Repair can be performed at the retail stores or repair centres.
- Products such as computers, mobile phones, washing machines are suitable for repair.

Refurbishing:

- The aim of refurbishing is to bring used products to a specified quality.
- Refurbishing needs similar processes to repair. It involves disassembly of used products into modules, inspection of the modules and then fixing and/or replacing some modules.
- Approved modules are then reassembled into refurbished products.
- The quality of refurbished products is often lower than that of new products.
- Products such as houses and caravans can be refurbished.

Remanufacturing:

- The aim of remanufacturing is to bring used products up to quality standards that are as good as those for new products.
- The processes involved are similar to those of refurbishing. Used products are often completely disassembled into modules and parts. There will be extensive inspection of modules. Worn-out parts or modules are replaced. Repairable parts are fixed and extensively tested. Approved parts and modules are re-assembled into remanufactured products.
- It is popular for products such as copiers, engines, car parts, machine tools, etc.

Cannibalization:

- The aim is to recover a limited set of reusable parts from used products or components.
- Only a small proportion of the parts of used products are recovered for reuse, remanufacture or repair of other products and components.
- Involves selective disassembly of used products and inspection of potentially reusable parts.
- The remaining parts are recycled or disposed of.

Recycling:

- The aim is to reuse materials from used products or components.
- The recovered materials are separated into categories.
- The materials can be used to produce original products and components if their quality is high. Otherwise, the materials can be used to produce other products.
- Examples are milk bottles, soft drink bottles, etc.

Upcycling:

- This is different from recycling; it requires creative reuse.
- The aim is to produce something new and better than the old items.
- The end product is typically one of a kind, handmade and sustainable.
- It is based on a 'buy low, sell high' business model.
- For example, worn T-shirts are used to make cleaning rags; many unwanted items are now used to make bags, notebooks, etc.

The above concept of upcycling has generated some attention recently because it transforms low-value unwanted items into high-value, highly sought-after items. Many new enterprises have emerged due to the opportunities for upcycling lots of unwanted items. For example, TerraCycle Inc is a world leader in the collection and reuse of consumer packaging products. Playback Clothing transforms trash such as plastic bottles and clothing scrap into great-looking eco-clothing. IceStone makes high-design surfaces from recycled glass instead of quarried stone. Kallio is a New York-based company that makes old clothes young again. Sword & Plough works with veterans to repurpose military surplus fabric into stylish purses and bags. TRMTAB collects leather scraps from factories around the world to create limited-edition, refined leather goods for tech devices. Loopworks is a social enterprise that rescues high-quality, unused material and turns it into limited-edition, hand-numbered goods. Blue Jeans collects old denims, transforms them into cotton fibre state and upcycles them into denim insulation. As of 2016, the company has upcycled more than 600 tonnes of denims, diverted more than a million denims from landfill, and produced over 2 million insulations. Even Ikea has started to consider collecting furniture to turn it into other types of furniture or appliances, and some clothing companies have already been incorporating recycled plastics into the design of their new clothes.

There are some main differences between the above recovery options. In terms of the level of disassembly, used products are disassembled at product level for repair, module level for refurbishment, part level for remanufacture and cannibalization, and material level for recycling. The quality of upcycled or remanufactured products is the highest (as new), and the quality of repaired and refurbished will be lower. By using the repair option, some parts are fixed or replaced by spares. By refurbishing, some modules are repaired or replaced and potentially there is a need for upgrade. By remanufacturing, used and new modules/parts are combined into new products with some potential upgrade. Upcycling is a new approach to remanufacturing that can significantly upgrade the value of unwanted items. Cannibalization is quite different; it reuses some parts and the remaining product is recycled or disposed of. Recycling is working at material level; that means parts are reprocessed into raw material form.

One of the very first steps to developing an effective PRM is to acquire adequate information. First, there is a need to understand the composition of products. The manufacturers should be able to identify each part and component of their products based on the bill of material and product/material technical specification. A manufacturer with a proper environmental management system (EMS) will have a system to gather knowledge about the materials used to make each part or product and the legislation governing the end-of-life management of such materials. They can therefore identify which parts/modules/products, depending on the quality of returned products, are suitable for reuse, repair, refurbishment, remanufacture, upcycling, recycling or recovery.

Different incentives can be provided to encourage customers to return used products. For example, used laser printer cartridges can be returned easily because customers are provided with cartridge boxes marked for free return shipment. Credits toward future purchases are given to encourage participation in product recovery. Sliding scales of prices to be paid by customers for products with different residual quality levels encourage customers to take better care of the products and subsequently help to increase the average quality of recovered products. Some companies offer free recycling services to customers who purchase a new product from them. Lexmark offers a 'pre-bate' discount to customers who agree to return their Lexmark printer cartridges to Lexmark for remanufacturing (Streitfeld, 2003, after Toffel, 2004). The scheme has not only increased return rates, it has also positively improved Lexmark's brand image. Many companies have even started to provide free take-back services by working closely with their distributors and third-party logistics service providers. Even though setting up own-product recovery or reverse logistics networks helps to ensure returned product quality, many manufacturers offer multiple return channels to increase recovery rates. Incentives for retail companies to collect end-of-life products can in some instances increase product recovery rates as well as sales of new products.

When choosing suitable product recovery options, several factors need to be considered. First, not all used products are technically suitable for reuse, repair, remanufacture or recycling. For example, food packaging may not be suitable for reuse, but it may be recycled. Second, there is a need to investigate if there is a constant supply (from the 'disposal' market) of suitable used products and components. This depends on the efficiency of the product return logistics flow, the willingness of consumers to return used products, and the

Table 7.1 Collection schemes

Collection scheme and incentive	Definitions and operating principles
Deposit fee (advanced)	When customers make a purchase an advanced deposit fee on the product is charged. The deposit fee will be returned to the customers when the used products or packaging materials are returned to the collection centre in the right condition. This is an effective scheme to ensure return of used products or recovery packaging materials. It is common to charge deposit fees for bottled beverages in some European countries.
Take back	Retail companies or original equipment manufacturers offer to take used products back for repair, remanufacture, refurbishing, etc. It could be free or there may be a fee involved. This scheme demonstrates the producers' responsibility to assure customers there is a reverse logistics system in place when the customers are making a purchase decision. The customers, OEMs or third-party service providers might be involved in physically returning the products. Take-back schemes are popular for copy machines, printers, batteries, automotives, etc. Products purchased under leasing agreements are often offered take-back schemes.
Trade in (rebates)	Used products may be returned to the retail stores for trade in, meaning customers have to purchase another product in exchange. There is an agreed value for the used products so that the customers do not need to pay the full price for the new product. Trade-in schemes are commonly used for cars and mobile phones.
Pick up system	Used products may be picked up at the customer's location, often for a fee. This collection scheme is often operated by local authorities (municipals) and charities for households, and also commercial waste management companies for industries.
Public recycling centres	Offered by the local authorities (municipals), households are given the opportunity to bring their used products to public recycling centres. This scheme is normally free of charge but customers have to be happy to return the used products themselves.

quality of the returned products. Sometimes participation in product return can be motivated by monetary incentive, regulation, as well as ease of participation. Ease of participation depends on the design of collection schemes (see Table 7.1); design of collection schemes and location of collection centres determine the magnitude of the return flows. The quality of returned products depends greatly on the design of the products and components, as well as the incentives given to customers to maintain the products while they are in use.

Third, there is a need to ensure that there is a constant demand for reprocessed products, components and materials. A better option is to re-route the recovered products to the forward logistics flows for reuse. In some cases, the (secondary) markets for reprocessed products could be thousands of miles away from the sources of the used products. Since the cost of reprocessing plastic is expensive in Europe, a significant amount of recycled plastic collected in Europe is shipped to China or other developing countries to be reprocessed, and the reprocessed plastic could be then shipped to Europe for making new plastic products.

The last consideration is economic and environmental costs and benefits. The value of the products, parts and materials indicates if there is any economic value for setting up or investing in a PRM. Since most reverse logistics systems contain many actors, with a fragmented structure and a lack of supply chain leadership, the efficiency of the system is often constrained by the least profitable parts of the chain. It is therefore important to understand the costs and benefits of each actor in the entire reverse logistics system. To understand the economic value of PRM, a new concept called value recovery (VR) was introduced by Srivastava (2008), naming collection, inspection/sorting, preprocessing and logistics, and distribution network design as four important functional aspects of value recovery. The dimensions used to characterize the value environments are returns volume, returns timing, returns quality (grade), product complexity, testing and evaluation complexity, and remanufacturing complexity. Value recovery strategies and programmes can result in increased revenues, lower costs, improved profitability and enhanced levels of customer service leading to better corporate image (Carter and Ellram, 1998; Stock *et al*, 2006).

Choosing the right recovery options and developing efficient PRM are onerous tasks and not everyone can make it economically viable. Others aim to become the leader in product recovery and environment within the industries they are operating in. Xerox, for example, attempts to achieve environmental leadership. The case study below illustrates how the extended responsibility and environmental leadership provided by a producer can significantly improve a reverse logistics system.

Xerox Corp's environmental leadership

Xerox is a leader in document technology and services, and is among the world's leading enterprises for business process and document management. It also offers global services such as claims reimbursement, automated toll transaction, customer care centres and HR benefits management. The mission of Xerox is: 'Through the world's leading technology and services in business process and document management, we're at the heart of enterprises small to large, giving our clients the freedom to focus on what matters most: their real business' (www.xerox.com).

Xerox aims to achieve zero waste for its products. The aim is 'waste-free products manufactured in waste-free factories to enable customers' waste-free workplaces'. Launched in 1991, Xerox's environmental programme achieved the 2-billion-pound milestone by waste avoidance in two areas: (1) reuse and recycling in imaging supplies, and (2) product take-back and recycling and parts reuse. Next, Xerox's Energy Challenge 2012 programme began with the goal of lowering greenhouse gas emissions (GHG) from worldwide operations by 10 per cent from 2002 to 2012. Recognizing the obligation to do even more, in 2007, Xerox set a new and challenging goal 'to reduce our GHG emissions by 25 per cent by 2012, from a 2002 baseline'. Figure 7.2 illustrates Xerox's closed-loop supply chain.

Figure 7.2   Xerox's closed-loop supply chain

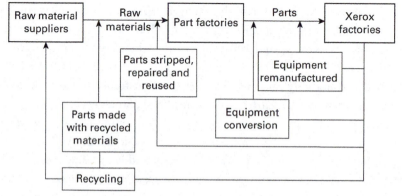

During product design, Xerox focuses on minimal use of hazardous substances and efficient use of materials. Reuse and recycling of parts and components are seriously considered. The product lifecycle costs are estimated and reduced by considering the extended life of parts, easy disassembly, part reusability and material recyclability. The products are designed in such a way that some major parts (eg frames) will last longer and could be repaired or used for remanufacturing to another product. To achieve this effectively, the product design team developed a product lifecycle cost model, material guides and disposal coding. The product lifecycle cost, material usage and recovery options for each part and component are discussed in a mandatory review during the product design process. Training is provided to ensure all staff involved are capable of executing such robust product design processes.

The manufacturing processes are also designed to create waste-free factories. The focus is to achieve low emission and efficient use of energy during the production processes. The possibility of using low-emission and low-energy production processes is considered during the product design stage. Another unique feature of Xerox factories is that they are designed not only to build new products but also to remanufacture used products. The production lines are designed to be able to build new products by using some of the major parts recovered from the used products.

More importantly, Xerox recognizes the significance of energy usage during customer use. In addition to paper-saving features, a lot of research has been devoted to the design of copy machines which consume the least energy while in use or in energy-saving modes. According to Xerox, 'standby' is a waste. When the copy machines are not in use, better energy saving options such as 'low power', 'sleep' and 'auto-off' can be used. Recognizing the need for some heat to fuse toner onto paper (making copies), a lot of research has been conducted to make the printing process work under lower temperatures to achieve the optimal use of energy during use and in energy-saving modes. As a result, it is possible achieve to energy-saving modes 80 per cent of the time. Since 1993, Xerox has worked with EPA and the industry together to set criteria for energy-saving copy machines. Xerox Energy Star products are internationally recognized. To meet the stringent requirements, common procurement requirements were launched, and in 2010, 100 per cent of newly launched eligible products achieved ENERGY STAR standard.

Another focus is on improving the customer return process. Return experience has been improved via enhancements at the Xerox Green World Alliance recycling website (www.xerox.com/gwa). There are three different return methods: (1) single-item return programme, (2) bulk returns on a pallet, and (3) Eco Box.

- Single-item return is a programme for customers to return a single item, for example a cartridge. Customers can submit a cartridge return label request and receive a label for shipping the cartridge by post free of charge. Depending on the types of returned products and the locations of the customers, Xerox decides which recycling centre should receive the returned products.

- Bulk returns on a pallet is a return programme for those who have more than 30 items to be returned. The Xerox Pallet Returns process allows customers to download the Xerox Bulk process, which contains instructions on how to prepare your times and schedule a pickup.

- Eco Box is a programme where customers may order kits of three boxes each at no cost, bundle items together in the box, download a pre-paid label, and return them to the returns partner. In Europe, 'Close the Loop' is a company, like Xerox, dedicated to zero waste to landfill recycling. The company takes cartridges that Xerox cannot reuse, and through its patented recycling process, separates cartridges into plastics, toner powder, metals, and other materials, then cleans and processes them for return to the market as raw materials or new products.

Since copy machines contain chemical (eg toners) the cleaning process has to be hazardous. Advanced technology for cleaning and predicting part reliability has been developed. Instead of traditional solvent-based cleaning and non-hazardous terpenes, Xerox uses automated CO_2 blasting to clean up used parts. Advanced technologies are developed to determine range for noise, heat and vibration during use, so that reusable returned parts are selected for reprocessing. Platform design is adopted and parts commonality is emphasized. These features enhance the predictability of field return. Xerox has further extended the concept of remanufacture to product conversion. The new-build remanufacture processes are integrated with the conversion processes. For example, the reusable parts and machine frames of end-of-life machines are used to build new (or 'reman') machines, for example Document Centre 220 becomes Document Centre 440.

> Xerox also extends its recovery channels further upstream by involving parts suppliers and raw material suppliers, as shown in the above diagram. Machines for remanufacturing and conversion are sent back to Xerox factories. Parts that can be reused are sent to part factories where they are stripped, repaired and reused; parts that cannot be reused but can be recycled are sent to part factories as raw materials. Recycled materials are sent to raw material suppliers to be reused.

Other companies, such as IBM, BMW, Mercedes-Benz, Fujifilm, Kodak, Dell, and many others have been constantly improving their reverse logistics systems to achieve environmental sustainability.

- IBM has to decide how to organize the collection of product returns, and which parties to involve depending on the processes required. In many countries, IBM has a take-back programme allowing business customers to return used products on top of the take-back responsibility that IBM has for the consumer market. IBM has set up a business unit dedicated to the management of recovery, with 25 facilities steering repair, remanufacturing and recycling (also with the involvement of third parties).

- BMW has been conducting recycling research in a pilot vehicle disassembly plant in Landshut, Germany since 1990. There are three main focused issues, the first being the recycling of materials from existing cars. BMW aims to reuse 80 per cent of all plastics, and has been able to incorporate recycled plastics into certain components such as luggage compartment lining and recycled bumpers. The second focus is the reuse of high-value parts from existing cars with the aim of remanufacturing high-value components such as engines, starter motors and alternators. Remanufactured parts are sold as 'exchange parts' for 50 – 70 per cent of new product prices. The third focus is the design and modification of future cars by avoiding composite materials and marking parts and components to ease sorting tasks. Further, design for disassembly is used to allow parts to be disassembled within 20 minutes. The use of two-way fasteners instead of screws and glue is considered.

- Mercedes-Benz accepts and disassembles EOL Mercedes vehicles to harvest and sell spare parts to both consumers and commercial customers at a significant discount compared to virgin spare parts (Toffel, 2004).

- Companies such as Fujifilm and Kodak, which sell single-use cameras, launched a take-back programme that recycles more than 90 per cent of such cameras and reversed the product's poor environmental image (Toffel, 2004). Detailed descriptions of the product return strategies of the Fujifilm Quicksnap camera are presented in Grant and Banomyong (2010).

- Dell attempts to increase recovery rates and end-of-life products and energy efficiency by endorsing a global Electronics Industrial Code of Conduct (EICC), providing low- to no-cost convenient recovery programmes and working with the Forest Products Stewardship (FPS) Initiative.

- Other cases such as Hewlett-Packard (Guide *et al*, 2005), Infosys in India (Srivastava, 2008), jet engine components (Guide and Srivastava, 1998) and cellular telephones (Jayaraman *et al*, 1999) provide good examples of the development of reverse logistics and recycling systems in different industries.

As illustrated by the Xerox case, hazardous materials are one of the major problems of reverse logistics for certain products. CRT (cathode ray tube) and LCD (liquid crystal display) are classified as hazardous because they contain lead glasses and mercury. PCs contain printed circuit boards with heavy metal and rechargeable lithium batteries. Other major waste from electronics goods includes plastics which can be toxic when they are burned. One of the problems for photocopiers is the emission of waste volatile organic compounds (VOCs) and other hazardous substances (Tischner and Nickel, 2004) and therefore there is a need for the development and dissemination of environmental handbooks for product development, and education programmes and information for employees, customers and waste managers.

Reverse logistics

Essentially, the systems required to take care of waste in a responsible, effective and sustainable way can be broadly called reverse logistics systems. Reverse logistics differs from the concept of forward logistics as it concerns mainly the reverse direction of a typical supply chain. Reverse logistics is about movement of goods from a consumer towards a producer in a channel of distribution (Murphy and Poist, 1989). Reverse logistics is almost synonymous with material recycling and waste management in an effort to minimize cost, retrieve value from reverse flows, and fulfil legislative and environmental requirements. Reverse logistics is a broader concept for overall supply chain optimization, the aim of which is to support the closed-loop character of supply chains by affecting activities like product design, supply chain design and product recovery. Reverse logistics plays the role of logistics in product returns, source reduction, reuse of materials, materials substitution, waste disposal, recycling, refurbishing, repair and re-manufacturing (Stock, 1992; 1998). From a process management point of view, reverse logistics is defined as:

> the process of planning, implementing and controlling the efficient flow of materials in process inventory, finished goods, and related information from the point of consumption to the point of origin for the purpose of recapturing value or proper disposal. (Rogers and Tibben-Lembke, 2001, p 130)

Or:

> the process of planning, implementing and controlling the efficient, cost-effective flow of raw materials, in-process inventory, finished goods and related information from the point of consumption to the point of origin for the purpose of recapturing value or proper disposal. (Grant, 2012, p 220)

Reverse logistics is an important concept both for companies that organize the recycling systems and the companies that have to pay for disposal of rundown or waste products (Carter and Ellram, 1998). It is sometimes considered as the backbone of 'sustainable development' in its economic and environmental footprint on business practices (Stock, 1992; 1998). It is considered an instrument of sustainable development and a driving force in sustaining the economy and environment. Reverse logistics is a crucial element of a closed-loop supply chain, which are supply chains with typically forward flows of materials from suppliers to end customers as well as reverse flows of products (post-consumption) back to the manufacturing or distribution supply chains. Reverse logistics prevents the disposal of end-of-life products into the less environmentally friendly channels such as landfill and incineration.

The management of reverse logistics requires some specific knowledge and skills. First of all, there is a need to understand what (the product) and who (the actors) are involved, the recovery processes, and the reasons or drivers behind the involvement of the different actors (de Brito and Dekker, 2004). The following are the typical actors involved in the recovery processes:

- Retail companies primarily offer reverse logistics services to manage product returns, repairs and warranties. Such services are often associated with the product warranties offered by original equipment manufacturers (OEMs), and may include the resale and redistribution of unsold products and product warranties. Some retail companies provide consumer packaging collection facilities voluntarily or following governmental request. A significant quantity of recycled materials can be collected by retail companies during the distribution process.

- As with retail companies, original equipment manufacturers (OEMs) may offer services for product returns, repairs and warranties. Manufacturers generally do not have stores, so they could own or outsource return centres to third-party logistics service providers, or provide channels (such as retail stores or postal services) for consumers to return used products to.

- Governmental agencies or local authorities normally offer waste collection and disposal services, generally to households and shops. In many countries, most household waste is collected by government agencies or local authorities. However, the extent to which the reverse logistics systems facilitates reuse, recycling, recovery and disposal may vary greatly depending on the collection and reprocessing systems provided.

- Private waste management and product return companies are third-party logistics service providers specializing in return management and acting on behalf of retail companies, original equipment manufacturers and government agencies. These companies normally also sort collected products and sometimes reprocess used products. In some countries, there are also individuals (scavengers) who collect reusable materials or products from garbage sites.

- Traders are companies that purchase and sell recovered products or recycled materials collected by government agencies, retail companies, waste management companies and scavengers. They play a significant role in aggregating and distributing recovered/recycled products to the reprocessors.

- Reprocessors are companies or individuals who disassemble, repair, remanufacture, refurbish, recycle and reprocess products and materials from the 'disposal' market and transform them into (re-)usable forms. Unless the products can be reused without the need of reprocessing, most recovered products need to go through the reprocessors. These businesses have to be commercially viable and therefore require a constant supply of recovered/recycled products and materials, as well as a constant and profitable demand from the markets.

- Customers are the last but most important actors in the reverse logistics loop. They form the 'reuse' markets: the consumers, commercial companies and non-profit organizations. Charities are also major customers of recovered products. There are also companies which distribute and sell used spare parts or remanufactured products. Without demand from these actors, the reverse logistics systems will not be economically viable.

Even though many actors are involved in waste management and reverse logistics activities there is often a lack of efficiency and visibility. While providing reverse logistics services, many manufacturing and retail companies are still more concerned about warranties and after-sales customer service than environmental sustainability. This is partly due to lack of regulatory pressure and producer responsibility. However, in recent years, more commercial companies are establishing reverse logistics systems to recycle, but also reuse, refurbish and remanufacture. Product-recovery activities can actually strengthen brand image (Guide and van Wassenhove, 2002). Driven by increased environmental awareness, many electronics manufacturers, for example, have transformed their product safety and occupational health organization units from those with a focus on purely regulatory compliance to those with a comprehensive environmental policy. Nowadays most computer and mobile phone manufacturers offer attractive product recovery services simply because customers only purchase new products from those who are capable of removing used products from them responsibly. The following case studies illustrate how multinational computer and mobile phone original equipment manufacturers (OEMs) utilize and adapt existing forward international distribution networks as reverse logistics systems.

Revolutionizing the reverse supply chain in emerging markets

Most manufacturers prefer to focus on manufacturing and distributing their products to the market instead of product recovery or reverse supply chains. Several factors motivate manufacturers to engage in product recovery: reducing production cost, enhancing brand image, meeting customer demand, protecting aftermarkets and pre-empting regulations (Toffel, 2004). Products may be returned at different stages in the product lifecycle and based on this the process can take different paths. Alternatively, new enterprises are created to fill the gaps. Nowadays there are new enterprises that collect unwanted items and turn them into something valuable and commercially viable. There are many such examples in Europe, North America, Latin America, Africa and Asia.

Reverse logistics is driven more by regulation in Europe and by profit in North America. In India, society is more price-sensitive and so it is driven more by quality and value than by environmental concerns (Srivastava and Srivastava, 2006), and functions in a more unorganized way. This phenomenon happens to be true for most emerging economies. The scale and size of the industry in the United States are such that for every 100 products moving forward to the consumer, on average, 10 come back to the manufacturer, whereas in India, for every 100 items going forward, about four of five come back across all categories. Accounting for all the goods produced in India, the opportunity market size for reverse logistics is US $15–20 billion.

This case study is based on an innovative company, Green Dust, which has tried to derive value out of this proposition by trying to convert an unorganized sector into a more organized one. Green Dust is based on a unique hybrid retail model where reverse logistics is used as a sourcing engine. The company takes rejected, defective, unsold or returned products from OEMs, refurbishes them, provides a year's warranty from their side, and sells them as factory seconds through their brand, Green Dust. By managing their (the clients') returns, the unwanted products are pushed back into the market using Green Dust through an online and offline model. They are still OEM-branded products, for example LG or Whirlpool, but with a Green Dust stamp on them. Consciously, through its branding exercise, it has altered the perception of refurbished products and stresses the extended life of the products and low maintenance costs. Selling refurbished products contributes to the 'green' initiative of the OEMs in managing the 'cradle-to-grave' lifecycle of products. This represents a restoration cycle according to the circular economy framework.

Essentially the reverse supply chain can be divided into product acquisition, logistics, inspection, disposition and sales. These items can be considered perishable and speed is a major proposition for value creation. Green Dust has created various values for its customers including reducing supply chain costs by 25 per cent (including warehousing, people, transportation, etc), increasing cash flow from systematic asset recovery, improving asset recovery by 50 per cent, not cannibalizing the new product sales channel from returned items, and increasing productivity by 10 per cent.

Green Dust enables manufacturers and retailers to become environmentally conscious and to comply with e-waste regulations by facilitating the 4 Rs – Reduce, Reuse, Repair and Recycle. Instead of allowing them to be dumped, Green Dust brings the rejected items to life and use by testing and repairing them. By providing them with a new home, it has reduced the amount of dead scrap which contributes to polluting the environment. Until now the company has prevented over **300,000** products from becoming scrap. It also hopes to cover all possible product categories, since the potential of this business is not limited to electronics and consumer appliances. Some of the products it collects will not be refurbished or resold, but the model supports eco-friendly destruction of such items. Products sold by Green Dust may have dents, scratches and aesthetic damages, but they will be functional. The products will not carry an OEM Warranty, but Green Dust offers a functional warranty of one year on all Green Dust-Certified products, unless otherwise specified.

Contributed by, Prof. Mohita G. Sharma, Fore School of Management, India.

SOURCES Sharma *et al*, (2016); Toffel, (2004); Srivastava and Srivastava (2006).

Recycling

Not all products can be reused, refurbished and remanufactured; however, their materials can be recycled and recovered (for energy). It is possible to design a product recovery system to extend the life of a product or material. Recycling plays a major role in extending the life of materials, and is a big business. To illustrate how recycling networks work, let's first examine metal recycling. Metal recycling is a £5.6 billion UK industry, processing ferrous and nonferrous metal scrap into vital secondary raw material for the smelting of new metals (www.recyclemetals.org). The UK is one of the five largest metal scrap-exporting countries in the world, with iron and steel making up the majority of the recycled metal. In the United States, of the 132 million tonnes of metal supply, recycling contributed 67 million tonnes (DoITPoMS, nd). Virtually all metals can be recycled into high-quality new metal. Scrap metals can be primarily recycled from:

- Packaging materials – some 2 billion aluminium and steel cans are recycled every year.
- Vehicles – over 75 per cent of a car is metal. Around half of the material processed by metal recycling shredders comes from vehicles.

- Electrical and electronics products – the industry already recycles most discarded household appliances. Electronic and telecommunications goods are significant consumers of nonferrous metals.

- Batteries – even before the EU Directive came into effect in 2008, the metal recycling industry were already recycling most lead and acid from vehicle and industrial batteries.

Metal recycling is a 'pyramid' industry which includes many small, family-owned companies as well as large international businesses. SIMS Metal Management (uk.simsmm.com) is one of the largest metal recycling companies in the UK. The company focuses on non-hazardous scrap metal recycling such as end-of-life cars and metal waste from manufacturing processes, WEEE and fridges. The company recycled over 14.3 million tonnes of metal in 2011, enough to off-set the carbon emissions of almost 3.3 million people (based on the average global emissions of carbon per person being almost 4.5 tonnes). Metal recycling companies carry out a range of functions, often including several of the following activities, with smaller operators supplying partially or fully processed metals to larger operators and traders:

- Collection, weighing, sorting and distribution of metals: dealing with a wide range of suppliers, including engineering industries, small traders such as plumbers or vehicle dismantlers, local authority collection sites, and householders disposing of domestic appliances.

- Shearing is required to reduce the size of large pieces of metal by cutting.

- Baling/compacting is required to improve ease of handling and transportation.

- Shredding of recycled materials helps to reduce feedstock to fist-sized lumps, separating metals from other materials using magnets and air classification methods. A large shredder can process a car in less than 10 seconds.

- Media separation is required to further separate any remaining nonferrous metals using liquid density and hand or mechanical sorting methods.

- Melting is the final process which aims to return the recycled materials into the various metal compositions and qualities.

In theory, all metals can be recycled. Lead, zinc, copper, aluminium and steel are the most commonly recycled metals. In addition to the cost of collection and separation, the economic viability of recycling metal relies on the energy saved by reprocessing a kilogram of recycled metal compared to the energy used to produce the same amount of metal from ores. According to the British Metals Recycling Association, energy savings from recycling of metals are as high as 62–74 per cent for steel, 87 per cent for copper, 63 per cent for zinc and 60 per cent for lead.

Plastics are other important materials for recycling; the use of plastics as opposed to papers and other materials has always been controversial. Should supermarkets ask customers to use plastic or paper bags? As far as packaging is concerned, the use of plastics is indeed much more environmentally friendlier than paper. According to *Science World* (2008), the production of every tonne of paper bags consumes four times more energy, and more air- and water-borne pollution than the production of plastic bags. Furthermore, the recycling of paper consumes 85 times more energy than the recycling of plastic bags. Packaging using plastics contributes to about 63 per cent of end-of-life quantity of products such as processed food, vegetables and fruits (*PlasticEurope*, 2009).

The use of plastics has become more popular nowadays because they are durable, strong, resistant to corrosion and above all, require low maintenance. Plastics are used for making packaging materials, building and construction, electrical and electronics, automotive and many other products (Wong, 2010). There are several basic types of plastics: polyethylene terephthalate (PET), high-density polyethylene (HDPE), polyvinyl chloride (PVC), low-density polyethylene (LDPE), polypropylene (PP), and polystyrene (PS). They are used to produce the following products:

- PET is typically used to make soft drink bottles, cooking oil bottles and peanut butter jars.
- HDPE is one of the most recycled plastics; it is used to make bottles, milk jugs, detergent bottles, margarine tubs, grocery bags, nursery pots, pesticides, and oil containers.
- PVC (or vinyl) is used for products such as pressure pipes, outdoor furniture, food packaging, shrink wrap, and liquid detergent containers.
- LDPE is used to produce films or bags, bin liners, food storage containers and stretch wrap, and to make clothing.
- PP is used in products such as yarn, fabrics, food packaging, meat trays and nursery pots.
- PS is used to make yogurt pots, egg cartons, meat trays, disposable utensils, video cassettes, televisions, packaging pellets or Styrofoam peanuts.
- Several types of the above plastics can be combined together to make different products, such as the popular 'Tupperware'.

Plastic waste can be recycled by two major processes – mechanical recycling and feedstock recycling. Mechanical recycling involves melting, shredding or granulation of plastic waste. Feedstock recycling breaks down polymers into their constituent monomers, which in turn can be used again in refineries, or petrochemical and chemical production. Plastic bottle recycling (eg HDPE and PET bottles) has been quite successful, but other remaining rigid plastics composed of PP and PS are not yet widely recyclable.

Plastics recycling in the UK

In the UK, post-consumer plastics are largely collected by local authorities. Recycling of plastic bottles from households is one of the most significant solid waste collection activities of the UK's local authorities. Based on the responses of 380 local authorities in the UK, WRAP (2008a) reported that 525,300 tonnes of plastic bottles were consumed in households throughout the UK in 2007. The total quantity of plastic bottles collected in the UK in 2007 was 181,887 tonnes. That means 35 per cent of plastic bottles consumed by households are collected. Since there has been a considerable increase in the total quantity of plastic bottles collected, mainly due to the increasing number of local authorities offering plastic bottle collection, the percentage of plastic bottle collection is expected to rise.

Figure 7.3   Household recycling in the UK

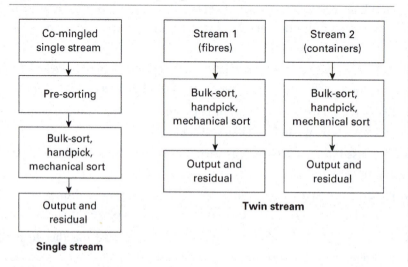

In some European countries, plastic bottles are collected by retailers, but in the UK, plastic waste is not managed by retailers or manufacturers of products. Local authorities in the UK typically collect dry recyclables from households using kerbside collection schemes and bring schemes. Figure 7.3 illustrates how the single- and two-stream collection schemes work. For the kerbside sort collection scheme, it is possible to ask households to sort recyclables into different groups. If it is difficult to get households to do the sorting, local authorities will then offer two collection systems. A single-stream system collects or co-mingles all dry recyclables in one container/vehicle. Co-mingled dry recyclables are then sorted and washed manually and/or mechanically. In some instances, pre-sorting is required. In a twin-stream system there are two co-mingled inputs, usually one co-mingled fibres (paper, card, etc) container and another container for bottles (HDPE, PET bottles, etc). It is possible to avoid pre-sorting and cross-contamination between fibre-based materials and containers in a twin-stream system.

A study of the cost of different collection schemes by WRAP (2008b) indicated that the net cost of twin-stream co-mingled collections was similar to the net cost of kerbside sort schemes. Kerbside sort schemes potentially have lower costs than single-stream schemes, taking into account the sales of recovered materials. There is actually no systematic advantage for one recycling system for the 'urban' and 'rural' nature of the areas served (WRAP, 2008b).

The UK's local authorities use different plastic bottle collection schemes. In 2007, approximately 147,450 tonnes (81 per cent) of plastics were recovered through kerbside collections, an increase of 77 per cent from 2006. In 2007, 14.4 million households were given kerbside collection services by 304 local authorities (WRAP, 2008a). Other collection schemes such as the bring scheme are less popular. At the moment, the main reason for not having a kerbside collection scheme for plastic bottles is lack of spare compartments in kerbside collection vehicles. Due to cost pressures, local authorities prefer to use a single vehicle to collect as many types of waste as possible, but the need to collect plastic bottles and other plastic waste would mean investment in new vehicles, adding costs. Another reason for the lack of investment in plastics collection schemes is the focus on heavier materials to hit recycling targets set by the central government. Recycling targets are set in terms of tonnage but plastics waste is lighter than other types of solid waste. Local authorities in the UK collected approximately 3.9 million tonnes of recyclables in 2007 and in terms of tonnage only about 5 per cent of those were plastic bottles (WRAP, 2007; 2008b). This explains why local authorities complained that their plastic bottle recycling schemes were a significant additional cost to their activities.

Each UK local authority typically collected 1 to 2,562 tonnes of plastic waste each year (WRAP, 2008a). Some local authorities own and operate their own kerbside collection facilities and material recovery facilities (MRFs). Many contract sorting and baling operations to waste management companies or MRFs. Local authorities pay a 'gate fee' and 'sorting fee' for every load of waste sent to the MRFs. Gate fees are influenced by factors such as competition, landfill tax, quality and quantity of material, energy cost, size of facility, and others (WRAP, 2008c). Some local authorities have a contract with their MRFs and use spot markets to sell their plastics. Usually the contractors sell plastics on behalf of local authorities; in some cases, income from the sale of plastics goes to the local authorities so contracted MRFs may not have a great interest in selling the plastics at the best price. Some local authorities have revenue-sharing contracts with their MRFs, and to further encourage recycling, some pay their MFR contractors extra for any shortfall between the actual market price paid by the contractors for the recycling of sorted materials and the landfill charge. Another way to improve recycling quality is to charge MRFs extra for materials rejected from the material reprocessors. In addition, to encourage household recycling, the incentive mechanisms discussed above contain elements to further improve recycling efficiency and quality. A report published by AEAT on behalf of WRAP discussing contractual arrangements between local authorities and MRF operators provides more detailed information about this issue (AEAT, 2006).

Another good example of waste recycling is Germany's recycling system. Since 1991, Germany has been developing a comprehensive infrastructure called the 'Dual System', which ensures the nationwide collection, sorting and recycling of used sales packaging in densely populated cities and rural areas. A viable finance model called the 'Green Dot' has been established to give industry an incentive to develop and produce recycling-friendly packaging and hence to reduce consequential ecological costs.

Summary

Reverse logistics and recycling are crucial for maintaining a healthy environment, not only because of the increasing scarcity of natural resources, but also because of the adverse effects of putting end-of-life products into landfills. They enable the transformation towards a circular economy because they help to keep products, components and materials in use rather than being landfilled. However, due to the lack of regulatory and competitive pressure in some countries, not every producer is seriously engaging in reverse logistics and recycling of the products they produce. Not all end consumers are participating in reverse logistics and recycling, or are aware of the consequences of their throw-away habits. Due to the lack of involvement of original equipment manufacturers (OEMs), reverse logistics and recycling activities have, in the past, been carried out by governments and incentivized recycling industries instead.

In recent years, due to increasing regulatory and competitive pressures, some industries have started looking into alternatives to simply allowing end-of-life products to be landfilled. More companies are now building the reverse logistics infrastructures and practices required to reduce, reuse, recycle and recover the products they produce. Some companies embracing environmental leadership have demonstrated that it is possible to create a truly closed-loop supply chain without becoming more expensive than their competitors. The regulation of extended producer responsibility will further drive investment in reverse logistics and recycling, which will in turn drive further innovation and investment. Consumers' purchasing and recycling behaviours will change when they realize they need to pay for reverse logistics and recycling of the products they get rid of. With the rise of new enterprises making reuse, refurbishing, sharing, remanufacturing, upcycling, recycling and energy-from-waste commercially viable, we now see many more possibilities for creating a circular economy.

References

AEAT (2006) *Contractual arrangements between local authorities and MRF operators*, final report for Waste and Resources Action Programme (WRAP), AEAT

Carter, C R and Ellram, L M (1998) Reverse logistics: a review of the literature and framework for further investigation, *Journal of Business Logistics*, **19** (1), pp 85–102

De Brito, M P and Dekker, R (2004) A framework for reverse logistics, in R Dekker, K Inderfurth, L van Wassenhove and M Fleischmann (eds), *Reverse Logistics: Quantitative models for closed-loop supply chains*, Springer, Berlin

Defra (2010), EU Landfill Directive, *Defra* [online] available at: https://www.gov. uk/government/uploads/system/uploads/attachment_data/file/69347/pb13563-landfill-directive-100322.pdf [accessed 31 December 2016] http://www. doitpoms.ac.uk/tlplib/recycling-metals/what.php

DoITPoMS (nd) What metals can be recycled? University of Cambridge [online] available at: https://www.doitpoms.ac.uk/tlplib/recycling-metals/what.php [accessed 31 December 2016]

EC Environment (2012), Waste, *European Commission – Environment* [online] available at: http://ec.europa.eu/environment/waste/index.htm [accessed 31 December 2016]

Ellen MacArthur Foundation (2015) Towards a circular economy: business rationale for an accelerated transition [online] available at: https://www. ellenmacarthurfoundation.org/assets/downloads/publications/Ellen-MacArthur-Foundation-Towards-the-Circular-Economy-vol.1.pdf [accessed 31 December 2016]

EPA (2011) Municipal solid waste generation, recycling, and disposal in the United States: facts and figures for 2010, United States Environmental Protection Agency, Washington, DC

Grant, D B (2012) *Logistics Management*, Pearson

Grant, D B and Banomyong, R (2010) Design of closed-loop supply chain and product recovery management for fast moving consumer goods, *Asia Pacific Journal of Marketing and Logistics*, 22 (2), pp 232–46

Guide Jr, V D R and Srivastava, R (1998) Inventory buffers in recoverable manufacturing, *Journal of Operations Management*, 16, pp 551–68

Guide Jr, V D R, and van Wassenhove, L N (2002) The reverse supply chain, *Harvard Business Review*, 80 (2), pp 25–26

Guide Jr, V D R, Muyldermans, L and van Wassenhove, L N (2005) Hewlett-Packard company unlocks the value potential from time-sensitive returns, *Interfaces*, 35 (4), pp 281–93

Hoornweg, D, Bhada-Tata, P and Kennedy, C (2013) Environment: Waste production must peak this century, *Nature*, 502, pp 615–17

Jacobs, B and Subramanian, R (2009) *Impacts of sharing responsibility for product recovery across the supply chain*, Working Paper Series, College of Management, Georgia Institute of Technology

Jayaraman, V, Guide Jr, V D R, Srivastava, R (1999) A closed loop logistics model for use within a recoverable manufacturing environment, *Journal of Operational Research Society*, 50 (5), pp 497–509

Kroon, L and Vrijens, G (1995) Returnable containers: an example of reverse logistics, *International Journal of Physical Distribution & Logistics Management*, 25 (2), pp 56–68

Murphy, E (2012) *Key Success Factors for achieving Green Supply Chain Performance; A study of UK ISO 14001 certified manufacturers,* unpublished PhD Thesis submitted at the University of Hull

Murphy, P R and Poist, R P (1989) Managing of logistics retromovements: an empirical analysis of literature suggestions, *Transportation Research Forum,* **29** (1), pp 177–84

PlasticEurope (2009) The compelling facts about plastics 2009 – an analysis of European plastics production, demand and recovery for 2008, *PlasticEurope* [online] available at: www.plasticseurope.org [accessed 01 January 2017]

RLA.org (2013) Company History, Reverse Logistics Association, RLA [online] available at: http://www.reverselogisticstrends.com/company_history.php [accessed 31 December 2016]

Rogers, D S and Tibben-Lembke, R (2001) An examination of reverse logistics practices, *Journal of Business Logistics,* **22** (2), pp 129–48

Rubio, S, Chamorro, A and Miranda, F (2008) Characteristics of the research on reverse logistics (1995–2005), *International Journal of Production Research,* **46** (4), pp 1099–1120

Science World (2008) Paper or plastic? *Science World,* **64** (13), pp 14–15

Sharma, M G, Das, J K and Singh, K N (2016) *Greendust: Revolutionizing the returns process,* Ivey Publishing, London, Ontario, pp 1–6

Srivastava, S K (2008) Value recovery network design for product returns, *International Journal of Physical Distribution & Logistics Management,* **38** (4), pp 311–31

Srivastava, S K and Srivastava, R K (2006) Managing product returns for reverse logistics, *International Journal of Physical Distribution & Logistics Management,* **36** (7), pp 524–46

Stock, J R (1992) *Reverse Logistics Programs,* Council of Logistics Management, Oak Brook, IL

Stock, J R (1998) *Development and Implementation of Reverse Logistics Programs,* Council of Logistics Management, Oak Brook, IL

Stock, J, Speh, T and Shear, H (2006) Managing product returns for competitive advantage, *MIT Sloan Management Review,* **48** (1), pp 57–62

Streitfeld, D (2003) Media copyright law put to unexpected uses; companies are using legislation meant to restrain web piracy to try to shut down rivals, *Los Angeles Times,* February 23, p 3

Thierry, M, Salomon, M, Van Nunen, J and Van Wassenhove, L (1995) Strategic issues in product recovery management, *California Management Review,* **37** (2), pp 114–35

Tischner, U and Nickel, R (2004) Eco-design in the printing industry – life cycle thinking: implementation of eco-design concepts and tools into the routine procedures of companies, *The Journal of Sustainable Product Design,* **3,** pp 19–27

Toffel, M W (2004) Strategic management of product recovery, *California Management Review,* **46** (2), pp 120–41

United Nations (2016) Sustainable development goals, Goal 6: ensure access to water and sanitation for all, *un.org* [online] available at: http://www.un.org/sustainabledevelopment/water-and-sanitation/ [accessed 26 December 2016]

UNEP (2015) *Global Waste Management Outlook*, United Nations Environment Programme

Wong, C Y (2010) *A Study of Plastic Recycling Supply Chain: Seed-corn 2009–10 project*, Chartered Institute of Logistics & Transport (CILT)

World Health Organization (2007) New country-by-country data show in detail the impact of environmental factors on health, *who.int* [online] available at: http://www.who.int/mediacentre/news/releases/2007/pr30/en/ [accessed 26 December 2016]

WRAP (2007) *An analysis of MSW MRF capacity in the UK*, WRAP, 1–12, pp 1–332

WRAP (2008a) *Local Authorities Plastics Collection Survey 2008*, WRAP, 1–65

WRAP (2008b) *Kerbside Recycling: Indicative cost and performance*, WRAP, 1–34

WRAP (2008c) *Comparing the Cost of Alternative Waste Treatment Options*, WRAP, 1–4

Risk, resilience and corporate social responsibility

08

Background

Extending supply chains globally is an effective way to expand customer base and gain access to cheaper materials and labour. However, this means multinational companies are facing greater supply chain risks and problems associated with ethical, environmental and corporate social responsibility issues. Sometimes it is inevitable to have to source raw materials and products from countries facing more frequent disruptions owing to natural disasters, man-made disasters or the like. Some unexpected disruptions can be very costly. For example, the lightning strike on 17 March 2000 which caused a fire at a local plant owned by Royal Philips Electronics, NV led to a loss of US $400 million in sales to one of its major customers, Telefon AB LM Ericsson (Chopra and Sodhi, 2004). In addition, natural disasters such as earthquakes, tsunamis, storms and flooding can affect supply chain operations for months. Others find themselves losing billions of dollars due to negligence in managing health and safety. The accident at the oil rig called Deepwater Horizon not only caused BP billions of dollars in legal fees, compensation and fines, there were further losses of future business from damage to brand reputation. Since then, more efforts and research have gone into developing more proactive, sustainable and resilient approaches to managing global supply chain risk and corporate social responsibility.

Even though economic benefits due to global sourcing and distribution are irresistible, companies involved are facing a lot of ethical issues. This is particularly true for companies operating in countries troubled by internal conflicts and lack of regulations to protect workers, society, children, and the environment. Such problems are normally revealed by non-governmental organizations (NGOs), creating a new type of risk called reputational risk.

Cases such as the use of child labour at Nike's factories and its suppliers' factories in Indonesia raise a question about who should be responsible for the welfare of the community when a company sources a product from such countries. The issues of child labour in the chocolate industry are further revealed by various reports such as the 2010 documentary *The Dark Side of Chocolate*. Issues about animal welfare have also been highlighted. For example, the 'KitKat Killer' campaign by Greenpeace accused Nestlé of cutting down trees causing animals such as orangutans to lose their homes (see the case study on the chocolate industry later in this chapter).

Then there are issues concerning how natural resources such as water and land should be used for whose benefits. Protests against the use of water resources by the production facilities of Coco-Cola in India raise a question about who should be responsible for the depletion of natural resources that leads to difficult living conditions for local communities. Furthermore, it is debatable who should pay for the pollution created by the parts of supply chains where regulatory enforcement is rather weak. While global, well-known clothing brands make profits out of the cheap clothing they source from countries such as China, Bangladesh and Indonesia, the costs of pollution problems in their major rivers due to the discharge of chemicals by textile factories have actually been largely paid by the local workers, communities and governments. Consequently, reports such as 'Dirty Laundry' and the 'Detox' campaigns by Greenpeace (Greenpeace, 2011a; 2011b) are putting pressure on global clothing brands to clean up their supply chains. This is why corporate social responsibility (CSR) becomes important for supply chain management and managers need to understand and learn how they can be more ethical and responsible in their decisions and actions.

This chapter first explains how risk in logistics and supply chains can be managed by making the supply chains more resilient. Some of the risks originate from the markets but others are associated with social, ethical and environmental issues. To better understand and manage issues related to responsibilities around the social, ethical and environmental impacts of global supply chains, this chapter outlines some useful frameworks for managing corporate social responsibility and business ethics.

Risk and resiliency in logistics and supply chains

Risk can be understood from different perspectives. Risk means potential danger, probability of occurrence, and variability of outcomes. Risk is generally defined in the academic literature as 'the variance of the probability of the distribution of outcomes'. Risk is present in our everyday life. From a business management point of view, risk involves variability in terms of returns or outcomes of a particular decision or action. Supply chain disruption is a major risk facing logistics and supply chain functions. It is defined as an unforeseen event that interferes with the normal flow of goods and/or materials within a supply chain (Ellis *et al*, 2010). Disruption in logistics and supply chain operations often cause loss of productivity, revenue, customers and even lives; 173 people were killed in the Tianjin explosion in August 2015 (BSI, 2015). While supply chain disruptions often lead to additional cost, the true cost is hard to estimate. Just cargo theft alone is estimated to cost the world US $22.6 billion annually (BSI, 2015). Based on a survey of 525 companies in 71 countries, the 2014 Supply Chain Resilience Survey conducted by the Business Continuity Institute (BCI) reported that 23.6 per cent of companies suffered annual cumulative losses of at least €1 million due to supply chain disruptions (BCI, 2014). While 12.3 per cent of companies lost over €1 million due to just one incident, there have been single incidents that have cost over €50 million.

Types of logistics and supply chain risks

One way to understand risk in logistics and supply chains is to identify its sources and understand how it occurs. The sources of risk can be atomic and holistic. Atomic (or unsystematic) sources of risk affect a limited part of a supply chain. This may involve the breakdown of a production or IT facility for a component which will not disrupt the operations of the entire supply chain. Holistic (or systematic) sources of risk involve widespread disruption and multiple members of a supply chain. These are systemic disruptions that could not be eliminated easily by a single party. For example, the fluctuations of crude oil prices and supply during the last decade have created significant financial problems, particularly among European plastics raw materials producers, which in turn leads to a lack of plant maintenance and subsequently frequent supply shortages of plastics raw materials to plastics converters and the packaging industry. This problem has caused an increase in irresponsible pricing/inventory behaviours and unjustified declarations of force majeure within the industries, which has ultimately led to some very damaging effects on various industries and supply chains (British Plastics and Rubber, 2015).

Table 8.1 provides a comprehensive list of the different types (sources) of risk in a global supply chain. According to the 2014 Supply Chain Resilience Survey (BCI, 2014), loss of productivity remains as the top reported consequence of supply chain disruptions for the same survey over the last six years

Table 8.1   Types of logistics and supply chain risk

Type of risk	Sources	Consequences
Demand risk	Uncertainty in demand owing to variation in demand (fashion, seasonality, new product launch), demand distortion (or Bullwhip effect).	Variation in demand could mean higher cost of inventory and obsolete inventory, and lost sales.
Supply risk	Uncertainty or disruption in supply chain owing to breakdown at supply sides, design changes, quality issues, price fluctuation, supply shortage, shipping schedules and natural disaster.	This risk could lead to breakdown of production and inability to supply to customers according to promised delivery dates, and escalating costs to find and expedite alternative supply.
Operational risk	Breakdown of operations, poor production planning, natural disaster, changes in technology, process variability, industry action (strike), accident, IT and telecommunication outage, power shortage, etc.	This could lead to inability to supply to customers according to promised delivery dates, and escalating costs to find alternative capacity.
Competitive risk	Innovation from competitor, competitor's aggressive moves (discounts, special offers, price war), competitor's influence on customers.	Innovative products or changes in buying behaviour could lead to the unpopularity of a product and therefore the market share could be seriously affected.
Security risk	Infrastructure security, information security, terrorism, vandalism, crime, sabotage.	This risk could lead to the loss of sensitive data and crucial operating data, disruption of production, and poor employee safety.
Macro-economic risks	Economic downturn, governmental financial crisis, problems at the capital market, changes in wage rates, interest rates and costs.	This risk could lead to a drop in demand and price, escalating cost, and a shortage in money supply. Although this risk cannot be avoided there are ways to anticipate its occurrence and magnitude.

(Continued)

Table 8.1 (*Continued*)

Type of risk	Sources	Consequences
Policy risk	Changes in policies by national and international governmental bodies (treaty currency, quota restriction, taxation, sanctions, advertising restrictions, trading licences, environmental responsibility).	This risk could lead to changes and restriction of market access, escalating cost, loss of market share, tax advantage, cost/profit from currency exchange, increased competition.
Reputational risk	Public distrust, negative customer reactions, boycott and bad brand reputation created by serious misconduct or breach of trust with customers.	This risk could lead to difficulties in getting capital, liabilities and legal penalties. Poor brand image could lead to serious loss of market share.
Corporate fraud and criminal risk	Serious fraud, bribery, corporate crime, corporate shake-up, accounting fraud, unfair/illegal trading practices, misuse of corporate finance.	This risk could lead to heavy liability and penalty costs, as well as reputational damage. It could also lead to management shake-up which further disrupts the recovery of the organization.
Resource (sustainability) risk	Shortage or depletion of rare national resources (water, metal, mineral, rare earth, trees, fish stock, farms), manmade and national disaster affecting the supply of national resources, national resources from politically unstable regions.	This risk could lead to escalating costs of acquiring natural resources and frequent shortage of supply. Also, it creates the need to operate in regions which are politically instable and troubled by bad business practices.

(58.5 per cent). Increased cost of working (47.5 per cent) and loss of revenue (44.7 per cent) are also two other commonly reported consequences. The survey concluded that the primary sources of disruption to supply chains were unplanned IT and telecommunications outage (52.9 per cent), adverse weather (51.6 per cent) and outsourcer service failure (35.8 per cent). As a form of operational risk, IT, power and communication outages occur more often in less-developed countries but they can also cause serious damages in developed countries. Although they usually cause atomic disruptions, in some instances, IT, communication and power outages can create holistic disruptions. For example, a power outage at the global headquarters of Delta Air Lines in Atlanta, Georgia in the United States in August 2016 led to serious IT glitches that forced the company to cancel over 700 flights in various airports (*Daily Mail*, 2016). Such disruptions are often caused by the use of legacy IT systems with fairly primitive security and backup features based on a single IT infrastructure (eg server) in a single location. Moreover, many firms failed to set up a robust back-up system for power supply, IT infrastructure and a robust IT security system that could fight against fraud and different forms of cyber-attacks. Even though nowadays it is possible to use a Cloud-based IT system where servers can be located in safer locations and protected by more robust IT security systems, companies can still face disruptions owing to the instability of internet connections, fraud and cyber-attack.

Table 8.1 also includes other risks originating from parties outside a supply chain such as policy risk, macro-economic risk, operational and supply risk caused by natural disaster, and cyber breach or attack. In the age of digitization, there has been a significant increase in the reliance on internet- and mobile-based IT systems and applications. This has given rise to a new form of risk – cyber breach or attack. A series of studies carried out by the UK government shows that the majority of companies studied have no formal written cyber security policies or incident management plan, while the cost of cyber breaches could reach millions of pounds (Gov.uk, 2016). Adverse weather can also be very costly. According to the United Nations Office for Disaster Risk Reduction (UNISDR, 2015), 346 reported natural disasters in 2015 took 22,773 lives, affected 98.6 million people and cost the global economy US $66.5 billion. According to the report, the 2015 April earthquake in Nepal (8,831 lives), heatwaves in France, Belgium, India and Pakistan (7,162 lives), the landslide in Guatemala (627 lives), and floods in India (618 lives) were among the top deadly natural disasters. Many of these were high-impact, low-likelihood risk (HILP). In terms of economic damages, the United States topped the list ($24.88 billion), followed by the Republic of China ($13.66 billion), Nepal ($5.17 billion), the UK ($3.6 billion) and India ($3.3 billion). In the past, some costly natural disasters included the 2011 Earthquake/Tsunami in Japan ($223 billion), the 2005 Katrina Hurricane in the United States ($219 billion) and the 2011 flooding in Thailand ($42 billion).

There are some newly emerging risks that involve not only logistics and supply chain functions but also corporate governance and corporate social responsibility (CSR), including reputational risk, corporate fraud and criminal risk (terrorism), and environmental (sustainability) risk. For example, the German engineering group Siemens had to pay a record fine of US $800 million (£523 million) to the US authorities in December 2008 to settle a bribery and corruption scandal, and another €395 million (£354 million) to settle a case in Munich (Gow, 2008). A China Mobile executive received a death sentence due to a bribery scandal that involved Siemens. Including legal fees, Siemens paid billions of dollars due to the corporate criminal risk. Similar risks can be found in the banking industry. Barclays Bank was asked to pay at least US $450 million to US and British authorities to settle a probe into manipulation of the key interbank lending rate known as Libor. On the other hand, risk owing to terrorism is on the rise. According to the BSI Supply Chain Intelligence Report, the reintroduction of border controls following the November 2015 terrorist attacks in Paris could cost Belgian cargo owners US $3.5 million, and to permanently re-establish Schengen area border controls could cost the German economy US $25 billion (BSI, 2015).

Reputational risk and resource (sustainability) risk are emerging risks facing global multinationals in particular. Especially at risk are those with famous household brands, who could face serious reputational damage if they were caught being involved in serious fraud and criminal activities or failed to stop their supply chains from causing serious health, safety, environmental and social problems. Once trust with customers is breached, they might boycott the brands and cause a fall in market shares. Nowadays there are many ways in which companies that cause such problems can be publicized in the media and on the internet. For example, Greenpeace publishes a database called the 'Greenpeace International Black List' showing fishing vessels and companies that engaged in illegal, unregulated and unreported fishing; the 'Detox Catwalk' contains fashion brands that make the effort to clean up and also those failing to do so; and the 'Guide to Greener Electronics' ranks electronics manufacturers in terms of their environmental management performance. The list of Chinese companies caught and fined by the Chinese government due to offences in environmental management, published by a non-profit organization called the Institute of Public and Environmental Affairs (IPE) (Jun *et al*, 2010), has shaken many industries and led to the formation of the Green Choice Alliance. Such risks cannot be fully addressed by the logistics and supply chain functions; this is why they should be managed at a corporate level where corporate governance and corporate social responsibility (CSR) are driven.

Processes to mitigate logistics and supply chain risks

To mitigate logistics and supply chain risks, companies may refer to standards such as ISO 22301 Business Continuity Management, PAS 7000 Supply Chain Risk Management (Supplier Qualification), cyber security guidelines and standards such as PAS 555 and ISO/IEC 27035. Since certifications for such standards can be costly, there are other process frameworks for a company to adopt. Typically there are five steps for identifying and mitigating supply chain risk (Manuj and Mentzer, 2008), explained as follows.

Step 1: Identify risk

Different sources of risk (see Table 8.1) can be formally identified by a team of selected management and experts. Since different staff and functional departments have different knowledge about specific types of risk, it may be beneficial to divide the task into three teams: (1) operational, supply and demand risks that occur quite regularly; (2) macro-economic, policy, corporate governance-related and external risks; and (3) risks brought by catastrophic events such as war or terror attacks, and natural disasters such as earthquake, flooding and storms. While logistics and supply chain staff are familiar with the first group of risks they need to learn more about the other two groups, especially natural disasters and terrorism. Some large multinational companies appoint a chief risk officer in order to put risk management at the top of the corporate agenda and create a better understanding of risks facing different locations globally.

For companies with limited experience it would be ineffective to use the existing setup and knowledge to identify risks. It may be beneficial to invite experts from outside and to gather relevant case studies from within and beyond the industry and country. There are many sources of new knowledge and information. For example, it is possible to find knowledge databases and real-time updates about natural disasters from a 'climate service' or similar providers:

- The Emergency and Disaster Information Services (EDIS) operated by the National Association of Radio Distress Signalling and Infocommunications (RSOE) provides a rich knowledge database and updates every five minutes about natural disasters around the globe.

- The Global Disaster Alert and Coordination System (GDACS) is provided by United Nations and the European Commission to improve alerts, information exchange and coordination during the early phase and after major onset disasters.

- There are different internet-based software applications that provide real-time views of threat information, help identify events and situations that may threaten a company, and help monitor threat.

Some risks cannot be identified by human beings, for example cyber-attacks. Nowadays there are increasing chances of logistics and supply chain information systems being disrupted by cyber-attacks, which could lead to financial loss, loss of operational and sensitive data, theft of intellectual properties, and loss of reputation owing to disruption of customer services and even leaking of customer data. Cyber-attackers can be motivated by financial gain (eg valuable information), political and social causes, and industry- and nation-state-sponsored sabotage or theft of intellectual property. Cyber-criminals can hack and shut down a company website, compromise user accounts, and breach security defences to directly access the servers and systems of a company. Traditional IT security controls based on layered security strategy lack proactivity, speed and sophistication because they are often rather static in their defence. Traditional IP reputation-based technology cannot be updated as quickly as needed and cyber-criminals can easily mask IP addresses during their attacks. Furthermore, cyber-attacks could take place at suppliers' or providers' systems outside a company's IT systems, and when their accounts are compromised it is possible for cyber-criminals to access the company servers if the IT systems between the companies and outsiders are connected via the internet. To address such emerging threats, companies may consider installing more advanced and intelligent platforms that are live, contextual, adaptive and capable of detecting emerging IP risks.

While identifying risk, there are several biases that could lead to ignorance or the downplay of specific risks. The first is confirmation bias, also known as confirmatory bias, which is the tendency to search for, interpret, favour, and recall information in a way that confirms one's pre-existing beliefs and subsequently gives disproportionately less consideration to alternative possibilities. A company might believe that fire is a threat because similar companies in the same industry have been affected and therefore put more effort into identifying sources of fire threat, but then allocate less attention to the possibility of other threats such as flooding. Another similar bias is selective exposure, referred to as an individual's tendency to favour information which reinforces his or her pre-existing views while avoiding contradictory information. With the view that 'it won't happen to us', an individual might disregard emerging indications about a risk that is considered as impossible or improbable. For example, when selecting a new logistics service provider or unfamiliar route, one might disregard the possibility of cargo theft and damages arising from manual handling simply because of the belief that they are not going to happen. Consequently, a manager may choose a less comprehensive insurance cover without making any contingency plan. The third bias is the tendency not to report risk, which is often created by a company culture that discourages exposure of risks or problems (especially to the top management and customers) and a tendency to punish individuals who make mistakes.

Step 2: Assess and evaluate risk

Upon the identification of different types of risks, the selected team can be asked to assign the likelihood (frequency or probability of occurrence) and the consequences in terms of the impact (seriousness of damage, in financial terms if possible) of a particular risk based on past experience, historical data, case studies, external experts and any available forecast data. Practically, likelihood or probability of occurrence can be categorized into very unlikely, improbable, probable, or very probable. While there are some technical terminologies and maps showing risks such as flooding and earthquake provided by government agencies, there is a need to clarify some misunderstandings. A 100-year flood does not mean the interval must be 100 years. While it means a flood has a 100-year recurrence interval, it could still take place 30 years from now, 150 years later or any year in between. It actually means there is 1 per cent probability that a flood event occurs in any given year, and there is approximately a 63.4 per cent chance of one or more floods in any 100-year period. On the other hand, earthquake or seismic activity is often predicted in terms of the percentage of probability in a 50-year period. Practically, it is better to translate x-year recurrence intervals into percentage chance of occurrence. Flood insurance rates are typically estimated based on 1 per cent, 0.2 per cent or less than 0.2 per cent chance of occurrence, while potential damages are added into the consideration. Some might think a 1 per cent chance means something is less likely to happen, but in fact, properties located in a 100-year flood zone are considered to be high flood risk and face a mandatory flood risk insurance.

In terms of consequences of damages, categories such as insignificant, minor, serious and catastrophic can be used. The thresholds of such categories are relative to the value of the businesses (locations) being considered. A US $1 million loss can be serious for smaller companies but insignificant for very large companies. A flood could cause financial losses some companies could afford and recover from, while others might go bust immediately after the flood. When a group of experts are asked to evaluate risk, it is important to understand that people may have different reference points in terms of the thresholds for a serious risk. Since it is not possible to obtain official estimates of likelihood and especially consequences for all risks pertaining to a specific location, there is thus a need for collective wisdom. The Delphi method, where a panel of experts answers questionnaires in two or more rounds, can be used to reveal the individual perceptions of each member of the team without being affected by group effects. To avoid over-reliance on past events, there is a need to identify future changes (eg forecasts) in the business environment which may change the likelihood and impact of a risk.

The assessment and evaluation of supply chain risk is one of the most difficult tasks within the risk management process. One major problem is the assignment of the probability of occurrence of an event and the estimation of its potential damage, liability or cost. For example, from past experience, flooding may have taken place at a location 40 and 100 years ago, but the damages varied significantly for each flood. It is often too costly for a government to build a robust flood defence system for flooding that could happen once in every 200 years. In this case, there is a need to refer to the studies of weather and climate change and flood defence upgrades reported by the relevant environmental agency. It is also possible to work with a range of occurrence frequencies and consequences. Another main problem is how to choose or prioritize the types or sources of risk to be addressed; a more pragmatic approach is to use rough estimation. Another common approach is to compare the relative scores of likelihood x impact. A risk which has a high likelihood of occurrence but relatively low impact may be less critical than another risk which occurs less frequently but potentially leads to very serious consequences. This is done by plotting the likelihood and impact scores for each type of risk onto a risk likelihood–impact graph (see Figure 8.1).

Another issue facing the assessment of likelihood and impact comes from the inconsistency in the ways people make risky choices under varying probabilities. Prospect theory helps explain how people make choices among risky prospects. In particular, people usually underweight outcomes that are merely probable in comparison to outcomes that are obtained in certainty (Kahneman and Tversky, 1979). For example, when presented with a lower chance of suffering a higher loss compared with definitely suffering a lower loss (or with a higher chance), more people tend to worry more about the high-chance loss. That means loss due to a risk can appear to be greater when its probability of occurrence is high. This is called the certainty effect, which increases risk aversion in choices involving sure gain and risk seeking in choices involving sure losses. A likelihood–impact graph may help avoid this effect as long as likelihood and impact are realistically estimated.

Figure 8.1 Risk likelihood–impact graph

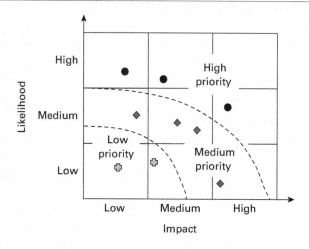

Furthermore, people often discard some components that are shared by all prospects in consideration. This is especially relevant to choosing potential outcomes. For example, more people are likely to choose an option that has a higher outcome with lower probability over a lower outcome with higher probability. This is called the isolation effect. The key here is to make comprehensive estimations, especially when it comes to impacts. Furthermore, one can scrutinize whether the probabilities of occurrence of two options are too unrealistically close to each other.

Many companies view risk identification and assessment as a one-off annual activity. Others have a risk register procedure but fail to use it to identify damaging risks. This problem could be created by ambiguity about the frequency of risk identification and assessment. Instead it is possible to differentiate the frequencies of risk identification and assessment by understanding the frequency and pattern in which a specific risk occurs. The answer to when to assess emerging risks is also dependent on the time and cost required to put in place additional mitigation measures. There are risks where frequencies of occurrence increase steadily, meaning it is possible to monitor frequencies and react at the right time. For example, long-term flooding risk can be identified once and addressed by purchasing suitable insurance, installing an appropriate flood defence system and putting in place other measures, whilst monitoring if there are more rainfalls or changes in weather systems on a need-be basis. Other types of risks emerge in an unexpected (interval) manner, giving less time to respond. For example, many operational health and safety risks can occur at any minute, so staff need to be vigilant and able to identify and address such risks all the time. The same goes for political and macro-economic situations that could change after being stable for a while. A long period of stability or lack of incidents can often lead to relaxation of risk identification and assessment frequency and vigilance. The second problem is that staff might not have the same understanding of how to assess and act on some emerging risks. The Ericsson case mentioned earlier in this chapter is a good example of where a supply risk was identified but no action was taken owing to the lack of a common approach to identifying and assessing risk.

Step 3: Choose appropriate risk management strategies

The choice of appropriate risk management strategies depends on the type of risks, likelihood of occurrence and extent of potential damage. There are five common types of risk mitigation strategies: (1) accept the risks and losses and do nothing; (2) buy insurance to offset potential losses; (3) invest in measures that can reduce losses, eg a flood defence system or a dual supply source that can be activated after the supply is disrupted; (4) prepare for recovery plans that take into account the breakdowns of various infra-structures; and (5) invest in measures that can reduce exposure to risks, eg change to a new and safer supplier or operating location. While the first strategy is suitable for low-likelihood and low-impact risks, the next three strategies are more relevant for low-likelihood, high-impact risks. The fifth strategy can be improper for high-impact risk if it is too costly to implement and the chance of such a risk occurring is rather small. For high-likelihood and high-impact risks there may be a need to combine the fifth strategy with the other three strategies.

Figure 8.2 illustrates a framework for selecting appropriate risk manage-ment strategies (Knemeyer *et al*, 2009). To facilitate appropriate decisions, first there is a need to decide what risk and loss to accept, reduce and prevent for risks identified in the likelihood–impact graph. As illustrated by the lower-left quartile in Figure 8.2 representing low-likelihood and low-impact risks, managers may choose to accept the potential risks and losses without investing in any countermeasures. For high-impact risks shown in the upper-left quartile of Figure 8.2 that are less likely to happen (eg flood-ing, earthquake) it may be impossible or too costly to build a totally robust protection system but there are some countermeasures that can be put in place in advance to reduce losses (eg insurance). For supply, demand and operational risks that occur rather frequently, safety stock, dual-source and sub-contracting for seasonal demand surge are often used to reduce losses. When a high-impact risk becomes more likely or frequent (shorter intervals)

Figure 8.2 Risk management strategies

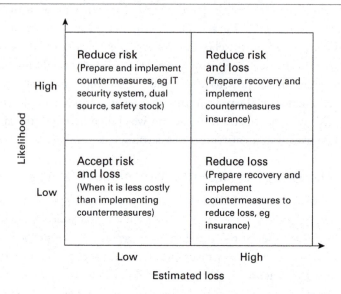

it may be necessary to consider reducing the risk by searching for alternative suppliers, locations and materials, and even redesigning the supply networks and systems. Sometimes it is too costly to put in place measures that prevent a high-impact risk that rarely happens. While Toyota suffered significant losses due to the 2011 earthquake/Tsunami, there is no evidence suggesting that this risk is becoming more likely or frequent. Therefore, earthquake/Tsunami is still considered a high-impact but low-likelihood catastrophic event. Subsequently, Toyota in Japan still relies on the just-in-time supply system to achieve cost efficiency and major suppliers remain located in earthquake areas while putting in place some additional upstream dual-sourcing arrangements and increasing capacities from their own foreign subsidiaries.

Different types of risks require different countermeasures. For macro-economy, competitor and policy risks, environmental scanning (eg market intelligence) is used to inform key product innovation, marketing and supply chain decisions. These risks can normally be transformed into demand, operational and supply risks and therefore require the top management and marketing staff to work closely with the logistics and supply chain functions. Similarly, corporate fraud and criminal risk require robust corporate governance systems but there are frauds, thefts and criminals that affect logistics and supply chain operations. Sustainability risk can be a supply chain issue and a wider corporate governance problem that cannot be addressed by a single corporation alone – industrial collaboration and multi-stakeholder initiatives with policy makers is one way forward, in addition to implementing codes of practice and governance structures. Many reputational risks originating from supply chains, especially the upstream suppliers, can be very tricky to mitigate. To address these issues, companies may need different multi-tier sustainable supply chain management strategies that specifically deal with upstream or lower-tier suppliers (Tachizawa and Wong, 2014):

- a 'don't bother' strategy where companies continue focusing on working with their first-tier suppliers and internal processes and pass on the blame to the lower-tier suppliers when something bad happens upstream;

- an 'indirect' strategy where companies do not work directly with the lower-tier suppliers but they provide their first-tier suppliers with sustainability requirements (eg codes of conduct, list of hazardous material, social and environmental responsibility codes), require first-tier suppliers to purchase from only certified lower-tier suppliers (eg ISO 14001) and assist first-tier suppliers on how to monitor lower-tier suppliers;

- another indirect strategy with a focus on 'working with third parties' by using information provided by third parties such as NGOs, local governments, competitors, customers, and suppliers' industrial associations, collaborating with them to develop new standards for the upstream industries (see global industrial initiatives discussed at end of this chapter), and even delegating responsibilities to such third parties;

- a 'direct' strategy whereby companies work directly with lower-tier suppliers by sourcing directly from them, monitor them directly, and provide information, requirements and assistance to them. This is usually done in conjunction with the indirect strategies.

Step 4: Implement supply chain risk management strategies

When a company has decided to do something to reduce exposure to logistics and supply chain risks and losses, there are three major phases of risk and disaster management to consider:

- Phase 1: Plan, prepare and implement risk mitigation before a risk happens.

- Phase 2: Responding to an emerging risk when it occurs, mainly to reduce losses and to temporarily recover the ability to resume normal operations.

- Phase 3: Longer-term recovery and reconstruction of the supply chains and preventing the same disaster from happening again, if possible.

The ability to address each of these three phases can be called organizational or supply chain resilience. The concept of resilience needs some clarification. Most scholars define resilience as the 'ability of a system to return to its original state or move to a new, more desirable state after being disturbed' (Christopher and Peck, 2004, p 2). Others argue this definition is too narrow because the ability to lessen losses is simply inadequate, and suggest the need for a more proactive approach to prevent disruption from happening in the first place. Particularly for high-likelihood and high-impact risks, companies may choose to invest in countermeasures prior to being disrupted; they need the ability to forecast, predict and monitor a future event. When such a proactive strategy becomes cost prohibitive or technically impossible, one has to rely on the ability to respond and recover.

The ability to manage the first phase (planning) is largely specified by standards such as ISO 22301 Business Continuity Management (BCM), PAS 7000 Supply Chain Risk Management (Supplier Qualification), cyber security guidelines and standards such as PAS 555 and ISO/IEC 27035. While such standards also specify how one might respond to and recover from emerging disruption, there are other standards that emphasize response and recovery. The management of the second phase (response) and third phase (recovery) requires some sort of disaster and emergency management system (DMES), specified by standards such as the ISO 22320: 2011 (Societal security: emergency management – requirements for incident management). Such a standard or DMES helps establish a foundation for the coordination and cooperation of all involved parties during an incident to minimize the risk of misunderstandings and ensure a more effective use of combined resources. It helps clarify the command and control, organizational structures and procedures, decision support, traceability and information management required to address an emergency. In particular, there is a need to establish the ability to account for employees and know their whereabouts after a serious incident. There is also a need to recover the IT communication infrastructure (or emergency communication system) that supports enquiries and sharing of reliable information. In an emergency, rule-based procedures for emergency responses (such as alert, warning, evacuation, assembly points, key infrastructures to be protected, roles and responsibilities) are often more effective because communications can break down. In terms of preparedness, there is a need to create a plan or the capability for establishing a dedicated emergency operations centre and a command team once an emergency or disaster occurs. Team members and roles during the emergency need not be the same as those in normal operations. People who have specific knowledge and skills for dealing with emergencies can be assigned to specific roles, such as commander, IT infrastructure, customer service, insurance claims, staffing, emergency procurement, and more. After identifying such roles there is a need to identify knowledge and skills gaps. New knowledge and skills can be acquired by attending special training and conducting exercises (simulation).

Most companies tend to create new programmes to prepare for risk mitigation after they have already suffered serious damages caused by a new risk. Somehow, many companies put less effort into rethinking their ability to address the first two phases. This reactive approach to mitigating risk may help if the same risk occurs again but it does not address other emerging risks or wider issues such as a lack of risk culture and organizational resilience. The main trick here is to make risk management a part of the routine, not a project or programme (Craighead *et al*, 2007). This is necessary because of the need to identify new emerging risk. Even though sometimes it is necessary to invest in physical infrastructure as part of the risk management programme, it is important to make sure the implementation programmes take into account the need to change risk culture within the company and supply chain and how day-to-day decisions are made by incorporating emerging risks.

Step 5: Mitigate risk and further identify risk

Even though we have specified ways for creating a routine to identify (Step 1) and evaluate risk (Step 2), the nature of risk is that it is unpredictable, and the best way to deal with this is to create a learning culture and the ability to confront and review one's assumptions. Here we are concerned with how new risks can be identified through risk management procedures. To enhance its ability to identify new risks, an organization has to learn to reduce its own bias, such as the confirmatory and selective exposure biases discussed earlier. This can be done in numerous ways. For example, one can assign people who have no operational responsibilities (risk management officers) or install an IT security system to identify new risks. With the use of a supply chain risk management system and dashboard supported by a global information system, some companies (eg IBM and DHL) are able to monitor their supply chain risks globally in real time. Such a system can provide real-time updates about risks associated with natural disasters, transport infrastructure, quality, suppliers, labour, and political and social issues. Similar supply chain risk management dashboards systems are offered by ERP solution providers (eg Oracle).

Many organizations fail to take appropriate action at the right time even though they have identified a new risk. A common cause is the tendency to cover up problems or blame employees. This is a trickier problem because such a cover-up or blame culture is usually created by top management themselves.

In some instances, management decided to go ahead with an operation even after being warned. NASA's second space shuttle *Challenger* underwent lift-off successfully nine times but exploded on its 10th lift-off in 1986. Despite warnings about cold weather, the space shuttle was instructed to launch according to schedule. An investigation (the Rogers Commission) concluded that the design of the O-ring that caused the failure was (knowingly) compromised by factors including the low temperature on the day of launch and design flaws being identified earlier without any action to rectify them. While avoiding blame for running behind schedule is a driver, in other instances, top management may pay less attention to some of the costly risk countermeasure systems and procedures (eg health and safety), especially when the industry is competing fiercely on cost. The Deepwater horizon oil spill is a good example. The relaxation of a procedure (eg safety features and number of back-up pumps) can be taken as a calculated risk because it is mistakenly viewed as an atomic risk that can be contained. Somehow, management often misjudges a potential holistic or systemic risk that could have major consequences as a form of atomic risk because they don't have the ability to understand how different parts of the system can affect each other and cause a serious disaster, or in some instances their decisions can be affected by an isolation effect.

A complex system also means there is a chance of failure in another part of the system coinciding with the failure of another procedure (ie the 'perfect storm'), and when this happens, cascading failures can accelerate out of control. While managers know different parts of a system can fail, it is the failure of several parts at the same time that can unexpectedly cause cascading failures. Most failures in different parts of a system (both technical failures and human errors) are 'normal' because they are not totally avoidable or predictable. Such an accident, called 'normal accident', often occurs in complex systems that are tightly coupled. While the assignment of external auditors or advisors and use of appropriate corporate governance structures could help, a systems approach is required to identify ways in which failures in different parts of a supply system can create catastrophic effects collectively.

Corporate social responsibility

The concept of corporate social responsibility (CSR) in the literature can be traced back to the 1950s in the book by Bowen (1953), *Social Responsibility of the Businessman*. It was recognized that the actions of large businesses should consider what is desirable in terms of the objectives and values of society. The earlier concept of CSR argued that production should be executed so that total social-economic welfare is enhanced; CSR concerns itself with business ethics. Businesses with CSR consider the ethical consequences of their actions on society. Even governmental agencies are involved in defining CSR. Notably, the Committee for Economic Development (CED) states: 'business functions by public consent and its basic purpose is to serve constructively these needs of society to the satisfaction of society.' In the public-sector literature, the concept of public responsibility, rather than social responsibility, is used to stress the importance of the public policy process and its impacts on the public.

It is worth noting that CSR is not just about charity. Businesses and individuals who donate a lot of money to charity after they have acquired a lot of wealth are not necessarily socially responsible. What really matters is that money is earned in a responsible manner. To be truly socially responsible they should be meeting social objectives while they are doing business. In addition, meeting social objectives mainly due to meeting legal requirements is not the same as meeting social objectives voluntarily. Social responsibility should be voluntary because there is no regulation that can force businesses to behave responsibly towards society. When social objectives are imposed on the corporation by law, the corporation exercises no social responsibility when it implements them just to meet the legal requirements (Manne and Wallich, 1972). Social responsibility is not an obligation; it is not just about responding to market forces or legal constraints. Self-regulation is always more progressive (King and Lenox, 2000). To qualify as socially responsible, a business must voluntarily allocate actual corporate expenditure to meet the objectives and values of society. The gradual acceptance of the importance of CSR among large corporations only started during the 1970s. The main purpose of most commercial companies in the past was 'to make as much money for their stockholders as possible', according to Friedman's (1962) view. In the more recent past, large corporations were told they should try to engage in social responsibility, and today, CSR is a must for all large and small corporations.

The reality is that businesses cannot just focus on social responsibility; they have to simultaneously consider multiple business objectives including market share, revenue, profit, competition, regulation, environment and social responsibility. To reflect this complex decision-making process, Johnson (1971, p 50) in his book, *Business in Contemporary Society*, refers to the conventional wisdom of a socially responsible firm as:

> one whose managerial staff balances a multiplicity of interests. Instead of striving only for larger profits for its shareholders, a responsible enterprise also takes into account employees, suppliers, dealers, local communities, and the nation.

Understandably, many businesses today still consider profit maximization as the most important objective. Under fierce competition, business managers have to make decisions to remain cost effective and competitive, in many circumstances trading off social and environmental responsibilities.

It is therefore argued that the definition of CSR should not ignore the responsibility to make profit, obey the law, and go beyond these activities. Based on this argument, 'the social responsibility of business encompasses the economic, legal, ethical, and discretionary expectations that society has of organizations at a given point in time' (Carroll, 1979). The inclusion of economic performance into CSR reflects the responsibility to produce goods and services that society wants and to sell them at a profit. A corporation that makes money will be able to continue providing employment and paying tax to the government. Businesses are expected to operating legally as well as responsibly. While society expects businesses to obey the law, ethical responsibility goes beyond the legal requirements. The ethical responsibility of a corporation is often left to individual managers' and corporations' judgement and choice, because society does not always provide clear-cut expectations of the corporation. Ethical responsibility encompasses those standards, norms, or expectations that reflect a concern for what consumers, employees, shareholders, and the community regard as fair, just, or in keeping with the respect or protection of stakeholders' moral rights (Carroll, 1991). Discretionary expectation refers to activities that help society, such as philanthropic contribution, training the unemployed, and conducting programmes to help disabled people. This responsibility is also called philanthropic responsibility. Table 8.2 further provides examples of the four responsibilities.

In order to make sure managers take into account all the above responsibilities in their day-to-day decisions, they must be embedded in the corporation's values and managerial practices. The pyramid of CSR proposed by Carroll (1979) attempts to illustrate how corporations view CSR in terms of a hierarchy of responsibilities (the pyramid of CSR):

- Economic responsibility is the foundation on which all other responsibilities rest. Economic responsibility means corporations need to be profitable.

- Legal responsibility is the second hierarchy of responsibility. Corporations need to obey the law because it is society's codification of right and wrong.

- Ethical responsibility is the third hierarchy of responsibility. It is about obligation to do what is right and fair and to avoid harm.

- Philanthropic responsibility is the highest hierarchy because it is about being a good corporate citizen.

Table 8.2 Different types of corporate responsibilities

	Economic responsibility	Legal responsibility	Ethical responsibility	Philanthropic responsibility
Primary drivers	Maximize earning per share.	Comply with expectations of government and law.	Meet expectations of societal norms and ethical norms.	Meet philanthropic and charitable expectations of society.
Primary objectives	As profitable as possible.	Comply with federal, state, and local regulations.	Prevent ethical norms from being compromised by other corporate goals.	Channel profits to philanthropic activities.
Reputation to be created	Be a very profitable company.	Be a law-abiding corporate citizen.	Be an ethical company that respects society.	Be a company that assists private and public education and improvement of the quality of life.
Logistics and supply chain roles	Achieve high level of efficiency and profitability.	Provide goods and services that at least meet legal requirements.	Make corporate integrity and ethical behaviour beyond mere compliance with law and regulation.	Participate or contribute to voluntary and charitable activities within the local communities.

While the pyramid of CSR helps to provide new meaning to CSR, it also exposes a complicated trade-off problem. Often there is an over-emphasis on profit maximization. Drucker (1954) suggested turning social problems into economic opportunity, economic benefit, productive capacity, human competence, well-paid jobs, and wealth. Johnson (1971) perceived social responsibility as a way to achieve long-run profit maximization. The trade-off between economic responsibility and ethical responsibility is still an ongoing debate. For example, the construction of production facilities in low-cost countries makes sense because it helps access to natural resources and low-cost labour, in addition to creating jobs and wealth. But if the production facilities pollute the surrounding environment, deplete the communities' access to natural resources, threaten the health of the communities, provide poor working conditions to workers and pay workers unfair wages, then this can be perceived as socially unfair and ethically wrong, even though these practices are considered legal in those countries involved. Efforts to reduce such harmful impacts may increase the cost of the production facilities, and subsequently competitiveness and profitability could be jeopardized. To constantly reduce costs (eg materials, labour, energy, legal compliance, ethical responsibility, etc) corporations tend to move their production facilities from one location to another, leaving behind the polluted environment, unemployment, and related social problems. This is equally ethically wrong.

Another emerging trade-off issue concerns the amount of profit a corporation should make, as opposed to the amount of wages its workers and suppliers should receive. Fairtrade is an example where large corporations pay at least the Fairtrade minimum price to Fairtrade-certified producers. This price aims to cover the costs of sustainable production for the producer, and is a safety net for the producers when market prices fall below a sustainable level. When the market price is higher than the minimum price, corporations must pay the market price. Producers are able to negotiate better prices based on factors such as quality. We have now seen the emergence of a wide range of Fairtrade products such as fruit, vegetables, tea, coffee, fruit juice, beverage, chocolate, confectionery, cotton, beauty products, and even gold. There is now emerging pressure facing some electronics manufacturers, who are accused of making very large profits whilst paying the lowest possible prices to workers and suppliers from low-cost countries. Just as with the questionable roles of exporters and traders in the chocolate industry (see following case study), people have started to ask the question, who actually adds value and who gets (fairly) paid?

Sustainability and corporate responsibility issues in the global chocolate industry

To understand the issues of sustainability and corporate responsibility facing the chocolate industry there is a need to trace the supply chain of cocoa beans from the farms where they are grown. Cocoa is the main ingredient for making chocolate, and one kilogram of cocoa beans produces approximately 40 bars of chocolate. Cocoa trees can be best grown in countries within 10° south and 10° north of the equator. Eighty-five per cent of the world's cocoa tree planting takes place on farms of less than two hectares with an average production of around one tonne per year (Fold, 2001) but the global production is 4 million tonnes per year (www.fao.org). Africa (countries such as Ivory Coast, Ghana, Nigeria, Cameroon) remains the world's leading cocoa-growing area. Indonesia, Brazil, Ecuador and the Dominican Republic are other large plantation countries.

Chocolate production starts with harvesting cocoa manually. The seed pods of cocoa will first be collected manually and transported to nearby processing sites. Each pod may contain up to 50 cocoa beans, which are collected by splitting opening the pods. Then the beans are selected and placed in piles, then placed in trays or covered with large banana leaves to undergo fermentation for five to eight days. During this process the beans turn brown, and they are then dried and packed into sacks ready for selling/ shipping. Until this stage, cocoa beans are largely processed by small growers, and due to lack of volume, market knowledge and finance, most growers are incapable of selling cocoa beans to the producer directly. Large exporters such as Cargill, ADM and Sal-Cacao are responsible for sourcing and washing cocoa, and selling it to the exchange market.

The remainder of the processing of cocoa beans is predominantly undertaken in Europe and North America, with the Netherlands and the United States the leading countries. The Ivory Coast is becoming a major producer. Typically, most cocoa-processing factories use machines to break down the cocoa beans into cocoa butter and chocolate. This process is called grinding. During this stage, cocoa beans go through winnowing and roasting processes and are then heated and will melt into chocolate liquor. Sugar and milk are added and then blended together with the chocolate liquor. There are millions of cocoa growers but 10 cocoa processors (mainly multinational companies) dominate about 70 per cent of the world's grinding output (www.fao.org). It is important to note that some processors source cocoa directly and perform trading of cocoa as well. The liquid chocolate is stored or delivered by tanker to the chocolate companies (eg Kraft Foods, Ferrero, Mars, Nestlé, etc) where flavouring, moulding, and packaging of the chocolates will take place.

Child labour is the major problem facing the chocolate industry. Responding to the problem, the main chocolate producers signed the so-called Harkin-Engel Protocol in 2001 (World Vision Australia, 2011). This protocol is a voluntary commitment which addresses the problem of forced child labour in West Africa and aimed to implement standards of public certification that cocoa has been grown without any of the worst forms of child labour by July 2005 (Chocolate Manufacturers Associations, 2001). This deadline was not met and a second deadline of 2008 was given, which was again not met. Failing to meet these deadlines has resulted in the breaking down of the trust relationship between the chocolate companies and their stakeholders, and has attracted the attention of the media and NGOs (see *The Dark Side of Chocolate*). In fact, the chocolate industry has made some progress in addressing the child labour issue. Cadbury and Nestlé in the UK have begun certifying their Dairy Milk and KitKat bars as Fairtrade. Mars announced its plans to use only sustainable cocoa for its products by 2020. Barry Callebaut, the world's largest chocolate producer, also announced they would focus more on certified Fairtrade products. However, Fairtrade chocolate occupies only about 1 per cent of the global chocolate market.

Another critique of the cocoa production concerns the lack of ecological sustainability because the expansion of the land used by farmers had led to monocultures, and this problem has been identified as the principal driver of the deforestation of the Guinean Rain Forest (GRF) of West Africa (Gockowski and Sonwa, 2010). The famous 'KitKat Killer' video clip produced by Greenpeace clearly highlights this issue. Today, the environmental sustainability of the chocolate industry is still an unresolved problem; the sustainability challenge facing the chocolate industry is very similar to other industries which involve farming and mining. Basically, such supply chains are controlled by large multinationals such as intermediaries, exporters, commodity exchanges, producers, and chocolate companies. Like many other commodities, cocoa beans are traded in many different complex trade channels but they are grown by mostly small farms. The cocoa exporters and traders make a lot more money than the growers but the real value they actually add to the supply chain is questionable. No one is responsible for the damage to the environment caused by the production of chocolate.

While global chocolate companies are facing a lot of pressure, the exporters, traders and grinders are 'invisible' and they have not yet participated in showing efforts for creating a sustainable supply chain. Furthermore, they are so dominant, even large chocolate companies are not able to influence or put pressure on them. The formation of cooperatives is a way to break down this power structure; the 'Cacaonica' cooperative consists of 350 members, receiving prices about 50 per cent higher than the market price due to the elimination of intermediaries. However, this solution is inadequate, and there are many other ethical and corporate responsibility issues facing the industry. In some cocoa growing countries, illegal trafficking of child labour is a more complex problem. Many years are required to establish certified products, and the chocolate companies remain unconvinced as to whether there is high demand for Fairtrade-certified chocolate. Although Fairtrade appears to be beneficial to small growers, these growers are facing other more serious problems such as security, fair and transparent legal systems, access to health and education, fair prices and timely payment, competitive wages for workers, and freedom from harassment and intimidation (Thomas, 2011). These problems are not directly created by the multinationals that source cocoa beans from these regions but should they not be responsible for providing a better life and working environment for the workers?

Ethical framework and codes of conduct

Should the goal of a business be solely to maximize shareholder value or profit? How about the health and safety of society, consumers and workers? The tainted milk incident in the People's Republic of China in 2008 demonstrates the serious consequences of running a business without ethical considerations. The incident affected thousands of victims, with some infants dying from kidney stones, others suffering from kidney damage and many others being hospitalized (Spencer, 2009). Melamine, an organic-based chemical used in the production of plastics and fertilizers, was added to milk to indicate a higher apparent protein content, but it can cause kidney stones and kidney failure. This is a perfect case example concerning corporate social responsibility, ethical and supply chain risk. Apparently, two milk dealers/middlemen sold milk containing Melamine to some major dairy companies in China who then failed to test whether the milk was pure and safe for human consumption. Furthermore, the chairperson of one of the dairy companies involved actually knew what had been illegally added to the milk. As a consequence, several criminal prosecutions took place, with two people being executed, another given a suspended death penalty, three receiving life imprisonment, two receiving 15-year jail terms, and seven local government officials, as well as the Director of the Administration of Quality Supervision, Inspection and Quarantine (AQSIQ), being fired or forced to resign. Over 20 companies implicated in the tainted milk were ordered by the Chinese government to pay a total of 1.1 billion Yuan (US $161 million; £97.5 million) to hundreds of thousands of consumers involved (Spencer 2009).

In order to truly be ethically responsible there is a need to understand the concepts of business ethics and morals. Ethics is generally defined as the 'inquiry into theories of what is good and evil and into what is right and wrong, and the inquiry into what we ought and ought not to do' (Beauchamp and Bowie, 1983, p 3). It is about what constitutes good and bad human conducts, including related actions and values (Barry, 1979). The main tools we need are principles or theories which guide what is good and evil or what we ought and ought not to do. There are many ethical theories and here are some which might be useful for business managers. The first group of theories, called consequential theories, urges managers to examine the consequences of their decisions and actions (Tsalikis and Fritzsche, 1989):

- The consequential theories (Egoism) argue that an act is ethical when it promotes the individual's best long-term interest. If an action produces a greater ratio of good to evil for the individual in the long run than any other alternative, then that action is ethical.

- The consequential theories (utilitarianism) suggest that we should always act so as to produce the greatest ratio of good to evil for everyone. This theoretical perspective emphasizes the best interests of everyone involved with the action.

The main problem of the above theories is that every individual has a different view on what constitutes good and evil, who is 'everyone' and how long is 'long term'. Alternatively, there are also theories which do not consider the consequences of the decision/action an individual makes (Tsalikis, and Fritzsche, 1989). These are called non-consequential theories:

- The single-rule non-consequential theories (golden rule) can be represented using a commonly accepted axiom – do unto others as you would have them do unto you. The main guiding principle is to treat others the way we would want to be treated.

- The single-rule non-consequential theories (Kant's categorical imperative) suggest that only when we act from duty do our actions have moral worth; we should act in such a way that we could wish the maxim or principle of our action to become a universal law.

- Rawls' principle of justice suggests that each person participating in a practice or affected by it should have an equal right to the greatest amount of liberty that is compatible with a like liberty for all.

- Ethical relativism argues that moral principles cannot be valid for everybody, and people ought to follow the convention of their own group.

In addition, there are theories that suggest the need to look at consequences as well as the rules, social norms and social obligations the decision makers ought to follow. Multiple-rule non-consequential theories argue that it is necessary to introduce consequences into ethical decision making but consequences alone do not make an act right; there are duties and obligations that bind us morally. Managers should be aware of the most obligatory duties (eg not lying, gratitude, justice, beneficence, self-improvement, non-injury). Garrett's principle of proportionality (Tsalikis, and Fritzsche, 1989) suggests that any moral decision involves three elements: what we intend, how we carry out the intention, and what happens (intentions, means, and ends). In additional to the legal punishment, a business person should consider the impacts of their actions on their individual integrity and professionalism. A business person may have the duty to maximize profit and, at the same time, be obliged to refrain from injuring people.

The terms 'ethics' and 'morals' are often used interchangeably. Taylor (1975, p 1) defines ethics as an 'inquiry into the nature and grounds of morality'. According to DeGeorge (1982, pp 13–15), morality is a term used to cover those practices and activities that are considered importantly right and wrong, the rules which govern those activities, and the values that are embedded, fostered, or pursued by those activities and practices. From a morality perspective, there are three kinds of business managers – immoral, amoral and moral.

- *Immoral managers* are those whose decisions, actions and behaviours are actively opposing what is deemed right or ethical. Such managers actively ignore what is moral in their decisions. Often they care about only the profitability and success of their organizations or themselves, and prioritize gains for the management group over even the shareholders. They see legal requirements as barriers which restrict their achievement of economic goals. Their strategy is dominated by the exploitation of opportunities for personal or corporate gain. The tainted milk incident previously discussed provides a good example of the behaviour of such managers.

- *Amoral managers* are neither moral nor immoral; they are simply insensitive to the moral obligations of the decisions they make. They lack ethical perception or awareness and often choose to meet only minimum legal requirements. Some of these managers may become amoral unintentionally. They may have good intentions but their decisions and actions could harm others. The use of plastic for packaging helps to reduce packaging cost, but it also unintentionally creates a waste disposal problem. There are also those who choose to be amoral intentionally because they believe ethical consideration is for private life, not for business. The selling of alcohol and cigarettes without providing adequate warnings to consumers is an example of the behaviour of intentionally amoral managers. They believe it is the consumers who should be responsible for the way they consume the products they choose to buy and consume.

- *Moral managers* are those who adhere to high levels of ethical norms and aim to be profitable while meeting legal requirements and ethical norms. They conform to high levels of professional conduct and apply sound ethical principles such as justice, rights and utilitarianism to guide their decisions. They prioritize short- and long-term shareholder interests and treat all stakeholders fairly and ethically. To achieve this, they demonstrate true commitment by establishing an ethical and responsible culture throughout the whole organization using an ethics committee, code of conduct and other management practices. They also provide leadership on ethical issues at the organizational and industrial levels.

In order to reduce immoral and amoral managers and to create more moral managers, corporations need to embed social responsibility, environmental responsibility and ethical culture into their organizations and their suppliers' organizations. Many commercial and non-commercial organizations and industrial associations have now developed their own ethical codes of conduct (CODs) or codes of ethics (COEs). Codes of conduct comprise the business principles a corporation expects its employees (and suppliers) to follow. Such codes may cover:

- Labour practices – employment (no forced labour, terms for termination), child labour, living wages, working hours, working conditions, health and safety, medical care, discrimination, human rights, gender equality, training, etc. One may refer to the International Labour Organization's labour principles for multinationals (ILO, 2014).

- Corporate governance – mutual respect, honesty, integrity, political contribution, charitable donation, legal compliance, bribery, corruption, fair competition, money laundering, working with governments and suppliers, conflict of interest, executive pay and bonuses, management of shareholder assets, confidentiality, share market trading rules, environment and safety, reputation, etc (for example refer to Siemens' compliance system at http://www.siemens.com/).

- Supplier practices – supplier responsibilities including contractual, labour, health and safety, environmental, society, legal compliance, transparency, reporting, confidentiality, etc (see the case study about the electronics industry later in this chapter).

- General moral and ethics – honesty, integrity, professionalism, mutual respect, collegiality, fairness, justice, legal compliance, etc.

Codes of conduct cannot be effective if the top management teams are unable to lead by example and demonstrate commitment by putting efforts into culture change within corporations and industries. Top management teams need to redefine the vision and mission of corporations by incorporating and clearly defining the importance of profit, people and planet (3Ps) or economy, environment and society (triple bottom line). These have to be filtered down to business objectives and targets with well-defined performance measurements for each metric; then there is a need to teach employees to engage in moral reasoning and to create a corporate culture in which ethical behaviour is both encouraged and rewarded. All these can increase the likelihood that a company's employees will act ethically. The following case study demonstrates how a company attempted to implement this new paradigm.

The Green Cargo story

Green Cargo (www.greencargo.com) is a national and international logistics company. The company has about 2,800 employees in over 100 locations throughout the Nordic region and Europe. It provides mainly rail-based logistics solutions for business in the Nordic region, and most of its revenue is generated from electric-powered rail-based freight. About a fifth of its revenue is generated from road transportation and third-party logistics services. As a transport company, environmental impact and social responsibility are two important issues. In addition, Green Cargo's business concerns many stakeholders: customers, employees, trade unions, suppliers, partners, government agencies, organizations, municipalities, neighbours and the media.

The core value of Green Cargo is sustainable development. This is reflected in their value statement: 'This should pervade everything we do: our products, our means of expression, the treatment of our customers and our conduct towards each other as employees.' To truly demonstrate commitment to social and environmental responsibility, the company has defined three routes (scoreboard) towards sustainable development:

- *Profitability* – measured in terms of finance (operating result, cash flow, return on capital, debt/equity ratio, cost per unit, efficiency) and customer performance (arrival reliability, customer index, availability).

- *Social concern* – measured in terms of employee (employee index, sick leave), safety (safety index, accident cost) and society performance (impacts on society).

- *Environmental performance* – measured in terms of environmental performance (carbon dioxide, energy consumption, environmental image).

Having set targets for the above performance metrics, the company developed several action programmes, starting in 2002 and 2003. The goals include the improvement of the financial results through increased revenues and reduced costs. However, this also meant staff needed to increase revenue through intensified sales operations such as offering road-based and third-party logistics services to the rail-based customers and vice versa. If not carefully managed, this could potentially increase emissions of carbon dioxide and non-renewable energy consumption.

To reduce operating costs, the company focused on reducing administrative costs through co-ordination and centralization. Next, the company optimized road-based operations through increased use of vehicles and a viable balance of owned and leased vehicles. To achieve efficient use of fuel and assets they established the Full Load Centre. The entire Green Cargo road-based operation was reviewed in terms of cost-effectiveness, customer needs and the environment. The company also attempted to optimize production resources through train 'pathing' and shunting to even out the 24-hour traffic flow and reduce production peaks. They attempted to fill more wagons by mapping out the empty wagon flow to identify business opportunities on sections currently running empty.

They learned that the constant attempt to improve the scoreboard has made a big contribution to the success of the action programmes. Performance measurements and key ratios have been integrated into targets at business unit level, and activities that could lead to target fulfilment are being defined in a clearer and more specific manner. Improvements in one target area have knock-on benefits for other areas and spur on the entire company to further efforts.

In terms of implementation, there is a need to fine-tune procedures for reporting, follow-up and control of the decision-making processes. There is also a need for a continuous improvement culture, in addition to the action programme. Such a culture allows daily operations to continue with further improvement and fine-tuning of procedures and tools for reporting, follow-up and control. This helps to shape guidelines for financial control within Green Cargo and the role of every business unit in the drive to achieve long-term sustainable profitability.

Global and industrial initiatives

While corporations learn to establish and implement codes of conduct and embed a corporate social responsibility culture, one can learn from multi-stakeholder initiatives and broad-based alliances at industrial and global levels. For example, the Global Compact is an initiative of the UN Secretary-General that promotes corporate responsibility by seeking to advance universal values. The underlying objective of the Global Compact is to enhance economic progress, foster corporate responsibility, global citizenship and institutional learning in addressing a variety of present-day issues.

By its efforts, the Global Compact creates a common forum for enterprises, labour and civil society organizations with the aim of expanding the benefits of economic development as well as limiting their negative impacts.

The Global Compact provides businesses with the challenge to adopt and apply 10 universal principles in the areas of human rights, labour and the environment and to integrate these principles into daily practices and management systems. These principles are based on the UN Universal Declaration of Human Rights, The International Labour Organization's Declaration on Fundamental Principles of Rights at Work, and the Rio Principles on Environment and Development. The 10 principles, listed below, have been adopted by various organizations as the basis for their ethical frameworks:

1 Businesses should support and respect the protection of internationally proclaimed human rights.

2 Businesses should make sure that they are not complicit in human rights abuses.

3 Businesses should uphold freedom of association and the effective recognition of the right to collective bargaining.

4 Businesses should ensure the elimination of all forms of forced and compulsory labour.

5 Businesses should ensure the effective abolition of child labour.

6 Businesses should ensure the elimination of discrimination in respect to employment and occupation.

7 Businesses should support a precautionary approach to environmental challenges.

8 Businesses should undertake initiatives to promote greater environmental responsibility.

9 Businesses should encourage the development and diffusion of environmentally friendly technologies.

10 Businesses should work against corruption in all its forms, including extortion and bribery.

Another new initiative concerns the disclosure of the social and environmental impacts of a company's activities. Back in the 1980s, the financial sector initiated a Social Investment Forum (SIF) to incrementally reform the existing economic system toward greater social responsibility through broad-based collaboration and alliance among investors, non-governmental environmental organizations, labour unions, etc. One of the initiatives of SIF was to develop, in partnership with environmental activist organizations, explicit codes of environmental conduct for industry, and ask companies to formally endorse them and report their performance on a regular basis. Some of the SIF activities later contributed to the establishment of the Global Reporting Initiative (GRI).

The Global Reporting Initiative (GRI) is a non-profit organization that promotes economic, environmental and social sustainability. GRI (www.globalreporting.org) aims to harmonize, standardize, clarify and unify practices of non-finance reporting, and to empower various societal actors with ways to access relevant information and use market and political mechanisms to demand from companies a certain level of accountability. GRI provides all companies and organizations with a comprehensive sustainability reporting framework that is widely used around the world. In the United States, other reporting initiatives such as the Public Environmental Reporting Initiative (PERI) and Global Environmental Management Initiative (GEMI) are used. Websites such as Accountability (www.accountability.org.uk) and CSRwire (www.csrwire.com) provide links to many corporations' CSR reports and case studies. There are also carbon disclosure initiatives focusing on reporting carbon emission. Such reporting initiatives can be beneficial to the companies as well as the public when there are clear guidelines on stakeholder inclusiveness, sustainability context, completeness and report quality (including balance, comparability, accuracy, timeliness, reliability and clarity). They can also be used as part of the company's corporate responsibility strategy, management approach and performance indicators.

The above 10 principles and reporting principles can be adopted by companies on a voluntary basis; there is no regulation covering all the principles as such. For companies truly serious in achieving sustainability leadership, there is a need to develop integrated management systems and processes toward sustainable development. For example, the 10 Ceres Principles (www.ceres.org) not only take into account human rights and sustainable natural resources, but also highlight the need for disclosure, management commitment, audits, reporting, and reducing the environmental, health and safety risks to their employees and their communities. International non-governmental organizations (INGOs) are also contributing to the development of codes of conducts for different industrial sectors, in addition to balancing the power between corporations and non-governmental or public interests. Instead of purely providing awareness and publication education, and engaging in lobbying and adversarial actions, INGOs work in partnership with companies to create initiatives such as the Marine Fisheries Councils, Rainforest Alliance, and many others. Many companies are participating in some of the above initiatives in order to develop their codes of conduct and improve their sustainability performance.

When it comes to supply chain risks and sustainability issues originating from suppliers, there are a lot of new approaches. Demanding that suppliers obtain certifications (eg ISO 14001) is an example; demanding they implement codes of conduct is another. This can be achieved by training and collaborating with suppliers to mitigate risks and/or to address sustainability issues.

Suppliers' codes of conduct in the electronics industry

Global electronics original equipment manufacturers (OEMs) have traditionally sourced the production of components from manufacturers in various countries. Health, safety and working conditions are critical issues for companies such as Hewlett Packard (HP), Apple Inc, etc. Even though such companies have codes of conduct, their social and environmental performance targets cannot be achieved without the involvement of the suppliers. The electronics industry's Electronic Industry Code of Conduct (EICC) was developed by Dell, Hewlett-Packard (HP), International Business Machines (IBM) and the electronic manufacturers Solectron, Sanmina-SCI, Flextronics, Celestica and Jabil.

This case study illustrates how HP implements the EICC to ensure that working conditions in the electronics industry supply chain are safe, that workers are treated with respect and dignity, and that business operations are environmentally responsible. The HP Suppliers Code of Conduct is based on the EICC and is independently maintained and updated to reflect HP standards and supplier operations. The scope of the codes is very wide – all suppliers involved in HP's manufacturing processes or in manufacturing HP's products, packaging, parts, components, subassemblies, and materials, or that provide services to or on behalf of HP, must comply with the EICC. It also applies to contingent workers – non-HP employees performing services at the direction of their respective employers for or on behalf of HP. The code is made up of five sections:

- *Section A:* Labour, including freely chosen employment, child labour avoidance, working hours, wages and benefits, human treatment, non-discrimination, freedom of association, etc.

- *Section B:* Health and safety, including occupational safety, emergency preparedness, occupational injury and illness, industry hygiene, physically demanding work, machine safeguarding, sanitation, food and housing.

- *Section C:* Environmental, including environmental permits and reporting, pollution prevention and resource reduction, hazardous substances, wastewater and solid waste, air emission, product content restriction, etc.

- *Section D:* Ethics, including business integrity, no improper advantage, disclosure of information, intellectual property, fair business, advertising and competition, protection of identity, responsible sourcing of mineral, privacy, non-retaliation etc.

- *Section E:* Management system, including company commitment, management accountability and responsibility, legal and customer requirements, risk assessment and risk management, improvement objectives, training, communication, worker feedback and participation, audits and assessment, corrective action process, documentation and records, supplier responsibility, etc.

HP provides training on the codes to its suppliers and expects them to train their suppliers. Suppliers are expected to sign a supplier social and environmental responsibility agreement with HP. Basically, suppliers are responsible for identifying any areas of operation that do not conform to HP's Supplier Code of Conduct and General Specification for the Environment, and for implementing and monitoring improvement programmes designed to achieve those requirements. HP may ask suppliers to submit a report describing actions taken and progress made and suppliers may be required to perform a self-assessment of their practices against the five sections of the codes. HP will be given access to suppliers' relevant records insofar as they relate to supply contracts, in order to verify information provided in the reports. HP in turn promises to use the reports and records only for the purpose of assessing the suppliers' progress in accordance with HP's codes.

The EICC Group further established a partnership with the Global e-Sustainability Initiative (GeSI) in 2005, which represents information and communications technology (ICT) companies in Europe, North America and Asia. The partnership was formed to develop common implementation tools for supply chain management and broaden the impact of this collaborative effort. With this technology, it is now possible for electronics OEMs to perform supplier risk assessment and self-assessment, apply a common audit methodology, and use a web-based platform to facilitate efficient and transparent information sharing among participants.

Supplier audit is an important practice in the electronics industry. The following example of Apple's approach illustrates how the audit may be conducted. Normally, an Apple auditor leads every onsite audit, supported by local third-party auditors who are experts in their fields. These experts are trained to use Apple's auditing protocol and assess requirements specified in Apple's supplier codes of conduct. There are annual audits for final assembly manufacturers and additional audits for suppliers posting certain risk levels. The auditors examine records, conduct physical inspections of manufacturing facilities, and evaluate management policies and procedures. The audits also take into account feedback from the community. There are surprise audits. Great emphasis is put on the correction and prevention of any violation of the supplier codes. Core violations such as involuntary labour, falsification of audit materials, worker endangerment, intimidation or retaliation against workers participating in an audit, or significant environmental threats could lead to termination of contracts and relationships with the involved suppliers.

In addition to the above, Apple also reports its environmental footprint. The total environmental footprint considers manufacturing, transportation, product use, recycling and facilities. Apple applies comprehensive lifecycle analysis to determine where its greenhouse gas emissions (GHGs) come from. The mapping of GHGs points to the need to address the manufacturing and product use processes. Manufacturing processes, including extraction of raw materials and product assembly, accounts for over 60 per cent of the total GHGs. This means a lot of collaboration with suppliers is required to address this issue.

Summary

Globalization means supply chains are facing greater risks and ethical dilemmas. New types of risks such as reputational and resource (sustainable) risks are becoming more critical. There is now an emerging realization that the types of businesses seen as desirable by society are those that behave responsibly towards shareholders, stakeholders, society and the environment. The public has started to realize the consequences of natural resource depletion. Companies are increasingly finding themselves competing for scarce resources. There are plenty of examples of companies being punished by the government, NGOs and customers for being negligent in taking care of health, safety, society and the environment. Companies are realizing that the pursuit of profits has to be balanced with the needs of society and the sustainability of the environment.

Even though some industries choose to create their own codes of conduct voluntarily, progress is not always satisfactory (for example in the chocolate industry). One of the main obstacles is that companies tend to see regulations as costly, and many managers see making money as their main job. Few companies see corporate responsibility and sustainability as a means to achieving sustainable competitive advantage. Most managers still see damage to the environment due to their supply chain activities as a reputational risk which could eventually reduce profitability, rather than seeing that such damages will eventually make the supply chain or business unsustainable. Incentives, regulations and pressures from NGOs do push industries forward but, as mentioned, great progress can only be made when social responsibility is viewed not just as an obligation but as part of the values of a corporation. Without such values, codes of conduct and regulations will not make much difference.

References

Barry, V (1979) Moral issues in business, in Danielle Beu and M. Ronald Buckley (2001), The hypothesized relationship between accountability and ethical behaviour, *Journal of Business Ethics*, 34, pp 57–73

BCI (2014) *Business Continuity Institute 2014 Supply Chain Resilience Survey*, Business Continuity Institute, Caversham

Beauchamp, T L and Bowie, N E (1983) *Ethical Theory and Business*, Prentice-Hall, Englewood Cliffs, NJ

Bowen, H R (1953) *Social Responsibility of the Businessman*, Harper, London

British Plastics and Rubber (2015) EuPC warns of 'damaging effects' of force majeure declarations, *British Plastics and Rubber*, 10 April, [online] available at: http://www.britishplastics.co.uk/News/-eupc-warns-of-damaging-effects-of-force-majeure-declarations/ [accessed 28 December 2016]

BSI (2015) 2014 SCREEN global supply chain intelligence report, *British Standards Institute* [online] available at: https://bsi.learncentral.com/ [accessed 28 December 2016]

Carroll, A B (1979) A three-dimensional conceptual model for corporate social performance, *Academy of Management Review*, 4, pp 497–505

Carroll, A B (1991) The pyramid of corporate social responsibility: toward the moral management of organizational stakeholders, *Business Horizons*, **34**, pp 39–48

Chocolate Manufacturers Associations (2001) Protocol for the growing and processing of cocoa beans and their derivatives products in a manner that complies with ILO convention 182 concerning the prohibition and immediate action for the elimination of the worst forms of child labor, signed on 19 September

Chopra, S and Sodhi, M S (2004) Managing risk to avoid supply-chain breakdown, *MIT Sloan Management Review*, **46** (1), pp 53–61

Christopher, M and Peck, H (2004) Building the resilient supply chain, *The International Journal of Logistics Management*, **15** (2), pp 1–14

Craighead, C W, Blackhurst, J, Rungtusanatham, M J and Handfield, R B (2007) The severity of supply chain disruptions: design characteristics and mitigation capabilities, *Decision Sciences*, **38** (1), pp 131–56

Daily Mail (2016) Second day of chaos for Delta passengers as the airline cancels 300 flights and struggles to find seats for customers who were unable to travel after a five-hour power outage yesterday, *Daily Mail* [online] available at: http://www.dailymail.co.uk/news/article-3731102/Second-day-travel-chaos-Delta-passengers-airline-struggles-seats-customers-flights-cancelled-five-hour-power-outage-yesterday.html [accessed 28 December 2016]

The Dark Side of Chocolate (2010) Film, directed by Miki Mistrati, *YouTube* [online] available at: https://www.youtube.com/watch?v=7Vfbv6hNeng [accessed 27 December 2016]

DeGeorge, R R (1982) *Business Ethics*, 2nd edn, Macmillan Publishing, New York

Drucker, P (1954) *The Practice of Management*, Harper & Row, New York

Ellis, S C, Henry, R M and Shockley, J (2010) Buyer perceptions of supply disruption risk: a behavioral view and empirical assessment, *Journal of Operations Management*, **28**, pp 34–46

Fold, N (2001) Restructuring of the European chocolate industry and its impacts on Cocoa production in West Africa, *Journal of Economy Geography*, **1**, pp 405–20

Friedman, M (1962) *Capitalism and Freedom*, University of Chicago Press, Chicago

Gockowski, J and Sonwa, D J (2010) Cocoa intensification scenarios and their predicted impact on CO_2 emissions, biodiversity conservation, and rural livelihoods in the Guinea rain forest of West Africa, *Environmental Management*, **48** (2), pp 307–21

Gov.uk (2016) Two-thirds of large UK businesses hit by cyber breach or attack in past year, *Department for Culture, Media & Sport* [online] available at: https://www.gov.uk/government/news/two-thirds-of-large-uk-businesses-hit-by-cyber-breach-or-attack-in-past-year [accessed 28 December 2016]

Gow, D (2008) Record US fine ends Siemens bribery scandal, *Guardian*, 16 December [online] available at: http://www.guardian.co.uk/business/2008/dec/16/regulation-siemens-scandal-bribery [accessed 28 December 2016]

Greenpeace (2011a) Dirty Laundry: unravelling the corporate connections to toxic water pollution in China, *Greenpeace* [online] available at: http://www.greenpeace.org/international/en/publications/reports/Dirty-Laundry/ [accessed 28 December 2016]

Greenpeace (2011b) The Detox Campaign, *Greenpeace* [online] available at: http://www.greenpeace.org/international/en/campaigns/detox/water/detox/intro/ [accessed 28 December 2016]

ILO (2014) Tripartite declaration of principles concerning multinational enterprises and social policy [online] available at: http://www.ilo.org/empent/Publications/WCMS_094386/lang--en/index.htm [accessed 28 December 2016]

Johnson, H L (1971) *Business in Contemporary Society: Framework and issues*, Wadsworth, Belmont, CA

Jun, M, Cheung, R, Jingjing, W and Qingyuan, R (2010) Greening supply chains in China: practical lessons from China-based suppliers in achieving environmental performance, *IPE/World Resources Institute* [online] available at: http://www.wri.org/sites/default/files/greening_supply_chains_in_china_en.pdf [accessed 28 December 2017]

Kahneman, J and Tversky, A (1979) Prospect theory: an analysis of decision under risk, *Econometrica*, 47 (2), pp 263–91

King, A A and Lenox, M J (2000) Industry self-regulation without sanctions: the chemical industry's responsible care program, *Academy of Management Journal*, 43 (4), pp 696–716

Knemeyer, A M, Zinn, W and Eroglu, C (2009) Proactive planning for catastrophic events in supply chains, *Journal of Operations Management*, 27, pp 141–53

Manne, H G and Wallich, H C (1972) *The Modern Corporation and Social Responsibility*, American Enterprise Institute for Public Policy Research, Washington, DC

Manuj, I and Mentzer, J T (2008) Global supply chain risk management, *Journal of Business Logistics*, 29 (1), pp 133–55

Spencer, R (2009) Two sentenced to death over China melamine milk scandal, *Telegraph*, 22 January, [online] available at: http://www.telegraph.co.uk/news/worldnews/asia/china/4315627/Two-sentenced-to-death-over-China-melamine-milk-scandal.html [accessed 28 December 2016]

Tachizawa, E M and Wong, C Y (2014) Towards a theory of multi-tier sustainable supply chains: a systematic literature review, *Supply Chain Management: An International Journal*, 19 (5/6), pp 643–63

Taylor, P W (1975) *Principles of Ethics: An introduction*, Dickerson Publishing Co Inc, Encino, California

Thomas, O (2011) *Sustainable Supply Chain Management in the Chocolate Industry*, GRIN Verlag

Tsalikis, J and Fritzsche, D J (1989) Business ethics: a literature review with a focus on market, *Journal of Business Ethics*, 8 (9), pp 695–743

UNISDR (2015) 2015 disasters in numbers [online] available at: http://www.unisdr.org/files/47804_2015disastertrendsinfographic.pdf [accessed 28 December 2016]

World Vision Australia (2011) Our guilty pleasure: exploitation of child labour in the chocolate industry – 10 years on from the Harkin-Engel Cocoa Protocol [online] available at: https://www.worldvision.com.au/Libraries/Reports/WVAReport_Our_Guilty_Pleasure.sflb.ashx [accessed 28 December 2016]

Sustainable logistics and supply chain management strategy

09

Concepts of corporate strategy

Corporate strategy is defined as:

> the direction and scope of an organization over the long term which achieves advantage for the organization through its configuration of resources within a changing environment, to meet the needs of markets and fulfil stakeholder expectations. (Johnson and Scholes, 1999, p 10)

It is accepted wisdom that if managers do not understand corporate strategy, they will be unable to make decisions that are consistently in the best interests of the firm as a whole. Thus, a corporate plan will always need to be developed in order to execute strategy and monitor progress against objectives.

Corporate plans usually contain three hierarchical levels. At the uppermost level, a firm's *strategic* plan considers its overall corporate mission objectives, service requirements, and how management intends to achieve its mission over the long term, ie greater than five years. This plan is very general and usually includes projected revenues and expenses, markets to enter or leave, lines of business or strategic business units (SBUs), expected relative share of business within the market, and sales and profits from existing lines of business compared with new lines.

At the next level, a *tactical* plan is often more specific than a strategic plan in terms of product lines and may be broken down into detailed quarterly revenues and expenses. A tactical plan usually has a time horizon of one to five years and should include a capital expenditure plan to indicate how much the firm will invest each year in new plant, equipment and other capital expenditure items.

Finally, the most detailed and lowest level plan is the *operating* or annual plan. This plan breaks out revenues, expenses, associated cash flows and activities by month for a one-year period. The operating plan is derived to guide the firm for the following year. Actual performance is monitored and compared to planned performance in order to anticipate problems and respond accordingly, and to communicate results to the firm's management.

The strategy planning process allows firms to develop their strategic, tactical and operational plans and consists of three elements: an analysis of its current situation, the implementation of its strategic choices, and its control and feedback mechanisms to ensure its strategy is working successfully. The current situational analysis involves the firm considering its internal Strengths and Weaknesses and its external Opportunities and Threats, and is commonly known as a SWOT analysis.

Further, the external analysis also requires consideration be given to the following external environments: Political, Economic, Social, Technological, and Legal. This analysis is commonly known by its acronym PESTL. However, as noted in Chapter 2, firms are now giving more consideration to the natural or ecological environment; this aspect has been included in the mix of external environments and the acronym has been amended to PESTLE. This analysis is often referred to as the 'where are we now' stage in the planning process.

After a situational analysis, the firm will develop various strategic, tactical and operational options for its business; these options comprise 'where are we going' and 'how do we get there' stages in the planning process. The firm then selects those options that best meet its criteria, which include return on investment, risk, and access to financial and non-financial resources, eg labour or human resources. Finally, the firm will implement these options and monitor and control its three plans to address the 'are we on course' stage of the planning process.

Much academic and practitioner work has been done on corporate strategy and strategic theories including examining competition through the threats of new entrants or substitutes or the bargaining power of customers or suppliers, considering product or SBU strategies relative to potential market growth rates and a firm's relative market share, and focusing on low-cost leadership or market differentiation are replete in the literature (Johnson and Scholes, 1999). An example of strategic, tactical and operational options related to the three major logistics and SCM activities of transportation (or 'Go') and warehousing and inventory management (or 'Stop') is given in the matrix in Table 9.1.

Table 9.1 Example of corporate strategy plans in logistics and SCM

Activity	Strategy	Tactical	Operating
Transportation	Choosing transport modes	Re-drawing warehouse delivery areas	Undertaking load planning or container fill decisions
Warehousing	Selecting the number, size and locations of warehouses	Redesigning internal warehouse layouts	Undertaking individual order picking and packing
Inventory management	Choosing a replenishment system and IT support	Adjusting safety-stock levels based on supplier risk profiles	Fulfilling individual orders

Natural environmental concerns or criteria related to the activities in Table 9.1 include the effect of different transportation options on emissions, fuel use and road congestion, energy use, emissions and land use related to warehousing and inventory management options. The complexity of these concerns or criteria is noted in the following box. Such complexity leads to a debate as to which concerns are the most important from the perspectives of both a firm and the natural environment. Further, firms need to know if there are existing frameworks or tools to evaluate these concerns properly.

Strategic sustainable choices for container shipping lines

The growth of container shipping over the past 30 years has also meant an increase in non-sustainable activities. What are some of the strategic choices and hence trade-offs facing shippers and ocean shipping lines as they endeavour to become more sustainable? Sustainability here means reducing the amount of CO_2 emissions from shipping activities, both in port and on the high seas, which results from shipping fewer containers, increasing container fill, shipping containers more efficiently and reducing movements and amendments, slow steaming, and switching fuels to lower-sulphur diesel.

McKinnon (2012) argued that by packing more products into containers, shippers could reduce the number of container movements and related CO_2 emissions. The pressure to minimize shipping costs would also give these firms a strong incentive to maximize fill. However, there are virtually no statistics in the public domain on the weight or cubic container (or cube) utilization of deep-sea containers.

McKinnon surveyed 34 large UK shippers and found that inbound flows into the UK were of predominantly low-density products bound for retail stores that 'cubed out' before they 'weighed out', ie 46 per cent of respondents importing containerized freight claimed that 90–100 per cent of containers received were 'cubed out'. On the other hand, weight restrictions were more of a problem for UK exporters, with 25 per cent of respondents reporting that 90 per cent or more of outbound containers were weight constrained, with 33 per cent of respondents 'weighing out' with more than 70 per cent of their containers. However, the composition of McKinnon's sample reflected a huge imbalance in the UK deep-sea container trade, with inbound containers outnumbering exports five to one. Thus, market flows inhibit the ability of shipping lines and customers to be more efficient in this area.

McKinnon also found that only around 40 per cent of the shippers have so far measured the 'carbon footprint' of their deep-sea container supply chains with just 6 per cent implementing carbon-reducing initiatives. The firms surveyed also assigned a relatively low weighting to environmental criteria in ocean carrier selection. So, while many shippers have the means to influence the carbon footprint of their maritime supply chains, the survey suggested that they are not currently using them explicitly to cut carbon emissions.

However, many of the measures that the UK shippers and their ocean carriers are implementing to improve economic efficiency, most notably slow steaming, are assisting carbon mitigation efforts. Slow steaming involves reducing the speed of a ship while at sea to reduce engine load and emissions. Slow steaming was mooted by the Maersk Line as a response to the 2008 economic recession as the spot-market price Maersk Line received in late 2008 for shipping containers from Asia to Europe or North America was around US $500 below their operating costs (Kolding, 2008). The relationship between ship speed and fuel consumption is non-linear and Maersk Line calculated that by redesigning their shipping schedules, using nine ships instead of eight to ensure customer volumes were handled and slowing their vessels' sailing speeds from 22 knots to 20 knots, they could reduce annual fuel consumption from 9,500 to 8,000 metric tonnes (Mt) and thus also reduce carbon emissions by 17 per cent from 30,000 to 25,000 Mt of CO_2. Maersk Line was also looking to make client processes more efficient as they had to make 1.6 million shipping amendments per year at that time, 80 per cent of which were due to client requests including booking cancellations of 20 per cent per year.

Finally, sulphur emissions as part of overall shipping-related particulate matter emissions is a problem for ships in port, as discussed in Chapter 1 (Corbett *et al*, 2007). Around 18 shipping lines signed the Fair Winds Charter (FWC) in 2010, which was an industry-led, voluntary, unsubsidized fuel-switching programme for ocean-going vessels calling at Hong Kong. The shipping lines committed to using fuel of 0.5 per cent sulphur content or less; however, if they all switched to the cleanest type of fuel available with 0.1 per cent sulphur, SO_2 emissions would drop by 80 per cent. The Charter expired at the end of 2014 as regulations mandating emissions control measures in port negated the need for it (Laursen, 2015).

In return for joining the scheme, ship operators got a 50 per cent reduction on port and navigation charges if registered vessels switched to burning low-sulphur diesel while berthed or anchored in Hong Kong. However, low-sulphur diesel is about 40 per cent more expensive than more heavily polluting marine 'bunker' diesel and the scheme only covered between 30 and 45 per cent of this higher cost. Thus, while shipping companies including Maersk Line, Orient Overseas Container Line (OCCL), Mitsui OSK Lines and Hyundai Merchant Marine registered fleets of 10–90 ships, other cost-conscious carriers were more reticent. APL and Hanjin Shipping were among the firms that signed the Fair Winds Charter, but neither registered any ships with the incentive scheme.

Thus, corporate strategic decision making for shippers and ocean shipping lines is not easy when it comes to sustainability in the face of thin profit margins, rising fuel and other operating costs and global economic uncertainty.

SOURCES Corbett *et al* (2007); Kolding (2008); McKinnon (2012); Wallis (2013); Laursen (2015).

Theoretical motivations underlying corporate and sustainable strategy

There are several theoretical motivations that underlie corporate and sustainable strategy, particularly in logistics and SCM, and the two major motivations are presented here. One is transaction cost economics (TCE) which contains four key concepts of bounded rationality, opportunism, asset specificity and informational asymmetry (Halldórsson *et al*, 2007):

1 Bounded rationality suggests that managers, while willing to do so, cannot evaluate accurately all possible decision alternatives to make a rational decision due to physical or other constraints.

2 Opportunism considers that managers will exploit a situation to their own advantage. This does not imply that all those involved in transactions act opportunistically all of the time; rather, it recognizes that the risk of opportunism is often present.

3 Asset specificity arises when one manager in an exchange invests resources specific to that exchange which have little or no value in an alternative use, and another manager in the exchange acts opportunistically to try to appropriate economic rent from that investment, economic rent being the additional amount over the minimum return the focal partner requires from the specific investment.

4 There is a relaxation of the perfect information assumption of neoclassical economic theory; many business exchanges are characterized by incomplete, imperfect or asymmetrical information.

Essentially, TCE describes the firm in organizational terms, or as a governance structure where decision makers respond to economic factors or transaction costs within the firm that affect both the structure of the firm and the structure of the industry within which it operates (Williamson, 1999). The increasing division of labour in a supply chain is determined by governance mechanisms and has been recognized as a means of competitiveness through terms such as 'strategic sourcing' or 'outsourcing'.

TCE, and the means of creating and developing resources and capabilities, can be applied to achieve supply chain improvement as the level of analysis moves away from the firm towards inter-organizational relationships (Halldórsson *et al*, 2007). This wider context of logistics and the supply chain, and in particular the adaptiveness of organizing economic activities under different economic conditions, has been investigated by

Williamson (2008) focusing on outsourcing. He considers how TCE should be operationalized, emphasizing the efficient alignment of transactions with alternative modes of governance. This cost–benefit view of governance and relationships supports the concepts of lean and agile logistics and supply chains presented in Chapter 1.

Another theoretical motivation is the resource-based view of the firm (RBV) from Penrose (2009), who in 1959 defined a firm as a collection of resources where growth is limited by its resource endowment. As the nature and range of these resources vary from firm to firm, so do the respective resource constraints. RBV suggests that a firm's resources and its capability to convert these resources to provide sustainable competitive advantage are the keys to superior performance (Grant, 1991).

In general, resources are referred to as physical, financial, individual and organizational capital for a firm and are necessary inputs for producing the final product or service forming the basis for a firm's profitability. They may be considered both tangible assets such as plants and equipment and intangible assets such as brand names and technological know-how. Resources can also be traded, but few resources are productive by themselves. They only 'add value' when they are converted into a final product or service (Grant, 1991).

Resources are also finite within the firm and are usually financed from internal resources, ie shareholder subscription or retained equity, or from external resources, ie debt financing. However, another option for developing more resources involves establishing relationships with supply chain partners to share resources or develop joint-resource activities to achieve a greater gain for both, ie the '1 + 1 = 3' notion of synergistic addition. This finite aspect of resources relates well to issues of sustainability.

Hart (1995) and Hart and Dowell (2011) proposed a natural resourced-based view of the firm (or NRBV) theory that argues a firm's resources and capability play an important role in the successful implementation of environmental supply chain practices. The NRBV considers there are three key strategic capabilities a firm should possess – pollution prevention, product stewardship and sustainable development – each generating their own sources of competitive advantage. However, key capabilities and competences also form part of Williamson's (1999; 2008) TCE view towards outsourcing, ie core competences are those activities unique to a firm that are non-replicable by other firms and which can achieve definable pre-eminence and provide unique value for customers. Thus, a firm that can identify its own core competencies regarding sustainability may be able to develop a competitive advantage.

Table 9.2   Five key competencies for sustainability

Competence	Concepts
Systems thinking competence	Variables/indicators, sub-systems, structures, functions. Feedback loops, complex cause–effect chains, cascading effects, inertia, tipping points, legacy, resilience, adaptation, structuration. Across multiple scales: local to global. Across multiple/coupled domains: society, environment, economy, technology. People and social systems: values, preferences, needs, perceptions, (collective) actions, decisions, power, tactics, politics, institutions.
Anticipatory competence	Concepts of time including temporal phases (past, present, future), terms (short, long), states, continuity (dynamics, paths), non-linearity. Concept of uncertainty and epistemic status including possibility, probability, desirability of future developments (predictions, scenarios, visions). Concepts of inertia, path dependency, including Delphi and future workshop interventions. Concepts of consistency and plausibility of future developments. Concepts of risk, intergenerational equity, precaution.
Normative competence	(Un)sustainability of current or future states. Sustainability principles, goals, targets, thresholds (tipping points). Concepts of justice, fairness, responsibility, safety, happiness, etc. Concept of risk, harm, damage; Concept of reinforcing gains (win–win) and trade-offs. Ethical concepts.
Strategic competence	Intentionality; transition and transformation. Strategies, action programmes, (systemic) intervention, transformative governance. Success factors, viability, feasibility, effectiveness, efficiency. Adaptation and mitigation. Obstacles (resistance, reluctance, path dependency, habits) and synergies. Instrumentalization and alliances. Social learning. Social movements.
Interpersonal competence	Functions, types and dynamics of collaboration. Strengths, weaknesses, success, and failure in teams. Concepts of leadership. Limits of cooperation and empathy. Concepts of solidarity and ethnocentrism.

SOURCE Adapted from Wiek *et al* (2011)

Wiek *et al* (2011) developed a set of five key competencies in sustainability for the express purpose of guiding academics in programme development. However, they are sufficiently generic that they are appropriate for other business and organizational sectors. Table 9.2 details these five key competencies along with the concepts underlying them.

Firms might be overwhelmed by Wiek *et al*'s call to acquire all these competences; four independent competencies and a fifth integrative competence. However, many of the concepts underlying these competencies already form part of a firm's strategy and its tactics. Thus it should be a relatively simple matter for the firm to include these competencies and concepts within their strategy, ensuring that similar ones are set into a sustainability context and incorporating new ones where appropriate.

The motivations of TCE and RBV, while appearing dissimilar, come together somewhat in the NRBV but more particularly are integrated in Elkington's (1994) model of the triple bottom line (TBL) of profits, people and planet as shown in Figure 9.1. The TBL posits that firms should focus not only on the maximization of shareholder wealth or economic value that they create in economies, but also on the environmental and social value that they add – or possibly destroy – in order to achieve long-term environmental security and egalitarian living standards for all human beings. The overlap of these three elements in the Venn diagram represents true sustainability from an economic, ecological and human perspective.

People or social performance pertains to fair and beneficial business practices toward labour and the community and region in which a firm conducts its business. Planet or environmental performance refers to sustainable

Figure 9.1 The 'triple bottom line'

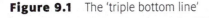

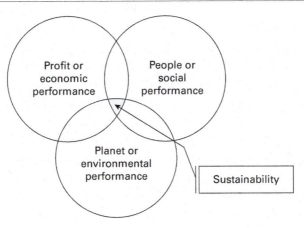

environmental practices. A TBL firm endeavours to benefit the natural order as much as possible or at least do no harm and curtail environmental impact. Finally, profit or economic performance is the bottom line shared by all commerce, conscientious or not. In the original concept, within a sustainability framework, the 'profit' aspect needs to be seen as the economic benefit enjoyed by the host society and is the lasting economic impact the firm has on its economic environment. This is often confused as being limited to the internal profit made by a firm. Therefore, a TBL approach cannot be interpreted as traditional corporate accounting plus social and environmental impact. The concept of TBL demands that a firm's responsibility should be to all stakeholders rather than only to shareholders.

Carter and Rogers (2008, p 368) defined sustainable supply chain management (SSCM) as:

> the strategic, transparent integration and achievement of an organization's social, environmental and economic goals in the systemic coordination of key inter-organizational business processes for improving the long-term economic performance of the individual company and its supply chains.

Their definition is based on the TBL as well as four supporting facets: risk management, transparency, organizational culture and strategy.

Risk management must go beyond managing short-term profits within an operational plan and also manage risk factors in the firm's products, waste, and worker and public safety through contingency planning and managing supply disruptions and outbound supply chains. Transparency not only includes reporting to stakeholders but also actively engaging them and supplier operations. Organizational culture for sustainability must be deeply ingrained and respect organizational citizenship and value and ethics. Lastly, sustainability must form part of an integrated corporate strategy. These four facets are not intended to be entirely mutually exclusive and thus interrelationships will exist among them.

It thus becomes clear that a firm's sustainable, environmental or 'green' agenda and corporate strategy will need to contain elements of the TBL and possibly other facets within whichever motivation a firm uses: TCE or RBV. However, it is also clear that an additional 'green' aspect, ie the colour of money, will emerge from achieving cost reductions through energy and emissions savings. Thus, like any other strategic business decision a firm will make, a sustainable or environmental agenda will be subject to its own cost-benefit tradeoffs. But how can a firm calculate all true and totals costs and benefits? Some form of performance measurement is required to fit into the three strategic plans.

Sustainable logistics and supply chain performance measurement

An old adage notes that 'you cannot manage what you cannot measure' and hence performance measurement is a staple in business for managing and navigating firms through turbulent and competitive global markets. They allow firms to track progress against their strategy, identify areas of improvement and act as a good benchmark against competitors or industry leaders. The information provided by performance measures allows managers to make the right decisions at the right times (Shaw et al, 2010).

Logistics and supply chain performance measures have conventionally been orientated around cost, time and accuracy. However, firms are now looking to include measures related to sustainability, ie the natural environment and corporate social responsibility (CSR). And yet there has only been limited research into incorporating a sustainability measure into the existing bank of logistics and supply chain performance measures.

Traditionally, logistics and supply chain performance measures have been quantitative and orientated around measuring cost, time and accuracy. Gunasekaran and Kobu (2007) identified almost 90 logistics and supply chain metrics, many of which overlap. The most widely used metrics identified were financial (38 per cent), but 60 per cent of all measures were functionally based. The proliferation of logistics and supply chain measures is a symptom of how supply chains are managed. Supply chains are complex structures and as a consequence practitioners have created numerous metrics to manage them, often duplicating the same metrics within and across supply chain nodes or sites.

Sustainable supply chain performance measures (SSCPM) have focused on greenhouse gas (GHG) emissions due to the importance attached to them in the fight against climate change that has developed from a historical perspective, as discussed in Chapter 2. To wit, the 2015 COP 21 Paris agreement legally bound industrialized nations to limit temperature rises to below 2 degrees Celsius.

The UK Department for Environment, Food & Rural Affairs, or Defra (2006), identified 22 sustainability performance indicators in four key categories that are considered to be significant to UK businesses: emissions to air; emissions to water; emissions to land; and natural resource use. To help manage these four categories, firms can adopt an environmental management system (EMS).

Environmental management systems

Environmental management systems include the International Organization for Standardization's ISO 14001 introduced in Chapter 6 (ISO, 2009) or the European Union's eco-management and audit scheme (EMAS, 2009) to provide guidance on mitigating their impact on the environment.

ISO has also developed ISO 14031:1999, an environmental performance evaluation tool which provides firms with specific guidance on the design and use of environmental performance evaluation and on the identification and selection of environmental performance indicators. This allows any firm, regardless of size, complexity, location and type, to measure their environmental performance on an ongoing basis (ISO, 2009). ISO 14031 divides environmental performance indicators into three classifications (Shaw *et al*, 2010):

- *Management Performance Indicators (MPI)*: an indicator of a firm's effort in influencing its environmental performance; for example, environmental costs or budget (dollars per year), percentage of environmental targets achieved, and time spent responding to environmental incidents (person hours per year).

- *Operational Performance Indicators (OPI)*: an indicator of an organization's operational environmental performance; for example, raw materials used per unit of product (kilograms per unit), hours of preventive maintenance (hours per year), and average fuel consumption of vehicle fleet (litres per 100 kilometres).

- *Environmental Condition Indicators (ECI)*: an indicator of local, regional, national or global conditions of the environment, which is useful for measuring the impact of an organization on the local environment; for example, frequency of photochemical smog events (number per year), contaminant concentration in ground or surface water (milligrams per litre), and area of contaminated land rehabilitated (hectares per year).

EMAS is the second most popular EMS standard in Europe. Structurally the ISO 14001and EMAS standards are very similar, but there are some fundamental differences between them (Murphy, 2013). For example, EMAS firms must be compliant with relevant environmental rules and regulations to guarantee their certification, and yet ISO 14001 states that although a commitment to compliance is required in the policy, compliance is not essential to keep their certification. Further, the evaluation of the EMAS standard is guaranteed by obligatory three-yearly audits where all cycles are checked and a statement is made public. ISO 14001 audits check for environmental system performance against internal benchmarks with no penalties for no improvements, and the frequency is left to the discretion of the individual firm. These differences are perhaps the reason that the number of ISO 14001 certifications in the UK is far greater, 14,346 in 2010, than EMAS registrants (289 in 2012); ISO 14001 appears to be the least demanding of the two standards.

From a broader perspective, the Global Reporting Initiative (GRI) developed in the late 1990s encourages the disclosure of sustainability performance data by organizations. GRI is very exacting over the calculation and reporting of these indicators, which enables standardization of outputs for benchmarking. GRI provides an alternative perspective on how organizations can measure and report on their environmental performance, designed as an external sustainable reporting tool to aid external benchmarking, and although it provides a useful guide of what to measure there is no indication of how this is applied to the end supply chain (Shaw, 2013). Similarly, Morana and Gonzalez-Feliu (2015) also propose a sustainability dashboard for measuring urban delivery performance. They identified a range of social, economic and environmental indicators, but the focus of their study was on the development of indicators rather than reporting.

Other country-specific reporting tools that exist include the UK's Carbon Reduction Commitment (CRC), which is a mandatory carbon emissions reporting and pricing scheme for large public and private organizations that use more than 6,000 megawatt hours (MWh) of electricity per year (Carbon Trust, 2016). In addition, other large global companies have demonstrated their green compliance to shareholders by being part of schemes such as the Dow Jones Sustainability Index or the FTSE Good Index. An example of a trade association's suggestions to help a firm make a business case for reducing emissions is discussed in the following box.

Making a business case for reducing emissions

The UK's IGD, formerly known as the Institute of Grocery Distribution, has developed a free online guide designed to help businesses understand what they can do to reduce their greenhouse gas emissions, and communicates it in a way that will provide the business case for investment in greenhouse gas (GHG) reduction initiatives. The guide uses numerous best practice examples from industry and offers links to tools and further sources of information to help organizations reduce their emissions. The guide focuses on three key drivers that organizations need to be aware of and address in order to reduce their GHG emissions and become a more environmentally sound business. These drivers are regulation, financial considerations and reputation. The guide also includes information on emissions regulation, financial benefits of reducing emissions, reputational benefits of emissions reduction, information on climate change and insight on future issues, and tools and resources.

Key UK regulations discussed in the guide include the Climate Change Act (2008), Climate Change Levy (CCL), Carbon Reduction Commitment (CRC) and Energy Performance of Buildings Regulations. IGD's hierarchy of steps to reduce GHGs in accordance with the various regulations is to calculate the amount of emissions or 'carbon footprint', avoid and/or reduce emissions by paying attention to emission sources and offset through suitable carbon trading schemes.

Regarding financial considerations, IGD notes that GHG emissions are likely to have negative cost implications due to taxation, restriction on activities with associated costs, and possibly fines for non-compliance. However, reducing emissions can result in financial savings such as energy costs from direct action or better working practices and a comprehensive list is provided regarding heating and lighting in offices, factories and warehouses. IGD also advises that there may be tax breaks for certain kinds of investments to reduce emissions that firms should be aware of.

Lastly, a firm's reputation may be at risk if it is not seen to be responsible in dealing with GHGs. There are various government and NGO indices and reports detailing the environmental performance of firms and firms also need to be aware of their existence and whether or not they are candidates to be on them.

While IGD's constituents are in the grocery sector, both manufacturing and retail, the guide is a good generic source for all sectors. Further, many businesses in the grocery sector and others are small to medium-sized enterprises (SMEs) and in this regards the guide also provides much helpful information and advice that SMEs may not be aware of or have access to.

SOURCE IGD (2012a).

There are a number of factors to consider when designing, implementing and evaluating an environmental management system. The most important factor is that no single approach is suitable for every firm; each firm has its own management systems and environmental impacts, organizational culture and structure. Further, the approach selected must also be responsive to all possible audiences such as management, employees, shareholders and the public. Many of the systems proposed by regulatory bodies are based on a plan, do, check and act framework. The planning stage is to set the targets and objectives and to detail how these will be attained through assigning individual responsibility. Implementing or 'doing' the system means providing the necessary resources to accomplish the objectives which have been set. Actions for checking and correcting areas which require attention include monitoring and measurement to determine how well the organization is achieving stated environmental goals. Finally, there needs to be a periodic review of the actions to ensure progress is as expected; the results from these reviews should also be documented as a log for continuous improvement (Murphy, 2013).

Lifecycle assessment

The all-encompassing method proposed for environmental performance measurement is the lifecycle assessment (LCA), also introduced in Chapter 6, which is a 'cradle-to-grave' approach for assessing industrial systems and supply chains (Curran, 2006). The LCA approach begins with the gathering of raw materials from the earth to create products for consumption, ie the premise behind the definitions of logistics and supply chain activities provided in Chapter 1, and ends at the point when all materials are returned to the earth, ie the premise of reverse logistics and product recovery management discussed in Chapters 1 and 5.

LCA evaluates all stages of a product's lifecycle from the perspective that they are interdependent, meaning that one stage leads to the next. LCA also enables the estimation of cumulative environmental impacts resulting from all stages in the product lifecycle, often including impacts not considered in more traditional analyses, for example raw material extraction, material transportation and ultimate product disposal. By including these impacts throughout the product lifecycle, LCA provides a comprehensive and holistic view of the environmental aspects of the product or process and a more accurate picture of the true environmental trade-offs in product and process selection (Grant, 2012).

The ISO 14000 series of standards formalize LCA components; according to ISO 14040, LCA consists of four phases: goal and scope definition for the LCA, ie can a firm do a true cradle-to-grave analysis; inventory analysis at each node in the industrial system or supply chain; the impact assessment at each stage; and interpretation of the findings. These phases are not simply followed in a single sequence as LCA is an iterative process in which subsequent iterations can achieve increasing levels of detail or lead to changes in the first phase prompted by the results of the last phase. LCA has proven to be a valuable tool to document and analyse environmental considerations of product and service systems that need to inform decision making for sustainability, and ISO 14040 provides a general framework for LCA.

However, no firm has complete visibility of its entire supply chain. Indeed, the simplified supply chain shown in Figure 1.1 represents a linear supply chain with only one tier 1 customer and supplier for the focal firm. In reality, the focal firm will have many tier 1 relationships, as will all the tier 1 customers and suppliers, and the concept of a focal firm's supply chain explodes into operational complexity. Further, the impacts of globalization discussed in Chapters 1 and 2 also add geographical and cultural complexity. Thus, a focal firm may only be able to perform an LCA across two tiers in either direction.

The UK retail grocery trade association, IGD, has developed an environmental sustainability matrix to assist the grocery sector in looking at important sustainability aspects across several tiers (IGD, 2012b). Its four key aspects are GHGs, water, packaging and waste and its six supply chain components are raw materials, manufacturing, storage, transport, wholesale and retail, and end user and end-of-life. These aspects and components are quite specific to this sector as food production and sales are about a 'plough to plate' perspective.

GHGs come from a variety of sources in food production and manufacturing such as fertilizers, animal methane gas and fossil fuels. For example, embedded GHGs in bread comprise 45 per cent for raw material production eg wheat, 23 per cent in manufacturing eg baking, 6 per cent in logistics, distribution and retail, 23 per cent in consumer use, and 3 per cent in recycling and disposal. Water of course is used heavily in agriculture and production but also in cleaning, cooking and sanitation by consumers. For example, one 150-gram hamburger, the same size as the yogurt pots discussed in Chapter 1, requires 2,400 litres of water. As noted in Chapter 2, IGD has also been at the forefront of water stewardship.

Packaging and raw materials waste from the UK food and drink sector per year is estimated to be 5.1 million tonnes. Efforts have been undertaken by IGD in conjunction with food manufacturers and retailers to reduce the amount of packaging waste used in the food supply chain. The use of reusable packaging and transport devices, such as plastic totes for fresh produce and roll cages for milk, has helped this situation. However, cardboard used in shelf-ready packaging for products such as crisps and snacks lends credence to the notion that efficient consumer response (ECR) initiatives and the need to time-compress replenishment of store shelves, ie logistics and SCM objectives, have driven the packaging agenda.

Lastly, food waste that is discarded throughout the supply chain amounts to 11.3 million tonnes per year, with 8.3 million tonnes or 74 per cent of such waste being generated by households. The discussion in Chapter 2 on social supermarkets presents one way of ensuring edible food is not wasted, while another use for waste food is presented in the following box.

Anaerobic digestion

Governmental waste policies, the increasing environmental agenda, the spectre of peak oil and rising fuel prices have focused attention on 'green' methods of energy generation such as wind, solar and anaerobic digestion. Anaerobic digestion is a resource recovery technology which allows organic matter, eg food waste, to decompose, generating biogas and digestate which can be then utilized for energy and fertilizer respectively. Anaerobic digestion thus has an additional benefit over other renewable energy sources as it helps reduce the amount of waste going to landfill.

The use of anaerobic digestion to produce biogas energy from food waste is a practical way to mitigate between 100 and 160 kilograms of CO_2 equivalent per tonne of food waste. The total renewable gas supply from UK-available biodegradable resources that could be recovered by anaerobic digestion represents 10 per cent of total UK energy demand and two-thirds of the UK government's 2020 renewable energy target.

The UK councils of North Lincolnshire and NE Lincolnshire in England requested a study of possible sites to build an anaerobic digestion plant (ADP) to service both councils and to minimize the costs involved in collecting and transporting food waste to the site as opposed to either incinerating it or delivering it to a landfill. A research team from the Logistics Institute at Hull University Business School used standard logistics and supply chain network and centre of gravity location modelling techniques to determine an optimal location that was cost efficient and operationally effective regarding customer service and food waste 'feedstock' availability.

The team first identified 1,394 firms within the two councils' areas that could provide appropriate feedstock for the ADP, including major firms such as educational establishments, hospitals, hotels, restaurants and cafes, and then qualified by a survey those firms who would be able to provide such feedstock. Two major food conurbations evolved around the port towns of Grimsby and Immingham and the inland town of Doncaster. However, businesses, motivated by cost reduction, are already very good at waste reduction; thus households appear to provide the largest source of feedstock. The amounts of food waste at postcode sector level were then used in the modelling process.

The logistics and supply chain decision factors for the ADP included locations of supply sources, locations of a potential ADP plant, supply forecast by source of supply, transportation costs between pairs of sites, and desired response time. Three potential locations were identified based on the availability of land and the need to be close to a substation to feed energy into the UK national energy grid. Feasibility scenarios were then modelled based on prices from feed-in tariffs (FITs) from the operators of the energy grid, and the costs to build and operate the ADP including costs to obtain and transport feedstock.

The study showed that North Lincolnshire and North East Lincolnshire councils could have separate feasible anaerobic digestion facilities as long as the costs of additional collections were avoided. However, the best solution appeared to be a combined site feeding biogas into the grid with the site being located at the centre of gravity for one of the councils. This study is an example of how logistics and SCM can make a positive impact on sustainability.

SOURCE Menachof et al (2010).

Assessing sustainable choices and initiatives

Once a firm selects a framework or technique to include sustainability into its corporate strategy, eg a TBL, EMS or LCA approach, it will then need to assess such matters as the economic viability, technological feasibility and environmental sustainability of that strategy. Economic development, for example a port expansion, will invariably increase environmental pressure, some of which will be ameliorated through specific management actions. For example, increasing a port's area will cause the loss of estuarine habitats such as mudflats or salt marshes or disturb overwintering wading birds or fish such as eels and salmon migrating between the sea and the catchment.

Such relationships between the impacts on the environment by society and in this case logistics and SCMs, and responses to such impacts, can be formalized through the development of a systems-based approach.

Integrated environmental management requires many aspects to be combined into a holistic system. The problems caused by materials (eg pollution) or infrastructure added to or removed from the system (eg aggregates, wetland space) require a risk assessment framework. This is then managed using actions through vertical integration of governance and the horizontal integration of stakeholder action. Those actions are required to ensure the natural system is protected and maintained while at the same time the benefits required by society are delivered (Elliott, 2014).

Consideration of these interactive environmental relationships first gives rise to assessing whether the strategy or strategic option fulfils various criteria related to environmental management. Barnard and Elliott (2015) proposed the '10 tenets' of environmental management to facilitate such assessment so that management of and a solution for an environmental problem will be sustainable and not environmentally deleterious. Further, they should fall within what is possible in the real world while taking note of the socio-economic and governance aspects. Finally, fulfilling the 10 tenets would also mean that environmental management would potentially be seen by wider society as achieving sustainability and in turn would be more likely to be accepted, encouraged and successful. The 10 tenets are listed below and are self-explanatory.

Ten tenets of environmental management

1 **Socially desirable/tolerable.** Environmental management measures are required or at least are understood and tolerated by society as being required; that society regards the protection as necessary.

2 **Ecologically sustainable.** Measures will ensure that the ecosystem features are functioning and the fundamental and final ecosystem services are safeguarded.

3 **Economically viable.** A cost–benefit assessment of the environmental management indicates (economic/financial) viability and sustainability.

4 **Technologically feasible.** The methods, techniques and equipment for ecosystem and society/infrastructure protection are available.

5 **Legally permissible.** There are regional, national or international agreements and/or statutes which will enable and/or force the management measures to be performed.

6 **Administratively achievable.** The statutory bodies such as governmental departments, environmental protection and conservation bodies are in place and functioning to enable successful and sustainable management.

7 **Politically expedient.** The management approaches and philosophies are consistent with the prevailing political climate and have the support of political leaders.

8 **Ethically defensible.** How costs of acting are determined and calculated for current and future generations.

9 **Culturally inclusive.** Notwithstanding actions that are desired and tolerated by society there may be some cultural considerations taking precedence.

10 **Effectively communicable.** Communication is required among all the stakeholders to achieve the vertical and horizontal integration encompassed in the foregoing nine tenets.

SOURCE Barnard and Elliott (2015).

Next, a framework is required for the setting and structuring of environmental problems. The DAPSI(W)R(M) framework (Scharin *et al*, 2016) encompasses *Drivers*, which are the key demands of society (for example a desire for economic growth) that have *Activities* which are responsible for creating *Pressures* (for example a proposed port development and the associated changes such as loss of habitat, influences on water quality and stressors such as noise or light pollution, etc). Such *Pressures* in turn give rise to *State Changes* in the environment, (for example a loss of habitat and ecological structure and functioning). If these adverse changes are not addressed they then lead to *Impacts* on human *Welfare* together representing changes to the receiving environment (for example direct human interaction with the environment). In order to prevent or remedy these adverse changes, a *Response* by society is required that can be verified as *Measures*, such as economic instruments or legal constraints. Hence the DAPSI(W)R(M) approach gives the framework for defining, scoping and then addressing environmental problems.

Figure 9.2 Application of the 10 tenets, DAPSI(W)R(M) and bow-tie techniques for environmental management

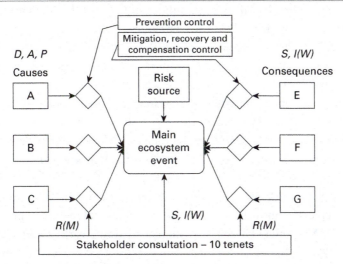

SOURCE Adapted from Grant and Elliot (2016).

To integrate the DAPSI(W)R(M) approach and the 10 tenets criteria Grant and Elliot (2016) adopted a bow-tie risk management analysis (Ferdous *et al*, 2012) that combines fault tree analysis (FTA) and event tree analysis (ETA) as shown conceptually in Figure 9.2.

FTA provides a graphical relationship between the undesired event and basic causes of such an occurrence while ETA is a graphical model of consequences that considers the unwanted event as an initiating event and constructs a binary tree for probable consequences with nodes representing a set of success or failure states. The follow-up consequences of the initiating event in ETA are usually termed as events or safety barriers, and the events generated in the end states are known as outcome events. Both techniques use the probability of (eg failure or success) basic events and events as quantitative inputs and determine the probability of occurrence for the top event as well as outcome events for likelihood assessments. It is a combined concept that integrates both techniques in a common platform, considering the top event as a critical event or risk source.

Like FTA and ETA, bow-tie analysis also uses the probability of failure of basic events as input events on the FTA site and the probability of occurrence (either failure or success) of events as input events on the ETA site for evaluating the likelihood of critical and outcome events. For quantitative bow-tie analysis, the probabilities of input events are required to be known either as precise data or defined probability density functions (PDFs) if uncertainty needs to be considered. The bow-tie analysis method can be further developed with quantitative modelling; for example, Bayesian Belief Network modelling based on probabilities of cause and effect has recently been linked to bow-tie analysis (Stelzenmüller *et al*, 2015).

Linking this method to a DAPSI(W)R(M) approach based on the 10 tenets criteria enables scoping, identification and analysis of the causes (based on the *Drivers, Activities* and *Pressures*) leading to the main events; anticipatory prevention measures (the *Responses* using *Measures*), including those limiting the severity of the main event; the consequences of the events (the *State Changes* and the *Impacts* on human *Welfare*); and mitigation and compensation measures (ie the *Responses* using *Measures)* aimed at minimizing those consequences.

The corporate strategy that a firm develops should include sustainability to meet increasing business, societal and governmental requirements as part of a good CSR policy. There are a number of frameworks and techniques such as TBL, EMS and LCA that a firm can use to consider sustainability holistically within its corporate strategy. Further, the DAPSI(W)R(M), 10 tenets and bow-tie analysis techniques discussed in this section allow the firm to ensure that its sustainability strategies meet its objectives and those of its stakeholders. While this section has discussed these latter tools on a conceptual basis, the following box provides a concrete example of their use for an upcoming major offshore wind farm that is intended to provide increased renewable energy use in the UK market by 2020.

Assessing offshore wind energy in the UK

The UK government's 2009 Renewable Energy Directive set a target for the country to achieve 15 per cent of its energy consumption from renewable sources by 2020, compared to 3 per cent in 2009. Offshore wind is expected to contribute to that energy target and the sector has made steady progress since. At the end of 2015, the European Wind Energy Association reported that of the 11.0 gigawatts (GW) of offshore wind capacity in Europe, 46 per cent or 5.0 GW was in UK waters.

The UK Crown Estate, which owns most of the UK's seabed out to a 12-nautical-mile territorial limit, has allocated and leased sites for offshore wind exploitation through three series of rounds. All 14 Round 1 projects are already in operation and generated almost 1.2 GW of clean electricity in 2014. Eight out of 15 Round 2 projects have also been fully commissioned and generated 2.4 GW in 2014, and there are seven Round 3 projects to be commissioned by 2025 (Danilova *et al*, 2016). Several manufacturers have expressed interest in developing manufacturing facilities in the Humber River Estuary for the wind turbines required for these farms. A study carried out as part of a University of Hull research project investigating the Humber's economic future found that increased economic activity in the Yorkshire and Humber region due to offshore wind developments is estimated to be between £4–10 billion gross value-added (GVA) per year and 8,000–15,000 new jobs through to 2020 (Wong *et al*, 2013). The study considered this potential development in terms of six of the 10 tenets for development and environmental management. Following are the assessments of the six tenets:

1 *Ecological sustainability*: different impacts on the environment were identified: impacts on marine mammals (mortality through collision with increased ship traffic, leaving the area due to disturbances, noise damage, and disruption of normal behaviour); fish (electromagnetic field, habitat loss, alteration of species composition); and birds (mortality through collision and disruption of feeding grounds, disruption of migration routes). However, wind energy is unlimited, unlike fossil fuels, non-polluting and safe. Moreover, eventual environmental disruptions are almost site-specific and temporary. Thus, a development score of 7 was awarded. On the other hand, habitat recreation (creation of seabed/ surface area, water column and air space) is a valid compensation scheme and if supported by specific characteristics of implementation (providing shelters as a fish aggregating device, turbine installation in areas with low levels of bird movements and away from conservation zones) positive effects can be greatly enhanced. Similar methods have been used in the past, tested on similar offshore structures (oil rig platforms) and in similar environmental circumstances. Moreover, costs related to site preparation are capital and require little maintenance. Thus, an environmental management score of 7 was awarded.

2 *Social desirability*: there is a general perception that an offshore wind farm is less constrained by social acceptance because visual impacts and noise problems, if sufficiently distant from the coast, are minimized. Although offshore sites are not simply and automatically preferred to onshore sites, approval rates for offshore wind farms have been around

90 per cent with consent periods of 22 months compared to 51 per cent and between 20 and 52 months for onshore wind farms. Moreover, offshore wind is generally seen as an unrepeatable opportunity to generate an increase in jobs and investment in the Yorkshire and Humber region where the unemployment rate is among the highest of the English regions. It therefore seems plausible to affirm that the development of the proposed offshore wind farms (development score: 8) and relative measures for habitat recreation (environmental management score: 10) would be considered positively by the local population although eventual public inquiries resulting in consent delays should be taken into account.

3 *Ethical defensibility*: offshore wind power, like other renewable sources of energy, offers security against energy shortcomings from other sources, being clean, domestic, carbon dioxide emission free and not contributing to climate change. Moreover, it is capable of generating remarkable allied industries and activities both at regional and national level. Therefore, it is not an exaggeration to assume a high ethical defensibility value (development score: 8, environmental management score: 10).

4 *Cultural inclusivity*: site selection undertaken by the UK Crown Estates is based on a zonal approach (awarded to one development partner) and a cumulative impact is calibrated on an ongoing basis engaging holistically with stakeholders. Moreover, the marine resource system model (MaRS) used is a robust, transparent and rational approach to site selection and capable of identifying and resolving eventual planning conflicts and assessing the suitability of sites for specific projects by identifying areas of opportunity and constraint, detecting how different activities would interact in a particular area. It is thus clear that cultural traditions and local needs are taken into account before a final decision is taken and that, given the numerous variables and interests involved, changes, although minimal, should be considered unavoidable (development score: 8, environmental management score: 9).

5 *Effective communicability*: relevant documentation and updates are posted on websites of the industrial consortia developing the proposed offshore wind farms and local media, especially newspapers, constantly disseminate updates. Moreover, public consultations have been undertaken to ensure not only social acceptability but also

effective communication and wide public participation. Therefore, a high compliance is suggested (development and environmental management scores: 8).

6 *Political expedience*: national and local political commitment is clear and a deliberate support to the development of offshore wind farms is being pursued (development score: 8, environmental management score: 9).

While readers may want to deconstruct the scores and their respective rationales based on their own cultural values and beliefs, this analysis nevertheless provides a good illustration of the application of the assessment of the development and management tenets that have been developed for just such a purpose.

SOURCES Wong *et al* (2013).

Summary

Logistics (and SCM since the 1980s) has been recognized as an important business function over the past 50 years and has grown from a transaction-oriented, tactical function to a process-oriented, strategic function. Today, logisticians and supply chain managers have greater opportunities to participate actively in setting strategy, meeting challenges and contributing to the success of the firm. The two major strategic motivations are transaction cost economics and the resource-based view of the firm.

However, a strategic imperative to include sustainability as part of the 'triple bottom line' means that logistics and SCM firms will need to incorporate these three motivations in future. In order to operationalize this third motivation, firms will first need to develop sustainable logistics and supply chain performance measures. One way to do so is to adopt an environmental management system through ISO's 14000 series or the European Union's eco-management and audit scheme. Further, using tools such as a lifecycle assessment and confirming that any strategic option fulfils criteria such as the 10 tenets of sustainable management will allow a firm to ensure it is properly addressing the three mandates in the 'triple bottom line': sustainable maintenance of the natural environment, economic growth and development, and a regard for societal and human concerns on this fragile planet.

The rewards for recognizing and accepting these challenges in a creative and proactive manner should prove to be substantial. It is the hope and sincere desire of the authors that we have presented the materials in this book in such a way as to encourage readers to properly recognize and strongly consider these issues that are before us.

References

Barnard, S and Elliott, M (2015) The 10-tenets of adaptive management and sustainability: applying an holistic framework for understanding and managing the socio-ecological system, *Environmental Science & Policy*, 51, pp 181–91

Carbon Trust (2016) CRC energy efficiency scheme: how it works and advice on managing the CRC as a business opportunity [online] available at: https://www.carbontrust.com/resources/guides/carbon-footprinting-and-reporting/crc-carbon-reduction-commitment [accessed 26 May 2016]

Carter, C R and Rogers, D S (2008) A framework of sustainable supply chain management theory, *International Journal of Physical Distribution & Logistics Management*, 38 (5), pp 360–87

Corbett, J J, Winebrake, J J, Green, E H, Kasibhatla, P, Eyring, V and Laurer, A (2007) Mortality from ship emissions: a global assessment, *Environmental Science & Technology*, 41 (24), pp 8512–18

Curran, M A (2006) Life cycle assessment: principles and practice, *EPA/600/R-06/060*, US Environmental Protection Agency, Cincinnati

Danilova, J, Grant, D B and Menachof, D (2016) Enabling UK SME participation in the Humber offshore wind supply chain, Hull University Business School, Hull, UK

Defra (2006) Environmental key performance indicators, reporting guidelines for UK business [online] available at: http://www.defra.gov.uk [accessed 4 April 2009]

Elkington, J (1994) Towards the sustainable corporation: win-win-win business strategies for sustainable development, *California Management Review*, 36 (2), pp 90–100

Elliott, M, (2014) Integrated marine science and management: wading through the morass, *Marine Pollution Bulletin*, 86, pp 1–4

EMAS (2009) http://ec.europa.eu/environment/emas/index_en.htm [accessed 18 June 2009]

Ferdous, R, Khan, F, Sadiq, R, Amyotte, P and Veitch, B (2012) Handling and updating uncertain information in bow-tie analysis, *Journal of Loss Prevention in the Process Industries*, 25, pp 8–19

Grant, D B (2012) *Logistics Management*, Pearson Education Limited, Harlow, UK

Grant, D B and Elliott, M (2016) A proposed framework for managing environmental causes and consequences of ocean traffic and ports, Proceedings of the 7th European Decision Sciences Institute Conference, Helsinki, May, pp 204–17

Grant, R M (1991) The resource-based theory of competitive advantage: implications for strategy formulation, *California Management Review*, 33 (3), pp 114–35

Gunasekaran, A and Kobu, B (2007) Performance measures and metrics in logistics and supply chain management: a review of recent literature (1995–2004) for research and applications, *International Journal of Production Research*, 45 (12), pp 2819–40

Halldórsson, Á, Kotzab, H, Mikkola, J H and Skjøtt-Larsen, T (2007) Complementary theories to supply chain management, *Supply Chain Management: An International Journal*, 12 (4), pp 284–96

Hart, S L (1995) A natural-resource-based view of the firm, *Academy of Management Review*, 20 (4), pp 986–1014

Hart, S L and Dowell, G (2011) A natural-resource-based view of a firm: fifteen years after, *Journal of Management*, 37 (5), pp 1464–79

IGD (2012a) Making the business case for reducing emissions, [online] available at: http://www.igd.com/Research/Sustainability/The-business-case-for-reducing-emissions/ [accessed 16 May 2014]

IGD (2012b) Environmental sustainability matrix: understand sustainability issues across the supply chain [online] available at: http://www.igd.com/sustainability [accessed 12 December 2012]

ISO (2009) www.iso.org [accessed 7 June 2009]

Johnson, G and Scholes, K (1999) *Exploring Corporate Strategy* (5th edn), FT Prentice-Hall, Harlow, UK

Kolding, E (2008) Challenges and Opportunities, Presentation at the 25th German Logistics Congress, October, Berlin

Laursen, W (2015) The demise of the Fair Winds Charter, *Maritime Executive* [online] available at: http://www.maritime-executive.com/features/the-demise-of-the-fair-winds-charter [accessed 19 December 2016]

McKinnon, A (2012) The possible contribution of the shipper to the decarbonisation of deep-sea container supply chains, Proceedings of the 16th Annual Logistics Research Network (LRN) Conference, September, Cranfield University, Cranfield, UK, e-proceedings

Menachof, D, Adams, J and Faint, R (2010) *An Assessment of the Feasibility of an Anaerobic Digestion Plant in NE Lincolnshire (Project SHGAD1)*, Logistics Institute, Hull University Business School, Hull, UK

Morana, J and Gonzalez-Feliu, J (2015) A sustainable urban logistics dashboard from the perspective of a group of operational managers, *Management Research Review*, 38 (10), pp 1068–85

Murphy, E (2013) Key success factors for achieving green supply chain performance: a study of UK ISO 14001 certified manufacturers, unpublished PhD Thesis, University of Hull, Hull, UK

Penrose, E (2009) *The Theory of the Growth of the* Firm (4th edn), Oxford University Press, Oxford

Scharin, H, Ericsdotter, S, Elliott, M, Turner, R K, Niiranen, S, Rockström, J, Blenckner, T, Hyytiäinen, K, Ahlvik, L, Ahtiainen, H, Artell, J, Hasselström, L and Söderqvist, T (2016) Processes for a sustainable stewardship of marine environments, *Ecological Economics,* **128,** pp 55–67

Shaw, S (2013) *Developing and Testing Green Performance Measures for the Supply Chain,* PhD Thesis, University of Hull, Hull, UK

Shaw, S, Grant, D B and Mangan, J (2010) Developing environmental supply chain performance measures, *Benchmarking: An International Journal,* **17** (3), pp 320–39

Stelzenmüller, V, Fock, H O, Gimpel, A, Rambo, H, Diekmann, R, Probst, W N, Callies, U, Bockelmann, F, Neumann, H and Kröncke, I (2015) Quantitative environmental risk assessments in the context of marine spatial management: current approaches and some perspectives, *ICES Journal of Marine Science,* **72** (3), pp 1022–42

Wallis, K (2013) Shipping lines face host of obstacles in jump to cleaner fuel, 14 January, *South China Morning Post* [online] available at: http://www.scmp.com/news/hong-kong/article/1127309/shipping-lines-face-host-obstacles-jump-cleaner-fuel [accessed 15 January 2013]

Wiek A, Withycombe, L and Redman, C L (2011) Key competencies in sustainability: a reference framework for academic program development, *Sustainability Science,* **6,** pp 203–18

Williamson, O E (1999) *The Mechanisms of Governance,* Oxford University Press, New York

Williamson, O E (2008) Outsourcing: transaction cost economics and supply chain management, *Journal of Supply Chain Management,* **44** (2), pp 5–16

Wong, C Y, D'Amico, F, Ashani, N, Hennelly, P and Grant, D B (2013) Work package 3: Research on potential employment and value in offshore wind, *White Paper: The Humber's future economic and sustainable development,* Hull University Business School, Hull, UK, pp 36–41

INDEX

DATE DUE

| GAYLORD | | PRINTED IN U.S.A. |

CPSIA information can be obtained
at www.ICGtesting.com
Printed in the USA
LVOW13s2009070518

576285LV00022B/246/P

9 780749 478278